"We who make it our work to study nonprofit governance are fortunate to have this valuable resource to inform our work in these exciting and sometimes-paradoxical times"

Prof. David O. Renz, *Midwest Center for Nonprofit Leadership*

Non-profit Governance

Non-profit Governance offers 12 perspectives and analytical frameworks to facilitate the development of governance in non-profit organisations (NPOs). In this sector, governance is all the more important because it is often voluntary. Organisations therefore need to be supported in their management, accountability, and strategy. International standards (in particular ISO 37000:2021, dedicated to the governance of organisations) propose key principles to ensure value creation around stakeholder engagement, leadership, risk governance, social responsibility, and organisational sustainability. This book proposes to explore and adapt these principles to the non-profit sector. To do this, the book focuses on four facets of governance: the controls it puts in place, the stakeholders it must listen to and manage, the performance it must monitor, and, finally, the people it must lead and mobilise. The book also highlights the interest of governance mechanisms and processes in developing effective performance, ethics in NPOs and responsible management. Each chapter therefore takes one or more of the principles of ISO 37000:2021 in the non-profit context and builds an analytical framework around them. These 12 frameworks can thus be used by the organisations themselves to develop their governance practices and by researchers who will find original approaches to incorporate into their studies.

Guillaume Plaisance is an associate professor at the IAE – Bordeaux University School of Management and is the deputy-head of the Corporate Social Responsibility (CSR) axis of research in the Research Institute in Management Science (Bordeaux, France). He is the head of two master's programmes dedicated to the management of non-profit organisations and to the management of the social responsibility of organisations. He conducted a PhD thesis linking non-profit governance and performance management. His research themes focus on the governance and management of NPOs and the social and societal responsibility of organisations. He is the Vice-president of Recherches & Solidarités, an NPO composed of professional and scientific experts who study the third sector. He is one of the Associate Editors of the *Journal of Philanthropy and Marketing*.

Anne Goujon Belghit is a full professor at the University of Limoges (France) from September 2024. She is a member of CREOP laboratory research. Her academic research concerns four specific fields: ethical decision-making, the relationship to employment, the Territorial Social Responsibility (TSR), and management in non-profit organisations. She teaches organisational behaviour, human resource management, career management, CSR, TSR, and Social and Sustainable Economy (SSE) issues. She is in charge of the chair of human capital of Bordeaux, and she is editor for the academic journal *VSE* (*Vie & Sciences de l'Entreprise*).

Routledge Studies in Corporate Governance

Corporate Social Responsibility and Governance
Stakeholders, Management and Organizational Performance
in the European Union
Panagiotis Dimitropoulos and Efthalia Chatzigianni

Supply Chain Management and Corporate Governance
Artificial intelligence, game theory and robust optimization
Catherine Xiaocui Lou, Sardar M. N. Islam and Nicholas Billington

Corporate Governance and IFRS in the Middle East
Compliance with International Financial Reporting Standards
Muath Abdelqader, Tamer K. Darwish, and Khalil Nimer

A Modern Credit Rating Agency
The Story of Moody's
Daniel Cash

Governing the Firm in the Social Interest
Corporate Governance Reimagined
Catherine Casey

Corporate Governance in Japan
Historical Roots from the Yamato to the Tokugawa Eras
Magdalena Jerzemowska

Non-profit Governance
Twelve Frameworks for Organisations and Research
Edited by Guillaume Plaisance and Anne Goujon Belghit

For more information about this series, please visit www.routledge.com/Routledge-Studies-in-Corporate-Governance/book-series/RSCG

Non-profit Governance
Twelve Frameworks for Organisations and Research

**Edited by Guillaume Plaisance
and Anne Goujon Belghit**

NEW YORK AND LONDON

First published 2025
by Routledge
605 Third Avenue, New York, NY 10158

and by Routledge
4 Park Square, Milton Park, Abingdon, Oxon, OX14 4RN

*Routledge is an imprint of the Taylor & Francis Group,
an informa business*

© 2025 selection and editorial matter, Guillaume Plaisance
and Anne Goujon Belghit; individual chapters, the contributors

The right of Guillaume Plaisance and Anne Goujon Belghit to be
identified as the authors of the editorial material, and of the authors for
their individual chapters, has been asserted in accordance with sections
77 and 78 of the Copyright, Designs and Patents Act 1988.

With the exception of Chapters 7 and 9, no part of this book may be
reprinted or reproduced or utilised in any form or by any electronic,
mechanical, or other means, now known or hereafter invented, including
photocopying and recording, or in any information storage or retrieval
system, without permission in writing from the publishers.

Chapters 7 and 9 of this book are freely available as a downloadable Open
Access PDF at http://www.taylorfrancis.com under a Creative Commons
Attribution-Non Commercial-No Derivatives (CC-BY-NC-ND) 4.0 license.

Any third party material in this book is not included in the OA Creative
Commons license, unless indicated otherwise in a credit line to the
material. Please direct any permissions enquiries to the original
rightsholder.

Trademark notice: Product or corporate names may be trademarks
or registered trademarks, and are used only for identification and
explanation without intent to infringe.

Library of Congress Cataloging-in-Publication Data
Names: Plaisance, Guillaume, editor. | Goujon Belghit, Anne, editor.
Title: Non-profit governance : twelve frameworks for organisations and
research / edited by Guillaume Plaisance and Anne Goujon Belghit.
Description: New York, NY : Routledge, 2025. | Series: Routledge
studies in corporate governance | Includes bibliographical references
and index.
Identifiers: LCCN 2024018662 | ISBN 9781032599861 (hbk) |
ISBN 9781032607917 (pbk) | ISBN 9781003460572 (ebk)
Subjects: LCSH: Nonprofit organizations. | Corporate governance.
Classification: LCC HD62.6 .N6558 2025 |
DDC 658/.048--dc23/eng/20240709
LC record available at https://lccn.loc.gov/2024018662

ISBN: 978-1-032-59986-1 (hbk)
ISBN: 978-1-032-60791-7 (pbk)
ISBN: 978-1-003-46057-2 (ebk)

DOI: 10.4324/9781003460572

Typeset in Times New Roman
by KnowledgeWorks Global Ltd.

Contents

List of figures	*x*
List of tables	*xi*
List of contributors	*xii*
Foreword	*xvi*

Introduction	1
GUILLAUME PLAISANCE AND ANNE GOUJON BELGHIT	

PART I

Governance and controls: from disciplinary to cognitive approaches—Introduction 9

GUILLAUME PLAISANCE AND ANNE GOUJON BELGHIT

1 **From traditional to collaborative governance: A stakeholder environment framework**	13
MARC PILON AND FRANÇOIS BROUARD	

2 **Implementing and maintaining an effective risk management system in non-profit organisations: A conceptual framework**	29
ELISABETH BERTIN	

3 **The role of public actors in the governance of French non-profit organisations: Proposing an integrated governance analysis framework**	48
ERIC-ALAIN ZOUKOUA	

viii *Contents*

PART II
Governance and stakeholders: from regulation to alliances and collaboration—Introduction   65
ANNE GOUJON BELGHIT AND GUILLAUME PLAISANCE

4 New rules: how funding and control tools shape the relationships between social actions actors   69
PAULINE BOISSELIER

5 What strategic processes to meet the challenges of democratic governance? The case of mergers between non-profit organisations   83
ADRIEN LAURENT

6 Alliances for outcome evaluation and theory of change to generate impact: Integrating network level and organisational level effort via organisational learning   100
RONG WANG

PART III
Governance and performance: from financial survival to responsibilities—Introduction   119
GUILLAUME PLAISANCE AND ANNE GOUJON BELGHIT

7 Drama-free finance: structures and strategies for stability and growth in non-profit organisations   123
RENÉE A. IRVIN

8 Double or tandem movement? The emergence and evolution of non-profit social responsibility   139
SHAWN POPE

9 Social responsibility and sustainability in non-profit organisations: Towards a semantic and conceptual precision   154
GUILLAUME PLAISANCE

Contents ix

PART IV
**Governance and people: from human capital
development to beneficiary focus—Introduction** 173
ANNE GOUJON BELGHIT AND GUILLAUME PLAISANCE

10 **How to retain volunteers? A literature review and
a managerial proposal of a volunteer journey** 177
NATHALIE DUBOST

11 **Why meaning-making capabilities for non-profit
executives? Understanding the nature of non-profit
leadership between the general and middle-range
approaches** 194
SUNGDAE LIM

12 **Authentic beneficiary engagement in the aged care sector:
Advancing non-profit governance through care** 213
KYLIE KINGSTON, SARI ROSSI, BELINDA LUKE,
AND ALEXANDRA WILLIAMSON

Conclusion 230
GUILLAUME PLAISANCE AND ANNE GOUJON BELGHIT

Index *234*

Figures

I.1	A summary of ISO 37000:2021	5
1.1	Governance system and its environment	18
1.2	Collaborative governance system	25
2.1	The NP-RM Diamond	39
3.1	Framework for analysing non-profit organisation governance	60
4.1	(Im)balance between governance and performance	80
5.1	Overview of strategic processes within NPOs	95
6.1	Proposed framework: non-profit learning pathways	106
8.1	Changing emphases in the development of the movement for non-profit social responsibility	141
8.2	The appearance of "Non-profit" and "Non-profits" in a large corpus of English text	142
9.1	An illustration of the distinction between OSR, social responsibility, and sustainability in NPOs according to their link with the mission and the targeted time horizon	162
9.2	Articulation of the concepts of social responsibility, OSR, and sustainability with those of performance and resilience in NPOs	165
10.1	A model of volunteering according to the TPB	184
10.2	A model of long-term volunteering	187
12.1	Directions of accountability	222
12.2	A care-based accountability framework for enhanced engagement of beneficiaries	223

Tables

1.1	Internal and external governance mechanisms	15
1.2	Collaborative governance: some definitions	19
2.1	Levels of NP-RM integration	42
6.1	Two perspectives of Organisational learning	102
7.1	Monthly cash forecast (€)	128
7.2	Stabilising endowment payout with a moving average payout (€)	131
7.3	Financial stability and growth over time	136
8.1	The roles of non-profits in supporting the firm-directed CSR movement	146
8.2	Examples of the dimensions of non-profit social responsibility	151
9.1	Definitions of organisational social responsibility, social responsibility, and sustainability in NPOs	159
10.1	Examples of items of the motivation scales	180
10.2	The six functions fulfilled by volunteering	181
11.1	Meaning-making capabilities for non-profit executives in theory and practice	206
12.1	Qualities of ethics of care and ethics of rights/justice	215
C.1	Statement of the dimensions of ISO 37000:2021 covered by the chapters and the proposed frameworks	232

Contributors

Anne Goujon Belghit
University of Limoges
France
Anne Goujon Belghit is a Full Professor at the University of Limoges (France) from September 2024. She is a member of CREOP laboratory research. Her academic research concerns four specific fields: ethical decision-making, the relationship to employment, the Territorial Social Responsibility (TSR), and management in non-profit organisations. She teaches organisational behaviour, human resource management, career management, CSR, TSR, and Social and Sustainable Economy (SSE) issues. She is in charge of the chair of human capital of Bordeaux, and she is editor for the academic journal VSE (Vie & Sciences de l'Entreprise).

Elisabeth Bertin
University of Bordeaux
France
Elisabeth Bertin is an associate professor at the University of Bordeaux. Her research focuses on risk management, internal audit, and governance of organisations. She is responsible for a master's degree in management control and internal audit. She has served as an expert on the French government's Internal Audit Harmonisation Committee.

Pauline Boisselier
Université côte d'azur, GRM
France
Pauline Boisselier has been a postdoc researcher at Université Paris Dauphine-PSL since 2023. She defended her PhD in management control at Université Côte d'Azur, in France. Her research focuses on the tensions that surround non-profit organisations, with an emphasis on their funding and organisational identity. She employs qualitative methods and, more specifically interviews, to study their management and evaluation tools. Empirically, she explores various settings in the field of social and solidarity economy.

François Brouard

Sprott School of Business, Carleton University, Ottawa, Ontario
Canada
François Brouard, DBA, FCPA, FCA, is a full professor in the accounting group (taxation) at the Sprott School of Business, Carleton University. He is the Founding Director of the Sprott Centre for Social Enterprises (SCSE/CSES), is the co-director of Philab Ontario, and is a member of Philab on philanthropy.

Nathalie Dubost

University of Orléans
France
Nathalie Dubost is professor of management science and a member of the Vallorem laboratory. Her research focuses on services for vulnerable people and the governance of healthcare provision. In addition to her academic activities, Nathalie Dubost holds elected office in non-profit organisations operating in the social sector.

Renée A. Irvin

University of Oregon
USA
Renée Irvin, PhD (Economics), serves as Vice Provost for Academic Affairs at the University of Oregon. Her research centres on family foundations, non-profit financial stabilisation, and dark money organisations. Irvin is a Public Administration Review 75th Anniversary award winner and is past president of the Nonprofit Academic Centres Council.

Kylie Kingston

Queensland University of Technology
Australia
Kylie is a lecturer in the School of Accountancy at Queensland University of Technology (QUT), Australia. Her research focuses on exploring ways to improve social and organisational conditions for marginalised people and stakeholder groups, integrating critical perspectives on accounting, accountability, and evaluation.

Adrien Laurent

Dauphine Research in Management – University of Paris Dauphine-PSL
France
Adrien Laurent is an associate professor at Université Paris Dauphine-PSL. His research focuses on public management as well as the not-for-profit sector: restructuring, collective organisation in the sector and links with public policy. He has been scientific lead on a number of research projects and is developing a variety of participative approaches with practitioners in the field.

xiv *Contributors*

Sungdae Lim
Department of Political Science, Sam Houston State University, Huntsville, Texas
United States of America
Dr. Sungdae Lim is an assistant professor of Public Administration in the Department of Political Science at Sam Houston State University. Dr. Lim's research interests include public- and non-profit-sector leadership, innovation, and partnerships with emphases on social equity, community engagement, and social construction in public service governance.

Belinda Luke
Queensland University of Technology
Australia
Belinda is a professor in the School of Accountancy at Queensland University of Technology (QUT), Australia. Her research interests include accountability in the third sector and public sector.

Marc Pilon
Faculty of Education and Professional Studies – School of Business – Nipissing University
Canada
Marc Pilon, PhD, CPA, CA, is an assistant professor of accounting in the Department of Accounting at HEC Montréal. He teaches financial accounting and assurance courses. His research focuses on how accountability is managed within non-profit, healthcare, and public sector organisations.

Guillaume Plaisance
Research Institute in Management Science (IRGO EA 4190) – Bordeaux University, Bordeaux
France
PhD in management sciences at the University of Bordeaux, Guillaume Plaisance is an associate professor at the University and IAE of Bordeaux. His research themes focus on the governance of organisations, the management of "associations" and cultural organisations as well as the social and societal responsibility of organisations.

Shawn Pope
IÉSEG School of Management
France
Educated at Duke (BA) and Stanford University (MA, PhD), Shawn is an associate professor at IÉSEG School of Management in Paris, France. His has published in numerous "Financial Times 50" journals and in outlets for practicing managers, including *Harvard Business Review, MIT Sloan Management Review* and *Stanford Social Innovation Review*.

Contributors xv

Sari Rossi
Queensland University of Technology
Australia
Sari is a mixed methods researcher specialising in arts and cultural policy, accountability and tax expenditures. Her PhD from Queensland University of Technology examined fiscal arts support. Sari has also worked extensively in the non-profit parts of the arts sector in Australia and Finland.

Rong Wang
Department of Human and Organisational Development, Peabody College of Education and Human Development, Vanderbilt University
USA
Rong Wang (PhD, University of Southern California) is an assistant professor at the Department of Human and Organisational Development at Peabody College, Vanderbilt University. Dr. Wang researches collective action, open collaboration, and inter-organisational alliances that are designed to achieve collective goals.

Alexandra Williamson
Queensland University of Technology
Australia
Alexandra is an Adjunct Research Fellow at the Australian Centre for Philanthropy and Nonprofit Studies (ACPNS) at Queensland University of Technology (QUT). Her research focuses on philanthropic foundations, accountability, and place-based giving. Before joining academia in 2011, she had 14 years of involvement in philanthropic foundations and grantmaking.

Eric-Alain Zoukoua
University of Orléans
France
Eric-Alain Zoukoua's research focuses on the governance of non-profit organisations. He is particularly interested in how the institutional functioning of these organisations is transformed by the actions of their public funders. His research on these issues has also led him to take an interest in the performance of non-profit organisations involved in the entrepreneurial innovation ecosystem.

Foreword

It is indeed a pleasure and privilege to have this opportunity to acknowledge and celebrate the publication of *Non-profit Governance: Twelve Frameworks for Organisations and Research*, edited by Guillaume Plaisance and Anne Goujon Belghit. This book arrives at an important time in the progression of the study of non-profit governance, and I have great confidence it will make a significant contribution to the next generation to our theory, research, and understanding.

Recently, as we engaged in a review of the past 50 years of non-profit governance research, my colleagues and I were impressed by the exceptional growth and development of this field. As we wrote in that assessment (Renz et al., 2023), increasingly substantive and sophisticated insights and perspectives have emerged as scholars from a growing range of disciplines and fields have studied non-profit organisation boards and governance systems to learn more about how they are organised, the practices they employ, and the impact they have on non-profit performance and even their larger communities. Non-profit governance research has expanded across a broad range of levels, from the micro of individuals and groups to the macro of non-profit organisation and network governance systems – inclusive of yet not limited to boards as we more fully recognise the many others also involved in the process of non-profit governance. As a field, we have learned more about the individuals who are a part of the governance process: what motivates them, how they engage in their work, and the implications of their behaviour and performance for effectiveness. And at the opposite end of the spectrum, we have learned more about systems of governance that engage yet extend well beyond the scope of individual organisations as more and more non-profits embrace networks and alliances. And the work of the field has broadened to embrace a richer portfolio of theoretical and research traditions and perspectives as we continue to study and explain this complex and multifaceted phenomenon of non-profit governance. As Donnelly-Cox et al. (2021) chronicle in their recent book, the field has come to understand governance as a multi-level phenomenon; as polycentric

Foreword xvii

and engaged with highly complex economic systems that extend beyond the nation-state; and as a combination of organisation governance, governance in networks, and systems of co-governance.

Increasingly, we as a field have come to understand non-profit governance as a system in which multiple actors are engaged in multiple and varied ways (sometimes productively and sometimes not). We also have grown to appreciate that much of what is relevant to the nature and performance of our governance systems cannot be explained by formal and objective structures and characteristics alone; the field has embraced the call to examine the less obvious yet no less important behavioural aspects of governance. Thus, there is today widespread acceptance that governance research must embrace a broad range of theories and multi-theoretical approaches, working at multiple levels of analysis and studying a wider range of units of analysis. And, for all that we have learned, we also must acknowledge and recognise that we as a field have only begun to scratch the surface!

Thus, we must appreciate and welcome the work of Guillaume Plaisance, Anne Goujon Belghit, and all the authors who have invested their time and intellectual energy in the development of this next-generation resource for the community of scholars in the field of non-profit governance. Their work builds in creative and meaningful ways on the progress chronicled in the previous paragraphs and, in several important ways, offers a platform for taking our work to the next level. This volume, and all of the authors' work culminating in its publication, is dedicated to the continued development and application of a substantive set of theoretical and analytical frameworks that will help researchers and practitioners generate new and unique insights on effective non-profit governance, insights that will help us more fully and effectively understand and address the new dynamics and complexities that characterise the non-profit sector and its governance. An undertaking of this magnitude is inevitably very demanding, so we are fortunate the editors and authors have collaborated to create this unique and valuable addition to the literature of the field of non-profit governance.

Part of what makes this book so interesting is its overt focus on linking and bridging the world of non-profit governance scholarship with the global (in both conceptual and geographic senses) body of work that constitutes the shared insights, understanding, and standards of the International Organisation for Standards (widely known as ISO) in its recent development and publication of the ISO 37000 standards for "good governance." ISO 37000 was developed to provide formal guidance to organisational governing bodies and governing groups (and, by extension, their members and those who work closely with them) (ISO, 2021). Adopted in 2021, these standards reflect an emerging global consensus on what we should expect of systems of organisational governance for organisations of all three sectors (business and government, as well as

xviii *Foreword*

non-profit). ISO 37000 standards exist to advance "good governance," with the goal of enabling effective performance, responsible stewardship, and ethical behaviour in the governance of all organisations (ISO, 2021).

While ISO 37000 standards apply to organisations in all sectors, an especially creative and useful contribution of this book is that it explicitly applies these standards to the conditions and dynamics of the non-profit sector and specifically to non-profit organisations and networks of non-profits. I think this volume already has begun to realise a critical outcome for those of us studying non-profit governance. It enhances our appreciation for the relevance and application of ISO 37000, and the clarity of the standards as they are articulated, and this has great potential for further enriching our own theorising and analysis. And, taking this further, the chapters of the book articulate ISO-relevant frameworks (one in each chapter) and help us more fully consider them in the non-profit context. Indeed, there is excellent potential for two-way systemic learning as these concepts and constructs influence both the standards and our emerging perspectives on non-profit governance.

One of my hopes for the impact of this volume is that it will also help those who study business organisation governance develop a better grounded and more nuanced perspective on the non-profit governance and that there is greater appreciation for the significance of context and contingency when it comes to understanding non-profit governance. As non-profit research has progressed and developed, it has become increasingly clear just how important such complexity is. Further, this will be especially useful as we continue to study governance in less usual non-profit settings, such as governance of hybrid and socially entrepreneurial organisations, as well as those that blur the boundaries of sectors.

Finally, but no less significant for me, it is especially delightful to see that this volume brings together authors from multiple nations. There is no question that the body of non-profit governance literature is more inclusive than it was a decade and more ago (Renz et al., 2023), yet it remains equally true the field needs to learn from substantially more of the work of scholars from outside the United States. I found it very beneficial to learn from the array of studies and analyses presented by our French colleagues, as well as from the chapters prepared by our colleagues affiliated with universities of Australia, Canada, and the United Kingdom.

Guillaume Plaisance, Anne Goujon Belghit, and their colleagues are to be congratulated for preparing this special new resource. It is a welcome contribution to the literature of non-profit governance and, in a larger sense, to the literature of organisational governance overall. There is much to recommend this book to non-profit researchers and scholars, as well as to practitioners and non-profit leaders of all nations – especially nations whose national standards bodies are members of the ISO. These chapters are written by scholars and professionals who understand their topics very well, and they are organised and presented

Foreword   xix

in a way that challenges all of us to embrace and explore these important new ways to frame our next generation of inquiry into the dynamic and growing field of non-profit governance. We who make it our work to study non-profit governance are fortunate to have this valuable resource to inform our work in these exciting and sometimes-paradoxical times.

David O. Renz
Midwest Center for Nonprofit Leadership
Henry W. Bloch School of Management
University of Missouri–Kansas City
January 2024

References

Donnelly-Cox, G., Meyer, M., & Wijkström, F. (2021). Deepening and broadening the field: Introduction. In G. Donnelly-Cox, M. Meyer, & F. Wijkström (Eds.), *Research handbook on nonprofit governance* (pp. 1–25). Edward Elgar Publishing.

International Organization for Standardization. (2021). *ISO 37000:2021(en) governance of organizations — Guidance*. International Organization for Standardization. Online Browsing Platform: https://www.iso.org/obp/ui/en/#iso:std:iso:37000:ed-1:v1:en

Renz, D. O., Brown, W. A., & Andersson, F. O. (2023). The evolution of nonprofit governance research: Reflections, insights, and next steps. *Nonprofit and Voluntary Sector Quarterly, 52*(S), 241S–277S.

Introduction

Guillaume Plaisance and Anne Goujon Belghit

This book, dedicated to non-profit organisations and more specifically to their governance, aspires to be essential for better defining, understanding and managing their operating methods.

It seems essential to strengthen a theoretical field specific to this sector, as it is often associated by academics with either the private or the public sector. Salamon and Anheier (1992) propose to define non-profit organisations as entities that combine the following five characteristics: their private, formal legal status, non-profit activities, independence of management and the presence of volunteers. The international classification of the non-profit sector includes 12 distinct groups including the social and medico-social sector, culture, education, the environment and philanthropic activities. Their challenges vary according to their founding project and the values they defend. Non-profit organisations are sometimes assimilated to private structures at the service of the public sector (O'Neill, 1989) and can be considered as the "armed arms" of the public authorities in the territory.

In this, the non-profit sector needs to find its own paradigm, because it creates significant employment and carries out essential activities to maintain social stability and help the most vulnerable people in our societies. By way of illustration, the non-profit sector in France generates 2.38 million jobs, including 1.76 million in grassroots volunteer organisations alone (Tchernonog & Prouteau, 2019). More broadly, there are 2.8 million non-profit organisations in Europe, employing 13.6 million people. In the United States, this sector contributes to the creation of almost 10% of jobs. Since the global health crisis linked to COVID-19, the non-profit sector has adapted and evolved.

Goujon Belghit et al. (2021) highlight the need for non-profit organisations to regroup, to merge, in order to maintain their activities. They have to constantly reconcile three conflicting logics: improving the quality of the services offered to users, reducing operating costs and generating enough cash to meet a growing working capital requirement (WCR) due to the ever-lengthening payment delays imposed by regulators. Goujon Belghit et al. (2021) describe the process of a

DOI: 10.4324/9781003460572-1

2   *Guillaume Plaisance and Anne Goujon Belghit*

merger between two organisations operating in the social and medico-social sector in France. The non-profit organisation decided to merge a *foyer de vie* (with 26 employees) with a holiday village (with 14 employees). The challenges lie in the support of individuals, the ability to create a group dynamic between the two organisations and the strategic management of human capital. At the organisational level, the management faces a permanent tension between the need to rationalise costs and to improve the quality of the services offered to the beneficiaries. This example shows that the model of Mintzberg (2003), which stresses that the functioning of non-profit organisations is based on a missionary model, is deeply challenged. In fact, they are based on objectives set by public sponsors and not only on missions and values.

The governance of non-profit organisations is based on notions of otherness, gift, social exchange or even reciprocity. Anthropology and sociology, represented by authors such as Gouldner (1960), Mauss (1923/1924) and Blau (1964), are interested in the norms of reciprocity. Based on the idea that we all feel indebted to others and on the hypothesis of a "just world" (Lerner & Miller, 1978), i.e. a shared belief that the world is morally ordered and that everyone receives "what he deserves", it is necessary to study the rules of these social exchanges and the way in which they can be managed. The governance of non-profit organisations works with volunteers and collaborators committed to values, standards of reciprocity and giving.

This norm of reciprocity is expressed in two ways. Firstly, it is observed in a direct way when people give in the hope of receiving something in return in the future. Then it occurs in an indirect way, when the recipient gives back to members of society other than the original donor (Nowak & Sigmund, 2005). Reciprocity differs from altruism because it is not a form of unconditional generosity, but a response to engage in a social relationship following an action initiated by a donor (Fehr & Gächter, 2000).

Our book is an essential educational tool to show the specificity of the governance mechanisms of non-profit organisations. Classic academic works draw on Chandler (1977) to show the separation between owners and managers and the emergence of a new power: managerial power. They also refer to the work of Berle and Means (1932), Jenson and Meckling (1976) or those of Williamson (1979) to study the transactions and their associated costs between owners or strategic decision-makers and managers, directors of orchestras, in order to strengthen the power of owners and shareholders.

In parallel with this questioning of power and decision-making, complementary internal and external stakeholders are positioned (Freeman, 1984). The initial question of value creation and its distribution is broadened to include all stakeholders. Owner-shareholders are looking for solutions to strengthen their power and ensure access to reliable information to guarantee the profitability of their investments in organisations. In order to counter the asymmetry of information (Spence, 1973) and to control managers who are considered more or less reliable, shareholders turn to social rating agencies and ask organisations to provide additional information, especially non-accounting information. All these concrete developments, conceptualised over time, do not help to clearly identify the governance mechanisms specific to non-profit organisations. The fundamental objective is to generate partnership performance that is useful at the level of society, not financial value for shareholders or owners. The question of power, control and value creation has to be considered in a very different way in the non-profit sector.

The first step is therefore to agree on a definition of non-profit governance. This is a difficult task and there is no consensus. In their already seminal review, Renz et al. (2023) use Cornforth's definition: "the systems and processes concerned with ensuring the overall direction, control and accountability of the organisation" (Cornforth, 2014, p. 5). However, they immediately highlight the tendency in the literature to reduce non-profit governance to the board. This observation is supported by recent studies on the definition of governance: the vast majority of published articles directly equate non-profit governance with the board, despite increasing efforts and attempts to provide definitions (69 counted by Plaisance, 2023).

These 69 definitions have led to the emergence of four approaches (which are not mutually exclusive): governance based on control (in line with the overview of the classic management approach above), relational governance (which looks at processes and relationships), stakeholder governance and, finally, governance as a key player in strategy. Some definitions tend to deal with governance from all these angles, as do Willems et al. (2017, p. 1426): "the set of conditions that should be fulfilled and practices that should be applied in order to enhance the achievement of a non-profit organisation's mission and vision. A board, its attributes, its internal structure, and what its members do, can thus been seen as conditions and practices relevant to this definition, but are not the only elements that constitute non-profit governance. In other words, actors both inside and outside the boardroom, such as managers, staff, and advisory committees can contribute in various governance functions". Kreutzer (2009, p. 117) also suggested a global approach, but based on control: "the set of processes, customs, policies, and laws affecting the way in which a non-profit organisation is directed, administered, or controlled. It also includes the relationships among the many stakeholders involved, entailing the functions of setting direction, making policy and strategic decisions, overseeing and monitoring organisational performance, and ensuring overall accountability".

These few examples illustrate the diversity of approaches found in the literature. In order to pay tribute to all the research, this book is based on the synthetic definition proposed by Plaisance (2023, p. 645) thanks to a lexicometric analysis: "non-profit governance is a set of practices, rules and mechanisms for control,

4 *Guillaume Plaisance and Anne Goujon Belghit*

planning and decision-making in order to achieve organisational objectives. Non-profit governance distributes power and authority and includes a political dimension implying responsibility, transparency and accountability, regularly provided by a board of directors. It is mission-centred, overall performance-driven and stakeholder-oriented".

However, despite growing interest and a growing body of work, the field of non-profit governance needs to be enriched. As Renz et al. (2023) found in their survey, we need more studies on diversity and inclusion, on non-profit governance in times of turbulence, on networks and alliances, and on the impact on performance. Respondents also called for "alternative models of non-profit governance". This is the aim of this book: to use an international standard dedicated to the governance of organisations as a basis for future research and to provide practitioners with a basis for strategic thinking and governance. International standards are essential references for both researchers and practitioners. They provide organisations with guidelines for their practices, while delivering scholars with an often original perspective on the concepts or processes they address.

In the case of governance, the international standard is ISO 37000:2021, published in 2021. The fact that it was published so recently and in the context of a pandemic has led to a limited reception, despite the fact that it proposes an original vision of governance. Scholars are then encouraged to study this standard in order to critically examine international standards and collectively advance the professional and scientific literature (Steffek & Wegmann, 2021). The standard defines governance as a "human-based system by which an organisation is directed, overseen and held accountable for achieving its defined purpose" (p. 1). Even at the definition stage, the standard includes what it calls foundational governance principles. These principles are essential for governance to function properly.

All four serve the primary governance principle: the purpose, which is defined as "the organisation's meaningful reason to exist" (p. 4). In other words, governance is at the service of purpose and is underpinned by four key principles. The first is strategy, understood as the way in which the organisation is run so that the purpose is achieved in line with the value generation model. The second is logically the value generation, for which the standard insists on respect for the "natural environment, social, and economic contexts" (p. 10). The third principle is accountability, defined by the standard as the "obligation to another for the fulfilment of a responsibility" (p. 3) and it specifies that responsibility is the "obligation to act and take decisions to achieve required outcomes" (p. 3). Finally, the fourth principle is oversight, which focuses on monitoring performance, ethics and compliance.

Around these principles, governance can rely on enabling principles to make it more functional. Stakeholder engagement (in particular to ensure that their expectations are met), leadership and social responsibility are particularly relevant. Social responsibility is defined as the "responsibility of an organisation for the impacts of its decisions and activities on society and the environment, through transparent and ethical behaviour that contributes to sustainable development, including the health and the welfare of society; takes into account the expectations of stakeholders; is in compliance with applicable law and consistent with international norms of behaviour; is integrated throughout the organisation and practised in its relationships" (p. 4). This echoes another enabling principle, "viability and performance over time", which includes sustainable development. Finally, governance can be built on two principles that are more concerned with control: risk governance, in relation to uncertainty, and data and decisions, in particular their reliability. Each principle is then detailed in the standard to help organisations implement the right practices. The content of the standard is summarised in Figure I.1.

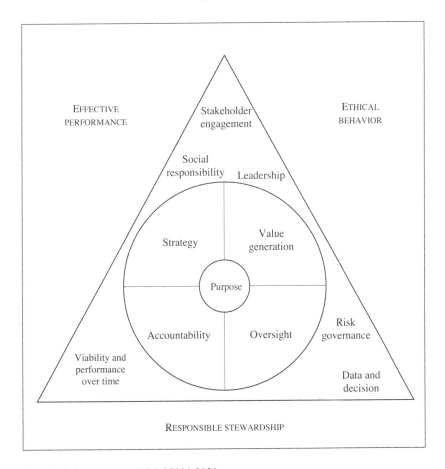

Figure I.1 A summary of ISO 37000:2021

6 *Guillaume Plaisance and Anne Goujon Belghit*

Assuming that governance is functional and effective, ISO 37000:2021 suggests that it should have three main effects according to:

1 effective performance: the organisation is true to its purpose, performs as required, generates value for stakeholders and remains in alignment with its policies and relevant stakeholder expectations

(p. 10)

2 responsible stewardship: the organisation makes use of resources in a responsible manner, effectively balances positive and negative impacts, considers the global context, ensures its contribution to sustainable development and engenders the trust and confidence of the communities within which it operates, and beyond

(pp. 10–11)

3 ethical behaviour: the organisation behaves in accordance with accepted principles of right or good conduct in the context of a particular situation and in a manner consistent with international norms of behaviour, including demonstrating an ethical culture, accountability through accurate and timely reporting on its performance and stewardship of resources, fairness in the treatment of, and engagement with, stakeholders, integrity and transparency in fulfilling its obligations, and commitments, and competence and probity in the manner in which it makes decision

(p. 11)

In addition to its interest in furthering the scientific literature, ISO 37000:2021 thus offers a new perspective on non-profit governance, in particular by taking an interest in all organisations, by focusing on the purpose and by incorporating the contemporary issues of viability and sustainability. In a pragmatic way, it highlights the mechanisms, benefits and impact of governance in all organisational contexts.

Because it is a fertile ground for both research and organisations, it has been chosen here as the basis for our book. This book thus offers 12 perspectives and analytical frameworks to facilitate the development of governance in non-profit organisations. As already seen, in this sector, governance is all the more crucial as it is often voluntary. Organisations must therefore be supported in their orientation, management, accountability and strategy. International standards (in particular ISO 37000:2021) propose key principles to ensure value creation in terms of stakeholder engagement, leadership, risk management, social responsibility and organisational sustainability: this book proposes to explore and adapt these principles to the non-profit sector. To do this, the book focuses on four facets of governance: the controls it puts in place, the stakeholders it must listen to and manage, the performance it must monitor and, finally, the people it must lead and mobilise. The book also highlights the interest of governance mechanisms

Introduction 7

and processes in developing effective performance, ethics within non-profit organisations and responsible management. Each chapter therefore adopts one or more of the principles of ISO 37000:2021 in the non-profit context, offers an in-depth analysis and finally provides an analytical framework. The adaptations of this international standard to smaller organisations may also inspire the authors to build their analytical frameworks. These 12 frameworks can thus be used by the organisations themselves to develop their governance practices, but also by researchers who will find original approaches to incorporate into their studies.

References

Berle, A., & Means, G. (1932). *The modern corporation & private property*, Transaction Publishers.

Blau, P. (1964). *Exchange and power in social life*. Wiley.

Chandler, A. (1977). *The visible hand. The managerial revolution in American business*. Belknap Press.

Cornforth, C. (2014). Nonprofit governance research: The need for innovative perspectives and approaches. In C. Cornforth & W. A. Brown (Eds.), *Nonprofit governance: Innovative perspectives and approaches* (pp. 1–14). Routledge.

Fehr, E., & Gächter, S. (2000). Fairness and retaliation: The economics of reciprocity. *Journal of Economic Perspectives*, *14*(3), 159–181.

Freeman, R. E. (1984). *Strategic management: A stakeholder approach*. Pittman.

Goujon Belghit, A., Cuenoud, T., Bretones, D., & Cherrad, O. (2021). Le management du capital humain selon une approche multipartite: Etude de cas dans le secteur médico-social. *Revue Recherches en Sciences de Gestion*, *2*(143), 233–265.

Gouldner, A. W. (1960). The norm of reciprocity: A preliminary statement. *American Sociological Review*, *25*, 161–178.

Jenson, M. C., & Meckling, W. H. (1976). Theory of the firm: Managerial behavior, agency costs and ownership structure. *Journal of Financial Economics*, *3*(4), 305–360.

Kreutzer, K. (2009). Nonprofit governance during organizational transition in voluntary associations. *Nonprofit Management and Leadership*, *20*(1), 117–133. https://doi.org/10.1002/nml.244

Lerner, M. J., & Miller, D. T. (1978). Just world research and the attribution process: Looking back and ahead. *Psychological Bulletin*, *85*, 1030–1051.

Mauss, M. (1923/1924). *Essai sur le don. Forme et raison de l'échange dans les sociétés archaïques*. Collection « les classiques des sciences sociales », Version numérique produit par Jean-Marie Tremblay.

Mintzberg, H. (2003). *Structure et dynamique des organisations*. Editions d'Organisation.

Nowak, M. A., & Sigmund, K. (2005). Evolution of indirect reciprocity. *Nature*, *437*(7063), 1291–1298.

O'Neill, M. (1989). *The third America: The emergence of the nonprofit sector in the United States*. Jossey Bass.

Plaisance, G. (2023). Governance in non-profit organisations: A plural or ambiguous research field? Bibliometrics and definitions of a broad concept. *International Journal of Business Governance and Ethics*, *17*(6), 619–653. https://doi.org/10.1504/ijbge.2022.10047033

Renz, D. O., Brown, W. A., & Andersson, F. O. (2023). The evolution of nonprofit governance research: Reflections, insights, and next steps. *Nonprofit and Voluntary Sector Quarterly*, *52*(1_suppl), 241S–277S. https://doi.org/10.1177/08997640221111011

Salamon, L. M., & Anheier, H. K. (1992). In search of the non-profit sector. I: The question of definitions. *Voluntas: International Journal of Voluntary and Nonprofit Organizations, 3*, 125–151.

Spence, M. A. (1973). Job market signaling. *Quarterly Journal of Economics, 87*(3), 355–379.

Steffek, J., & Wegmann, P. (2021). The standardization of "Good Governance" in the age of reflexive modernity. *Global Studies Quarterly, 1*(4), 1–10. https://doi.org/10.1093/isagsq/ksab029

Tchernonog, V., & Prouteau, L. (2019). *Le paysage associatif français: Mesures et évolutions*. Dalloz.

Willems, J., Andersson, F. O., Jegers, M., & Renz, D. O. (2017). A coalition perspective on nonprofit governance quality: Analyzing dimensions of influence in an exploratory comparative case analysis. *VOLUNTAS: International Journal of Voluntary and Nonprofit Organizations, 28*(4), 1422–1447. https://doi.org/10.1007/s11266-016-9683-6

Williamson, O. E. (1979). Transaction-cost economics: The governance of contractual relations. *The Journal of Law and Economics, 22*(2), 233–261.

Part I

Governance and controls: from disciplinary to cognitive approaches

Introduction

Guillaume Plaisance and Anne Goujon Belghit

Part I of our book takes a decidedly dual approach. We recognise that governance has often been seen as a disciplinary arrangement (to bring the organisation under control) in the sense that agency theory is one of the most widely used theories in non-profit organisations (Brown, 2005) and that it has been complemented by a partnership approach that integrates stakeholder and stewardship theories with agency theory (Van Puyvelde et al., 2012). In their comprehensive review of the literature, Ortega-Rodríguez et al. (2023) also show very clearly that there are four main reasons why non-profit organisations implement governance mechanisms: to prevent fraud, to ensure accountability to stakeholders, because of the growth of the sector (and the associated regulatory pressures) and to protect public trust. This is a disciplinary approach, meaning that governance seeks to discipline managers to act in the interests of members and funders in the case of agency theory, and in accordance with the requirements of stakeholders in the case of stakeholder theory. Stewardship theory makes the relationship between managers, on the one hand, and members and funders, on the other, more accommodating, but the aim of managers is still to serve those who give them power. Acknowledging this reality does not prevent us from arguing in Part I of this book for a shift towards a cognitive approach to governance. Here we refer to cognitive governance as a form of governance that moves away from a disciplinary vision and places managers in a position of cognitive coordination. The aim of managers is to develop knowledge and skills within the organisation so that it can best adapt to its environment. In other words, managers are supported by stakeholders to develop an internal and external cognitive space in which organisational learning is prioritised, mistakes are accepted and cognitive conflict between stakeholders is valued (because it allows new points of view, new ideas, etc. to emerge). Collaboration, adaptation and comprehension are preferred to the tensions highlighted by agency theory, for example. These are the three themes that run through the chapters of Part I.

DOI: 10.4324/9781003460572-2

10 *Guillaume Plaisance and Anne Goujon Belghit*

In Chapter 1, entitled "From traditional to collaborative governance: a stakeholder environment framework", Marc Pilon and François Brouard highlight the tension described above. The authors depict the traditional governance mechanisms, which can be found in the governance bodies (such as the general meeting of members, the board of directors or associated committees), in the management and control system and externally, depending on the structure of the environment and markets. As ISO 37000:2021 reiterates, governance does indeed have an oversight role over "the organisation's performance to ensure that it meets the governing body's intentions for and expectations of the organisation, its ethical behaviour and its compliance obligations" (ISO 37000:2021, p. 19). However, the authors go much further and emphasise the importance of collaboration, which leads them to formulate a third type of governance mechanism, known as collaborative governance mechanisms. Thanks to their specific analytical framework, the authors offer non-profit organisations a set of original mechanisms to implement in order to develop a collaborative culture adapted to the sector. This conception of governance also opens up an interface gap in the current design of governance mechanisms, which deserves consideration in new research.

In Chapter 2, Elisabeth Bertin proposes a conceptual framework for "implementing and maintaining an effective risk management system in non-profit organisations". The author has focused on the governance of risk, as defined by ISO 37000:2021, which assigns a specific role to the governing body: it should "ensure that it considers the effect of uncertainty on the organisational purpose and associated strategic outcomes" (ISO 37000:2021, p. 30). However, the author quickly encountered a number of difficulties inherent in the literature and the topic itself. Research on risk management in non-profit organisations is still in its infancy, and it seems difficult to ask these organisations to implement processes that are as formalised and standardised as those found in the for-profit private sector. The author also draws on the challenges of collaboration to suggest an approach that is appropriate to non-profit organisations in general, but also to each individual organisation. She suggests an understanding attitude towards organisations that do not always have the resources to implement such procedures and proposes an "NP-RM diamond" specific to risk management in the non-profit context. Organisations and researchers will thus be able to base their practices and reflections on the flexible approach proposed by the author.

In Chapter 3 by Eric-Alain Zoukoua, entitled "The role of public actors in the governance of French non-profit organisations: proposing an integrated governance analysis framework", the theoretical shift called for in this introduction to the section is translated into reality in the context of relations with public actors. The author points out that New Public Management, which is now being questioned by researchers, continues to spread within non-profit organisations. Faced with the many risks inherent in such a diffusion, the author calls for vigilance and offers theoretical and practical perspectives for renewing relations

Governance and controls: from disciplinary to cognitive approaches 11

between the public sector and the private non-profit sector. The analytical framework proposed reflects the cognitive issues at stake, and the author suggests that stakeholders (in this case, public actors) should work with non-profit organisations to develop appropriate governance mechanisms. This collaborative, comprehensive and adaptive approach should inspire both organisations and future research.

References

Brown, W. A. (2005). Exploring the association between board and organizational performance in nonprofit organizations. *Nonprofit Management and Leadership, 15*(3), 317–339. https://doi.org/10.1002/nml.71

ISO. (2021). *ISO 37000:2021 – Governance of organizations – Guidance*. International Organization for Standardization (ISO), ISO Technical Committee 309.

Ortega-Rodríguez, C., Martín-Montes, L., Licerán-Gutiérrez, A., & Moreno-Albarracín, A. L. (2023). Nonprofit good governance mechanisms: A systematic literature review. *Nonprofit Management and Leadership, 34*(4), 927–957. https://doi.org/10.1002/nml. 21598

Van Puyvelde, S., Caers, R., Du Bois, C., & Jegers, M. (2012). The governance of nonprofit organizations: Integrating agency theory with stakeholder and stewardship theories. *Nonprofit and Voluntary Sector Quarterly, 41*(3), 431–451.

1 From traditional to collaborative governance

A stakeholder environment framework

Marc Pilon and François Brouard

Introduction

Organisations operate in a situated environment with multiple forces influencing them and interacting with a number of stakeholders. From prior research, we know that governance is an important element of managing the demands of stakeholders (Pilon, 2019). It is also a mean of managing accountability (Pilon & Brouard, 2023). Governance may be useful to address the evolving organisational landscape, such as stakeholder engagement, performance, value generation, social responsibility and sustainable development (ISO 37000:2021).

The literature refers to two main groups of governance mechanisms: internal and external. However, collaborative governance may be viewed as a third group of mechanisms that needs to be taken into account. Collaborative governance could be defined as an "approach to governance in areas where organisations need to work closely together in order to achieve their goals" (Shaw et al., 2019, p. 61). As public, private and non-profit activities, and society in general, become ever more complex and intertwined, the prevalence of collaborative governance will only increase. Anecdotally, we hear of organisations being involved in several collaborative initiatives concurrently.

The need for a third group of governance mechanisms, collaborative governance, involves interdependency and trust. By introducing the concept of collaborative governance, the concept is defined, along with its ingredients and barriers. The future direction and complexity of collaborative governance make it important to understand its contributing factors.

This chapter will briefly review the literature on governance in relation to the constructs of stakeholder environments. The objective of the chapter is to examine organisational level governance system and to propose a collaborative governance stakeholder environment framework that integrates salient concepts.

This chapter is organised as follows. First, stakeholders and their environment are presented. Then internal and external governance mechanisms are described. Collaborative governance is examined focusing on the need, the process, the ingredients, the mechanisms and the barriers. Two frameworks are offered on

DOI: 10.4324/9781003460572-3

14 *Marc Pilon and François Brouard*

the governance system and its environment and on the collaborative governance mechanisms. Finally, concluding remarks are presented.

Macro-environment and stakeholders

This section examines stakeholders and their external environment. The environment could be divided into the external environment and the internal environment. The external environment includes the macro-environment and the stakeholders. The internal environment includes resources, culture, strategies, direction and structure (Brouard, 2004). Since the internal environment is specific to each organisation, the focus in this chapter is mainly on the external environment.

Macro-environment

Macro-environment includes different forces such as demographic, economic, technological, political, legal, ecological, geophysical, infrastructure, sociocultural, nature and ecology (Albrecht, 2000; Fahey & Narayanan, 1986; Kulieshova, 2014).

Various dimensions could characterise the external environment, such as homogeneity/heterogeneity, dynamism, connectivity, hostility, concentration/dispersion and turbulence (Fahey & Narayanan, 1986; Miller & Friesen, 1983).

Stakeholders

As Agle et al. (2008, p. 153) say: "the stakeholder idea is alive, well, and flourishing". Over recent years, discussion regarding stakeholders is more and more included in decision-making.

Stakeholders could be defined as "any individual, group, organisation, institution that can *affect* as well as *be affected by* an individual's, group's, organisation's, or institution's policy or policies" (Mitroff & Linstone, 1993, p. 141). Stakeholders could be individuals, groups, organisations or nature (Quattrone, 2022).

Among the stakeholders, a number of them could be listed, such as owners (shareholders/investors), members, volunteers, employees (executives, non-managerial persons), unions, customers/clients/beneficiaries/patients, suppliers/creditors, donors/foundations, media, competitors, society (public, citizens, local community), governments (national, provincial, regional, local), regulators, international organisations/agencies, advocacy groups, pressure groups, activists, professional associations, educators/researchers (university/college, think thank) and partners (Fassin, 2009; Mitroff & Linstone, 1993; Stamp, 1980).

A particular group of stakeholders is particularly relevant for collaborative governance; they create partnerships, cross-sector partnerships, alliances, public-private partnerships and networks. Those partnerships could be formal or informal.

Not all stakeholders (or interested parties) are created equally (Mitchell et al., 1997, 2015). Depending on the decisions or issues, hierarchy and prioritisation

From traditional to collaborative governance   15

of stakeholders could be decided, for example in determining salient stakeholders (Mitchell et al., 1997).

Internal and external governance mechanisms

This section examines internal and external governance mechanisms as described in Brouard and Pilon (2020). The distinction between internal and external adopts the perspective of a specific non-profit and what is external to it. Table 1.1 presents a summary of internal and external governance mechanisms. The list applies to non-profits, but is not exclusive to this sector.

Internal governance mechanisms

Internal governance mechanisms can be grouped into the following categories: (1) beliefs and values, (2) board of directors, (3) board of directors committees, (4) advisors board, (5) family groups and rules, (6) remuneration plans, (7) management systems and (8) financial/ownership structure.

Beliefs and values include beliefs and values system, code of values, code of conduct, code of ethics, conflict of interest rules, trust, culture and management philosophy.

Board of directors is probably the mostly cited mechanism in terms of governance. It includes numerous facets such as its establishment, its statutory and oversight role, its size, its composition, the frequency of meetings per year, the proportion of executive directors/non-executive directors on the Board, the proportion of independent directors on the Board, the proportion of independent directors with accounting and finance background on the Board, the proportion of directors external to the family on the Board of directors (especially important with a family foundation) and the mix of inside and outside directors.

Board of directors has various committees which cover numerous aspects of the governance of an organisation. Various names are used by organisations for

Table 1.1 Internal and external governance mechanisms

Internal governance mechanisms	External governance mechanisms
Beliefs and values	Market
Board of directors	Members/stakeholders
Board of directors committees	Employees
Advisors board	Legal system
Family groups and rules	Disclosure requirements
Remuneration plans	Accounting profession
Management systems	Results and performance
Ownership structure	Media pressures
	Societal ethics and morality

Source: Adapted from Brouard and Pilon (2020, p. 65).

those committees, such as audit committee, governance, fundraising, nomination, management, executive, finance, remuneration and benefits, pension, environment and health, human resources, investment, risk, regulatory, compliance and government affairs, public responsibilities, technology and innovation, sustainability and ethics.

Family groups and rules may be relevant for family non-profits. For example, a family foundation may be regulated by the family procedures and rules such as the establishment of a family assembly, the frequency of the family assembly meetings per year, establishment of a family council, the frequency of the family council meetings per year, the frequency of meetings per year between family members, the family business rules and family charter. The interconnection between the non-profit and the family, especially for private foundations, may be unofficially settled at the family meetings.

Remuneration plans may be a source of tension between donors and the non-profit. The level of remuneration is often cited in the media for charitable organisations. Examples include executive compensation structure, executive compensation level, CEO compensation, remuneration systems, and performance incentives.

Management systems includes a wide variety of mechanisms such as constitution, bylaws, policies and guidelines, vision and mission, strategic plan, accounting systems, budget, business plan, rules and procedures, internal controls, internal auditor, strategic intelligence, balance scorecard, risk management system, conflicts resolutions, whistleblower policy and tools, crisis management, continuity plan and insurance. Some of those management systems are integrated in the ISO (37000:2021) guidelines.

Ownership structure of a non-profit organisation may include the ownership structure with various or a handful of members, the ownership by a family and its use for other objectives. Sometimes corporate foundations act as the philanthropic arm of a for-profit corporation.

External governance mechanisms

The external governance mechanisms are: (1) market, (2) members/stakeholders, (3) employees, (4) legal system, (5) disclosure requirements, (6) accounting profession, (7) results and performance, (8) media pressures, (9) societal ethics and morality.

The market has less implication for non-profits compared to for-profit corporations. However, with social enterprises market is more involved. The financial market and subsequent transactions may be relevant when considering the asset management or transactions by non-profits. Other market-related facets may include debt/loan market (debt covenant), labour market, managers market, goods and services market and competition between organisations, especially for attracting donation dollars.

Members may have an impact at the general meetings of the organisations. It may be the member's meetings participation and their rights (vote, protection from abuse, proxy voting).

Employees may exercise a control over the organisation. The number of employees may be small for non-profits. The control might be increased with the presence of unions, which is quite rare in non-profits. The employees may have the possibility and right to elect directors to the Board of directors.

The legal system includes corporate law, securities legislation, labour law, environmental law, access to information legislation, privacy legislation, disclosure protection legislation (whistleblowing), lobbying legislation, other laws and regulations, governance codes and codes of best practices.

Disclosure requirements is a major component of demonstrating financial accountability, and includes financial statements, management and discussion analysis (MD&A), annual reports, governance reports, environmental reports, social responsibility reports, governmental reports, disclosures of remuneration and voluntary disclosures.

The accounting profession with the accounting standards – Generally Accepted Accounting Principles (GAAP) and the auditing standards (GAAS) – regulates the financial disclosure and the assurance of financial statements. For instance, the accounting profession regulates audit engagements, including auditor independence, the presence of two auditors and the proportion of services other than auditing offered by an auditor.

Results and performance could be measured in various ways. In addition to the net income or excess of revenues over expenses, performance could be measured on various aspects such as social impact and its reputation. It could be board performance reviews, staff performance assessment, volunteer impact and contributions evaluation.

Media pressures could play a role in the flow of information with media inquiry on various facets. Societal ethics and morality place a context of what is acceptable or not in a society. The #metoo movement and its implications is an example of the evolution of societal ethics and morality.

Governance system and its environment framework

The governance system includes three main governance mechanisms, i.e. external, internal and collaborative. The governance system is in interaction with the external environment, namely the macro-environment and the stakeholders and also the organisational internal environment, including resources, culture, direction and structure.

As the purpose of the book is to provide frameworks for academics and practitioners, Figure 1.1 presents a framework showing the governance system and its environment with the addition of the collaborative governance to the usual internal and external governance mechanisms.

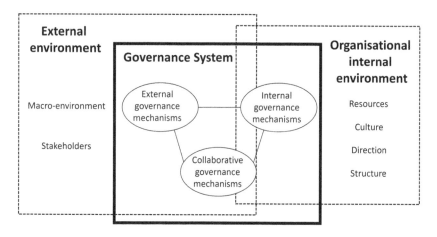

Figure 1.1 Governance system and its environment

Collaborative governance

While internal and external governance refers to a specific organisation, collaborative governance refers to the governance of multiple stakeholders interacting in the environment. For example, in a complex system, such as the health system, multiple stakeholders are involved to different extents. As the core element of this chapter, collaborative governance is examined within its environment. Justification for organisations to collaborate, definition of collaborative governance and process will be offered. To have a better chance of success, collaborative governance needs some ingredients, so the mechanisms could overcome the inherent barriers.

Need for organisations to collaborate

The need for collaborative governance emerges from the failures of agency-type governance mechanisms when an organisation realises that a problem cannot be tackled by the organisation acting alone. Many non-profits (small, medium and large size) may not have the capacity to achieve their goals on their own or it may be more beneficial for society as a whole to achieve those goals with other stakeholders. Haven't we heard the phrase attributed to Aristotle that: "The whole is greater than the sum of the parts?"

In collaborative governance, each participant aims to gain something from the resource investment, with the goal of achieving something that could not be realised by a single organisation acting alone: "the purpose of collaboration is to generate desired outcomes together that could not be accomplished separately" (Emerson et al., 2012, p. 14). In other words, organisations are incentivised to participate in collaborative governance because organisational outcomes are dependent on the participation of others.

From traditional to collaborative governance 19

For it to be attempted, participants need to perceive a benefit or value in collaborating (Sowa, 2009). The realisation of common purpose and interdependency is a catalyst to initiate collaborative governance (Emerson et al., 2012), where an organisation can work together to achieve more than what can be achieved independently. It is an alternative when adversarial approaches are ineffective, leading to efforts to experiment with collaborative governance. Collaborative governance is not about contracting out (agency): it is to achieve more than the sum of parts separately by working with others rather than against them. It therefore requires a shift from an agency perspective to stewardship perspective: "the goal is to transform adversarial relationships into more cooperative ones" (Ansell & Gash, 2008, p. 547).

Definition of collaborative governance

Definitions from the literature were gathered to identify common themes. Presented chronologically, Table 1.2 presents a sample of collaborative governance definitions found within the non-profit and public sector literature.

Table 1.2 Collaborative governance: some definitions

Author(s), year	Collaborative governance definitions
Gray, 1989	"a process through which parties who see different aspects of a problem can constructively explore their differences and search for solutions that go beyond their own limited vision of what is possible" (p. 5)
Huxham, 2000	"all forms of, and labels for, governance that involves people in working relationships with those in other organizations" (p. 339)
Ansell and Gash, 2008	"a governing arrangement where one or more public agencies directly engage non-state stakeholders in a collective decision-making process that is formal, consensus-oriented, and deliberative and that aims to make or implement public policy or manage public programs or assets" (p. 544) (definition within a public administration context)
Ansell, 2012	"a strategy used in planning, regulation, policy making, and public management to coordinate, adjudicate, and integrate the goals and interests of multiple stakeholders" (p. 498)
Emerson et al., 2012	"the processes and structures of public policy decision making and management that engage people constructively across the boundaries of public agencies, levels of government, and/or the public, private and civic spheres in order to carry out a public purpose that could not otherwise be accomplished" (p. 2)
Purdy, 2012	"processes that seek to share power in decision making with stakeholders in order to develop shared recommendations for effective, lasting solutions to public problems" (p. 409) (definition within a public administration context)
Cornforth Hayes and Vangen, 2015	"formalized, joint-working arrangements between organizations that remain legally autonomous while engaging in ongoing, coordinated collective action to achieve outcomes that none of them could achieve on their own" (p. 777)
Wodchis et al., 2019	"an approach to governance in areas where organizations need to work closely together in order to achieve their goals" (p. 56)

20   *Marc Pilon and François Brouard*

Based on the definitions in Table 1.2, three themes of collaborative governance are found in a majority of the definitions. The themes that emerge from the definitions above are that collaborative governance is (1) about engagement with stakeholders, (2) for collective decision-making through shared power and (3) to solve problems.

System and process

Collaborative governance unfolds within a governance system. Collaborative governance is a form of governance that is cross-boundary; in other words, it exists at the intersection of inter-organisational governance. Collaborative initiatives may also be called partnerships or networks (Cornforth et al., 2015).

Unlike distinct internal or external governance mechanisms, collaborative governance mechanisms straddle organisational boundaries and are an important (yet often overlooked) part of a governance system. A diverse range of governance mechanisms need to work together for a governance system to function properly. Like the mechanisms of a watch, no single component makes the system work, but rather, all pieces work together.

In all collaborative situations, the social aspect of people gathering is central to the endeavour. Collaborative governance is a mode of governance that "brings multiple stakeholders together in common forums [...] to engage in consensus-oriented decision making" (Ansell & Gash, 2008, p. 543). It is joint action (in conjunction with others) to solve complex problems. Stakeholders in a collaborative endeavour may be called participants, members, parties, partners or collaborators. From here out, the term participant will be used.

The collaborative process is iterative or cyclical (Ansell & Gash, 2008; Emerson et al., 2012), as the participants build trust, dialogue their needs, negotiate alternatives and a path to problem solving, in different orders at different intervals and to varying degrees of effort and success. Per Shergold (2008), collaboration goes beyond coordination, which is the process of informing others ex-post of decisions made, and cooperation, which is the process of sharing ideas and resources for mutual benefit. Collaboration is a shared creation.

It may be important to note that collaborative governance is not the governance of each individual organisations but the governance of the collaboration (Shaw et al., 2019).

Ingredients of collaborative governance

For collaboration to be effective several ingredients are necessary. We use the term ingredients to describe the conditions or dimensions under which one can expect collaborative governance to function. These common ingredients include joint purpose and motivation, trusting relationship, leadership and engagement, power balance and sharing, engaging forum, resources and capacity. Each of these ingredients is discussed next.

From traditional to collaborative governance   21

The historical context of the collaboration may have an impact on the collaborative governance (Shaw et al., 2019). Previous organisational relationships and individuals' personal relationships may accelerate or constrain the collaboration. Positive relationships may enable the collaboration, while negative ones may set back the collaboration on a more difficult track. Recognition of the history is a step to assess the situation.

Joint purpose and motivation

For collaborative governance to work, there has to be mutual benefit and shared goals (Emerson et al., 2012). The purpose is also the primary governance principle (ISO 37000:2021). There needs to be a common agreed upon purpose or objective. Any lack of clarity can frustrate participants and put at risk intended results. Two dimensions of the joint purpose could be raised, namely shared understanding and shared interest (Shaw et al., 2019).

A shared understanding is important regarding the overall purpose. However, the joint purpose is composed of many sub-goals which may also have to have a common understanding. Small steps and interim goals may be useful to solidify the collaborative relationship and to help in building a strong relationship. Participants need to have shared interest in achieving the collaboration. Without a clear interest for each participant, disengagement may happen sooner than later.

Shared motivation and incentives to participate are other key ingredients. Without motivation of the organisations and each leadership team, the collaboration will suffer, and commitment may disappear. The benefits need to be explicit for each participant. It is not only the motivation at the beginning of the collaboration, but also over its existence. Incentives could be "either internal (problems, resource needs, interests, or opportunities) or external (situational or institutional crises, threats, opportunities)" (Emerson et al., 2012, p. 9).

Interdependency

Recognition of interdependency is required. In an interconnected world, collaborative governance might be seen as an effective way or even the only way to address complex social problems. Therefore, it is a perception or realisation of interdependency that fosters a desire to participate (Ansell & Gash, 2008). Complexity of issues, for example regarding poverty or health care, is difficult to tackle by a single stakeholder. Collaboration may be a way to increase the chance in solving some problems or at least going in the right direction. A challenge of collaboration is the uncertainty around it, and collaboration may be a way to manage risks in achieving a purpose (Emerson et al., 2012).

Trusting relationship

Mutual trust is an important ingredient to collaborative governance. Collaborative governance requires mutual accountability, which is only possible through trust (Jing & Hu, 2017). Trust is a relational resource. If missing, it is a trust deficit or liability for which the participants need to rebuild for effective collaborative governance. The starting point of trust between participants "can either facilitate or discourage cooperation among stakeholders" (Ansell & Gash, 2008, p. 550). Whereas a history of cooperation will foster trust, a history of conflict will make trust harder to achieve (Ansell & Gash, 2008).

Trust can be damaged from changes in leadership, personality differences, poor prior outcomes, unfavourable changes to policy directives, miscommunications, lack of resources to carry out collaborative activities and many other negative factors. As such, the nurturing process must be continuous and permanent (Huxman & Vangen, 2008). If a participant is involved in collaboration for only vested (personal) interests rather than mutual benefit, the endeavour is less likely to succeed if hidden agendas are identified by the other participants, resulting in a loss of trust. As conflicts are inhibitors of collaborative governance, any aggressive participant will lead to distrust. Therefore, commitment on the process and in building trust is important (Shaw et al., 2019).

Leadership, engagement and commitment

Leadership, engagement and commitment to the collaboration is an "essential driver" (Emerson et al., 2012, p. 9). An identified leader should be present and committed. Leadership acts to make sure resources and capacity are allocated, acts fairly to the benefits of the collaborative relationship and all participants, and may assume the transaction costs when starting the collaboration (Emerson et al., 2012). Leadership could be pre-determined from the start or emerging organically (Shaw et al., 2019). The persons assuming the leadership of the collaboration should have enough power to be able to make decisions for the collaborative relationship.

Power balance and sharing

Collaborative governance only works among perceived partners, or when otherwise upward stakeholders share their power in the decision-making, as "traditional hierarchies do not exist in collaborative settings" (Huxman & Vangen, 2008, p. 39). Power is a resource that must be shared, so that the decision-making is made by the participants as a whole (Purdy, 2012). Therefore, participants who have authority must transfer or share their power for the collaborative endeavour to function (Purdy, 2012). Collaborative governance provides the opportunity for participants to dialogue and negotiate without one participant imposing their vision. All participants build knowledge and gain a better understanding of the complex problems and explore (together) ways of improving processes and achieving the collaborative objectives without coercion. Power imbalances may result in co-optation or coercion by the more powerful participants, resulting in a less effective, or altogether ineffective, collaboration process (Purdy, 2012).

Engaging forum

Collaborative governance brings stakeholders together in a collective forum to engage in consensus decision-making (Ansell & Gash, 2008). Specific mechanisms could be used for that purpose as discussed in the following Section, "Collaborative governance mechanisms". Collaborative governance goes beyond consultation, as it implies a two-way (or multiple-way) communication and the opportunity for participants to listen to each other, learn from each other and understand other participants' needs and constraints. Collaborative governance requires engagement through dialogue (Emerson et al., 2012). Constructive dialogue also helps to sustain trust and rectify any confusion or lack of clarity.

Resources and capacity

Collaborative governance requires the pooling of resources, as value of collaborative governance is derived from the resources that each participant provides to the endeavour. The resources need not be equal, but strategic in terms of each participant's unique situation. The resources may include financial funds, people and their time, technology and knowledge. Knowledge can be seen as the currency of collaboration (Emerson et al., 2012), whereas when knowledge is shared between participants, it facilitates problem solving that could not have been achieved independently.

The collaboration may bring a new capacity by combining "four necessary elements: procedural and institutional arrangements, leadership, knowledge, and resources" (Emerson et al., 2012, p. 14). A joint capacity is created which may not have been possible without the collaborative relationship.

Other ingredients

Other 'ingredients' for successful collaborative governance exist at the individual level – e.g. facilitative leadership (Ansell & Gash, 2008; Emerson et al., 2012), but these constructs are out of scope for this organisational level analysis.

In addition to the ingredients above, to be successful, collaborative governance needs to regenerate itself over time by redefining its purpose and reengaging with participants as a result of changing environments (Cornforth et al., 2015).

Collaborative governance mechanisms

The process of collaborative governance "involves respecting the circumstances in which collaboration takes place, committing to face-to-face meetings to establish trust, and respecting a process that all parties agree upon for making collaborative decisions. By responding to a series of questions informed by collaborative governance, organizations can orient their governance activities in a more collaborative way for more integrated care" (Wodchis et al., 2019, p. 56).

24 *Marc Pilon and François Brouard*

Collaborative process, policies and rules may be integrated in regular internal and external governance mechanisms. While not exhaustive, examples of collaborative governance mechanisms include:

- Clear and documented processes
- Regular meetings
- Joint committees
- Community advisory councils
- External and independent advisors
- Umbrella groups or working groups
- Limited companies or partnerships
- Multi-stakeholder joint roundtables
- Learning and continuous improvement procedures

Therefore, collaborative governance mechanisms are the actions taken to bring together the various stakeholders and advance the joining endeavour. By fostering the ingredients, an organisation will benefit from collaborative governance and contribute to the desired outcomes (Calò et al., 2024). By changing the dynamics from competition to collaboration, this may improve organisational legitimacy and the overall service delivery.

Barriers of collaborative governance

While collaborative governance offers many advantages, it is not without its drawbacks. The drawbacks include high transaction costs, a fragmentation of accountability and a loss of autonomy (Brandsen & Johnston, 2018; Jing & Hu, 2017; Purdy, 2012).

High transaction costs

Setting up and maintaining a collaboration can require more effort than advancing projects independently (Brandsen & Johnston, 2018). Success is dependent on other participants following through on their commitments (no freeloaders), and like other investments, it is done without the certainty of benefit. Moreover, collaborations require lots of work because of its complexity, and burnouts among its members can happen.

Fragmentation of accountability

Collaborative governance blurs the lines of organisational accountability. The more there are participants and the more the solutions (and resulting outcomes) are integrated among the organisations, the more responsibility is diffused. Ill-defined responsibility can make it difficult to hold participants accountable and result in accountability ambiguity (Brandsen & Johnston, 2018). Specific accountability needs to be established for collaborative governance to be effective.

Loss of autonomy

For collaborative governance to work, decisions need to be made in conjunction with the participants involved. Collaborative governance is not a 'winner-take-all'. Rather, the consensus required could be exhausting to participants as it requires a win-win process. This results in organisations being evermore dependent on others.

In addition, in instances of abuse of trust, some participants may self-servingly scheme to use collaborative governance improperly as a means to grow power over collaborators (Purdy, 2012). Therefore, collaborative governance is not costless.

Collaborative governance is also not for every situation. For example, it would likely not be the appropriate in situations that require quick decision-making or rapid implementation. Building a relationship is a long-term endeavour that takes time.

Collaborative governance mechanisms framework

By expanding on the collaborative governance mechanisms circle presented in Figure 1.1, Figure 1.2 summarises a collaborative governance mechanisms framework with examples of governance mechanisms, some ingredients and some barriers.

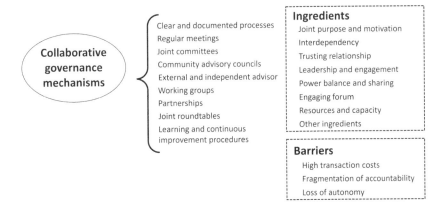

Figure 1.2 Collaborative governance system

Conclusion

The literature argues that collaborative governance is generally worth the effort and corresponding risk because the whole of what can be achieved together is greater than what can be achieved independently. However, the adoption of collaborative governance requires a change in culture and training for organisational leaders working to achieve their organisation's objectives when it is interdependent with others.

Collaboration and collaborative governance offer an opportunity to extend the governance to multiple stakeholders aiming to achieve a common objective or purpose. Some ingredients are necessary to achieve a success.

Some go so far as to argue "that unless potential for real collaborative advantage is clear, it is generally best, if there is a choice, to avoid collaboration" (Huxman & Vangen, 2008, p. 42). Therefore, in order to achieve its full potential, entering into collaborative governance should not be taken lightly. Ingredients such as joint purpose, mutual trust, engaging forum, power sharing and heterogeneous resources are important conditions of successful collaborative endeavours.

References

Agle, B. R., Donaldson, T., Freeman, R. E., Jensen, M. C., Mitchell, R. K., & Wood, D. J. (2008). Dialogue: Toward superior stakeholder theory. *Business Ethics Quarterly*, *18*(2), 153–190. https://doi.org/10.5840/beq200818214

Albrecht, K. (2000). *Corporate radar – Tracking the forces that are shaping your business*. AMACOM – American Management Association.

Ansell, C. (2012). Collaborative governance. In D. Levi-Faur & D. Levi-Faur (Eds.), *The Oxford handbook of governance* (pp. 498–511). Oxford University Press.

Ansell, C., & Gash, A. (2008). Collaborative governance in theory and practice. *Journal of Public Administration Research and Theory*, *18*(4), 543–571. https://doi.org/10.1093/jopart/mum032

Brandsen, T., & Johnston, K. (2018). Collaborative governance and the third sector: Something old, something new. In E. Ongaro & S. van Thiel (Eds.), *The Palgrave handbook of public administration and management in Europe* (pp. 311–325). Macmillan.

Brouard, F. (2004). *Développement d'un outil diagnostique des pratiques existantes de la veille stratégique auprès des PME*, DBA dissertation, Université du Québec à Trois-Rivières.

Brouard, F., & Pilon, M. (2020). Financial accountability and reporting of foundations in Canada. In P. R. Elson, S. A. Lefevre, & J.-M. Fontan (Eds.), *Philanthropic foundations in Canada – Landscapes, indigenous perspectives and pathways to change* (pp. 54–82, chapter 3). Alliance Publishing Trust.

Calò, F., Teasdale, S., Roy, M. J., Bellazzecca, E., & Mazzei, M. (2024). Exploring collaborative governance processes involving nonprofits. *Nonprofit and Voluntary Sector Quarterly*, *53*(1), 54–78. https://doi.org/10.1177/08997640231155817

Cornforth, C., Hayes, J., & Vangen, S. (2015). Nonprofit-public collaborations: Understanding governance dynamics. *Nonprofit and Voluntary Sector Quarterly*, *44*(4), 775–795. https://doi.org/10.1177/0899764014532836

Emerson, K., Nabatchi, T., & Balogh, S. (2012). An integrative framework for collaborative governance. *Journal of Public Administration Research and Theory*, *22*(1), 1–29. https://doi.org/10.1093/jopart/mur011

Fahey, L., & Narayanan, V. K. (1986). *Macroenvironmental analysis for strategic management*. West.

Fassin, Y. (2009). The stakeholder model refined. *Journal of Business Ethics*, *84*(1), 113–135. https://doi.org/10.1007/s10551-008-9677-4

Gray, B. (1989). *Collaborating: Finding common ground for multiparty problems*. Josssey-Bass.

Hurth, V. (2021). *ISO 37000:2021 – Governance of organizations – Notes accompanying 'in conversation' session*. International Organization for Standardization (ISO), ISO Technical Committee 309, December 15.

Huxham, C. (2000). The challenge of collaborative governance. *Public Management: An International Journal of Research and Theory*, *2*(3), 337–357. https://doi.org/10.1080/14719030000000021

Huxman, C., & Vangen, S. (2008). Doing things collaboratively: Realizing the advantage or succumbing to inertia? In J. O'Flynn & J. Wanna (Eds.), *Collaborative governance: A new era of public policy in Australia?* (pp. 29–44). ANU E Press.

ISO. (2021). *ISO 37000:2021 – Governance of organizations – Guidance*. International Organization for Standardization (ISO), ISO Technical Committee 309.

Jing, Y., & Hu, Y. (2017). From service contracting to collaborative governance: Evolution of government-nonprofit relations. *Public Administration and Development*, *37*(3), 191–202. https://doi.org/10.1002/pad.1797

Kulieshova, N. V. (2014). Factor model of the significant factors in the macro environment of tourism enterprises. *Problems of Economy*, *3*, 246–254.

Miller, D., & Friesen, P. H. (1983). Strategy making and environment: The third link. *Strategic Management Journal*, *4*(3), 221–235. https://doi.org/10.1002/smj.4250040304

Mitchell, R. K., Agle, B. R., & Wood, D. J. (1997). Toward a theory of stakeholder identification and salience: Defining the principle of who and what really counts. *Academy of Management Review*, *22*(4), 853–886. https://doi.org/10.5465/amr.1997.9711022105

Mitchell, R. K., Van Buren, H. J., Greenwood, M., & Freeman, R. E. (2015). Stakeholder inclusion and accounting for stakeholders. *Journal of Management Studies*, *52*(7), 851–877. https://doi.org/10.1111/joms.12151

Mitroff, I. I., & Linstone, H. A. (1993). *The unbounded mind – Breaking the chains of traditional business thinking*. Oxford University Press.

Pilon, M. (2019). *Accountability in Ontario's Health Care System: The Role of Governance and Information in Managing Stakeholder Demands*, PhD dissertation, Carleton University.

Pilon, M., & Brouard, F. (2023). Conceptualizing accountability as an integrated system or relationships, governance, and information. *Financial Accountability & Management*, *39*(2), 421–446. https://doi.org/10.1111/faam.12323

Purdy, J. M. (2012). A framework for assessing power in collaborative governance processes. *Public Administration Review*, *72*(3), 409–417. https://doi.org/10.1111/j.1540-6210.2011.02525.x

Quattrone, P. (2022). Seeking transparency makes one blind: How to rethink disclosure, account for nature and make corporations sustainable. *Accounting, Auditing & Accountability Journal*, *35*(2), 547–566. https://doi.org/10.1108/AAAJ-04-2021-5233

Shaw, J., Gordon, D., Baker, G. R., Wodchis, W. P., Steele Gray, C., & Kuluski, K. (2019). How can patient and caregiver needs be met by collaborative governance. In W. P. Wodchis, G. R. Baker, K. Kuluski, J. Shaw, & C. Steele Gray (Eds.),

28 Marc Pilon and François Brouard

How can we implement integrated care? Practice guide series. Health System Performance Research Network (HSPN).

Shergold, P. (2008). Governing through collaboration. In J. O'Flynn & J. Wanna (Eds.), *Collaborative governance: A new era of public policy in Australia?* (pp. 13–22). ANU E Press.

Sowa, J. (2009). The collaborative decision in nonprofit organizations. *Nonprofit and Voluntary Sector Quarterly, 38*(6), 1003–1025. https://doi.org/10.1177/0899764008325247

Stamp, E. (1980). *Corporate reporting: Its future evolution.* Canadian Institute of Chartered Accountants.

Wodchis, W. P., Baker, G. R., Kuluski, K., Shaw, J., & Steele Gray, C. (2019). *How can we implement integrated care? Practice guide series.* Health System Performance Research Network (HSPRN).

2 Implementing and maintaining an effective risk management system in non-profit organisations

A conceptual framework

Elisabeth Bertin

Introduction

Non-profit organisations (NPOs) face a variety of internal and external risks that can affect their ability to achieve their mission. According to ISO 37000:2021, the governing body should consider the impact of uncertainty on the organisation's purpose and results, and be accountable for the organisation's ongoing risk identification and response. The governance of NPOs should therefore be supported by appropriate frameworks, effective methods and tools for monitoring, analysing and managing risk.

Risk management has been widely discussed and studied for several decades, both in academic literature and in practice. Recent developments in this area have advocated a shift from a "silo" approach to a holistic, integrated approach to risk management ("enterprise risk management" or ERM). By definition, the silo approach develops an individualised and fragmented management of the organisation's key risks. Managers limit themselves to what is directly within their decision-making scope. In other words, they do not and cannot have a real understanding of the impact of each of these risks on the overall risk. On the contrary, by taking a holistic and integrated approach, an ERM framework ensures that each type of risk and opportunity does not receive excessive attention and resources, to the detriment of other risks and opportunities that are less well understood or not identified (Fraser & Simkins, 2016).

While ERM has become very popular in large corporations over the last two decades and is now considered a major paradigm of good corporate governance (Anton & Nucu, 2020), few authors have focused on the conditions, modalities and effects of its implementation in NPOs.

However such an approach is of considerable interest for this type of entity. NPOs differ from for-profit organisations in several ways. They are not driven by profit but by commitment to a particular cause. They have no shareholders, but rather a multiplicity and diversity of stakeholders, and a strong financial dependence on funders whose expectations differ from those of investors in the for-profit sector. These characteristics create specific risks, that if not managed,

DOI: 10.4324/9781003460572-4

30   *Elisabeth Bertin*

can damage the organisation's reputation and the trust of funders and beneficiaries. In addition, many experts[1] believe that the pandemic highlighted the extent to which the NPO sector was ill-prepared for a chaotic event of such magnitude, due to the absence or weakness of ERM programmes.

The aim of this chapter is to explore the extent to which the holistic and integrated approach to risk management can be implemented in NPOs and to propose an innovative conceptual framework for risk management in such organisations, which could be used as a guide by professionals wishing to establish or maintain an effective risk management system.

First, we consider ERM as a lever for creating societal value. The use of the terms "social value creation" and "societal value creation" can vary according to context, language and discipline, and it is not uncommon for them to be used interchangeably. Social value creation focuses more on aspects related to individuals and groups, while societal value creation is more global and focuses on society as a whole. We believe that the concept of societal value is more appropriate for NPOs. We then analyse the difficulties NPOs face in implementing a risk management system. Based on these findings, we develop a conceptual framework for an effective risk management system in NPOs. Our non-profit risk management diamond (NP-RM Diamond) takes into account both the relevant features of the ERM model and the management characteristics of NPOs. It should enable staff and volunteers to raise relevant issues and engage in a process of continuous improvement in risk management.

Enterprise risk management: A lever for creating societal value?

By their very nature, the ultimate goal of NPOs is not to create economic value, but to create societal value. Societal value creation is understood as the improvement of societal dimensions, namely social, environmental and governance issues (Davies & Doherty, 2019). It involves making a positive contribution to the well-being of individuals, the environment and the community. It can include actions such as sustainable development, organisational social responsibility (OSR), social innovation, etc. So, unlike businesses, NPOs do not consider societal value as a support to economic value, but as an end in itself. The aim of this section is to explore how ERM can be seen as a lever for creating societal value. After pointing out that ERM and its underlying principles are designed to take into account the interests of all stakeholders and to create societal value, we will look at the findings of research on value creation through ERM.

Enterprise risk management: A holistic approach designed to create societal value

ERM is an integrated and coordinated approach to the management of all significant events that could have a negative (downside risks) or a positive (upside

Implementing and maintaining an effective risk management system 31

risks or opportunities) impact on the organisation. ERM thus provides reasonable assurance that the organisation's objectives will be achieved. The consistency of risk management with the definition of the organisation's objectives is therefore crucial. ERM makes it possible to identify which risks should be avoided or reduced and which should be maintained or even increased. The portfolio view of all risks enables an understanding of the interdependencies and correlations between different risks, and is said to be more effective than fragmented (or "silo") risk management. Indeed, it is widely accepted that ERM has its origins in modern portfolio theory (Markowitz, 1952), which is based on the assumption that the effect of individual risks is greater than the effect of total portfolio risk.

ERM is more than just the processes and methods by which organisations identify events (risks and opportunities), assess them, determine a response and monitor the effectiveness of the decisions made about them. Above all, it is a coordinated, enterprise-wide process. The impetus and requirements for ERM come from the highest level of the organisation. Management is responsible for the design and implementation of the ERM approach. The governance body, i.e. the Board of Directors, understands and approves the ERM system and monitors the identified risks to ensure that the measures taken by management and risk owners are appropriate and meet the objective of creating value for all stakeholders. ERM therefore requires the commitment of all employees at all levels of the organisation.

To help organisations and individuals adopt and implement this approach systematically and effectively, several best practice guides have been published over the last 20 years. The most widely known are:

- A *Risk Management Standard* from the Institute of Risk Management (2002)
- The *ERM Framework* (COSO, 2004) and the *Enterprise Risk Management – Integrated Framework* (COSO, 2017) from the Committee Of Sponsoring Organisation of the Treadway Commission (COSO)
- ISO 31000:2018: *Risk Management Principles and Guidelines*

COSO's recent publications of guidance on applying its model to complex risks (such as environmental, social and governance risks, cybersecurity and artificial intelligence risks) demonstrate its ability to take contemporary societal issues into account.

Whichever framework we choose, the ERM approach has five essential components:

- An enabling context, particularly in terms of the organisation's culture and governance
- The integration of risk into strategic analysis and decision-making
- A rigorous methodology for identifying, assessing and managing risks

32 *Elisabeth Bertin*

- A formalised monitoring of the effectiveness of risk management and a continuous improvement mechanism
- A system of top-down, bottom-up and cross-functional information and communication, both internally and with stakeholders

The latest version of COSO emphasises the need to integrate the approach into the DNA of the organisation. The degree of this integration will vary depending on a number of factors, including the organisation's size, culture, implementation processes, operating models and external environment.

COSO's definition of ERM places a strong emphasis on value creation: "it is the culture, capabilities, and practices that organisations integrate with strategy-setting and apply when they carry out that strategy, with a purpose of managing risk in creating, preserving and realising value".

In this way, ERM leads to a better understanding of risk and greater transparency to external stakeholders (Liebenberg & Hoyt, 2003). Because ERM is a holistic approach, this encompasses all of an organisation's objectives, functions and activities and promotes alignment between risk, strategy and performance, it addresses all of the downside and upside risks that the organisation is likely to face. Its purpose is to create value for stakeholders and society as a whole.

Promising empirical evidence, but an underdeveloped area of research

In the academic literature, we will examine the extent to which the creation of societal value is one of the motivations for implementing ERM, and whether this approach actually contributes to the creation of societal value. We will also look at some very recent and promising work exploring the link between ERM and organisational social responsibility (OSR, including for for-profits, that is corporate social responsibility, CSR).

The vast majority of research that has attempted to examine the factors that influence the implementation and degree of maturity of ERM has focused on private sector companies. Although NPOs differ from enterprises in many ways, understanding the findings of this research is useful for identifying the determinants and potential effects of ERM implementation. In particular, they highlight the critical nature of organisational size (Beasley et al., 2005, 2015; Paape & Spekle, 2012; Pagach & Warr, 2011), industry sector (Beasley et al., 2005), financial leverage (e.g. Golshan & Rasid, 2012; Liebenberg & Hoyt, 2003; Pagach & Warr, 2011), governance characteristics (Beasley et al., 2005; Gates, 2006; Golshan & Rasid, 2012), the presence of institutional investors (e.g. Golshan & Rasid, 2012; Liebenberg & Hoyt, 2003; Paape & Spekle, 2012), the existence of a risk management policy, a risk committee and the publication of risk reports (Beasley et al., 2015; Kleffner et al., 2003).

Chen et al. (2019) conducted a research project in the non-profit sector, which confirms the findings of corporate studies, according to which structural and organisational factors (i.e. the existence of a risk committee, a risk management policy statement and a risk manager) influence the level of ERM maturity.

Lu et al. (2022) show that the best performing companies in terms of CSR are more inclined to adopt the ERM approach. Companies that choose to implement ERM therefore have expectations in terms of social and societal value creation.

Regarding the impact of ERM implementation, a large body of research demonstrates the influence of ERM on the performance and creation of financial and stock market value of private sector companies. Researchers highlight the crucial role played by the level of maturity of ERM, which is linked to the development of a risk culture within the organisation (Farrell & Gallagher, 2014), the presence of a chief risk officer (Beasley et al., 2008) or a risk committee (Florio & Leoni, 2017), the reporting level of the entity responsible for ERM (Grace et al., 2015) or the risk manager (Aebi et al., 2012), the degree of stakeholder involvement (Silva De Souza et al., 2012). The risk portfolio approach generates cost savings (Eckles et al., 2014). However, several authors (Li et al., 2014; McShane et al., 2011; Quon et al., 2012) have not demonstrated an increase in firm performance following the implementation of ERM. Gordon et al. (2009) show that the relationship between ERM and corporate financial performance depends on the fit between ERM and the following five factors that affect a firm: environmental uncertainty, industry competition, firm size, firm complexity and board control. The implication of these findings is that organisations should consider the implementation of an ERM system in conjunction with the contextual variables surrounding them.

Some researchers, arguing that stock market and financial performance are simplistic measures of the value created by an ERM approach, have introduced the notions of efficiency, flexibility and strategic value. They seek to demonstrate the extent to which the adoption and use of ERM can increase the efficiency and the flexibility of an organisation, or improve strategic decision making. For example, Al-Amri and Davydov (2016) showed that ERM reduced both the frequency and severity of operational risks. Arnold et al. (2011) demonstrated that implementing a strategic approach to ERM facilitated compliance with new regulations, due to the organisational flexibility it creates. According to the same authors (2015), a strategic approach to ERM also strengthens the relationship between flexibility and firm performance. The results also provide evidence that strong information systems integration is the mechanism through which ERM enhances strategic flexibility. Viscelli et al. (2017) find that even when the decision to adopt ERM is driven by strategic reasons, the integration of ERM and strategy is limited, due to issues related to culture, lack of training and insufficient ERM leadership. According to Meidell and Kaarbøe (2017), the ERM function is an organisational change agent, in that it informs and influences decision-making, over time, by promoting new ideas related to new risk management technologies to management and disseminating new knowledge to other departments while ensuring that it is integrated into their processes.

Furthermore, if being socially responsible means anticipating future stakeholder requirements in order to minimise the risk of not being able to meet future demands, having an effective ERM system is crucial for strengthening responsible interaction with stakeholders (Frederiksen, 2018). The findings of Pérez-Cornejo and Quevedo-Puente (2023) highlight that the quality of the ERM system has a positive impact on corporate reputation through the mediating effect of CSR performance. They conclude that companies should therefore use ERM to strengthen both their CSR and their reputation. In line with the work of Bundy et al. (2017), they show that high-quality ERM programmes reduce the likelihood of companies experiencing a loss of reputation following a severe crisis. The existence of such systems reinforces stakeholders' perceptions that the company has behaved responsibly towards them, thus eliminating blame when a negative event occurs. Naseem et al. (2020) also show that CSR is linked to risk management. But they reveal that ERM plays a partial mediating role in the relationship between CSR and firm performance. The active engagement of companies in CSR activities leads them to take into account the interests of all stakeholders, thus supporting ERM, which also takes into account the risks associated with all stakeholders (Boatright, 2011).

Most of the research analysing the link between ERM and value creation focuses on companies. They point to many positive effects, but sometimes come to different conclusions. This is partly due to the highly complex link between two multidimensional concepts and partly to the nature of the variables included in the models. They do not take into account all the components of an ERM system. And the creation of societal value is only considered in a very indirect way.

Nevertheless, the research that explores the link between ERM, CSR and reputation, and highlights the crucial role of ERM, is promising. It encourages us to continue our reflections on the adoption of ERM in NPOs, that have a societal purpose, and for which reputational risk is paramount.

NPOs deserve special attention because their managerial specificities can make the implementation of risk management difficult.

The delicate implementation of risk management in NPOs

In order to secure ongoing stakeholder support, NPOs need to demonstrate their ability to achieve goals and objectives that are aligned with stakeholder values. To this end, Power (2007) highlights the important role of mature risk management practices: risk management is no longer the preserve of experts, but is increasingly certifiable and visible because of its role in developing organisational virtue and legitimacy. Failure to manage risk can be perceived by stakeholders as a sign of failure to achieve goals and objectives, which can have a negative impact on the social legitimacy of NPOs and on their funding (Kummer et al., 2014). It has become necessary for NPOs to adopt more professional risk management behaviour (Maier et al., 2016). However, NPOs can face difficulties when it comes to adopting ERM (Power, 2009), and more generally risk management, especially adopting the famous Three Lines Model. Organisational culture then plays an essential role in the implementation of risk management.

Difficulties in applying the three lines model

The actors who participate in the process of creating societal value through NPOs may be different from those who capture that value. Driven by a variety of motivations that may be economic, strategic or symbolic, donors provide funds to NPOs to enable them to fulfil their societal missions, and beneficiaries benefit from the activities carried out by NPOs without paying for them. NPOs thus serve different stakeholders with multiple, variable and even conflicting interests. These stakeholders entrust oversight of their organisation to a governing body, which in turn delegates resources and authority to management to take appropriate action, including risk management. NPOs provide an indirect link between donors and beneficiaries, communicating with the latter about the societal impact of the activities they support.

In this context, these organisations need effective structures and processes to help them achieve their objectives, while strengthening their governance and risk management systems.

The Three Lines of Defence model was developed by the Institute of Internal Auditors (IIA) in 2013, then updated and renamed the "Three Lines Model" in 2020 to provide organisations with a standardised approach to governance and risk management.

According to the IIA (2020), management's responsibility for achieving the organisation's objectives encompasses the roles of the first two lines of the model. The roles of the first line are more directly related to the provision of products and/or services to the organisation's customers, and include support functions. The second line includes activities that support risk management (management control, internal control, risk management, compliance, ethics, quality assurance, etc.). Some second-line functions may be assigned to specialists who provide additional expertise and support to first-line staff. However, risk management remains the prerogative of front-line functions and is a management responsibility.

Internal auditors, who are responsible for reviewing all risk management processes and procedures, and providing reasonable assurance on the effectiveness of governance, risk management and internal controls, form the third line of defence. It supports the previous two lines, but must be able to operate completely independently, take an objective view and report directly to a management body, board or audit committee.

Together, all these roles are expected to contribute to both creating and protecting value, provided they are aligned with each other and with expectations of key stakeholders. Communication, cooperation and collaboration are essential to ensure the reliability, consistency and transparency of the information required for risk-based decision-making. Finally, the model is robust if the governance body provides independent oversight of the rigorous implementation of these three lines.

The way in which organisations apply the principles of the IIA to put in place appropriate structures and processes and to ensure risk management may vary from one organisation to another, depending on their needs and objectives.

However, many NPOs are small in size, and as a result, the second line is weak and the third line is often non-existent, reducing the level of protection against risk and failing to support the operational resilience of these entities. There is also an issue of risk management knowledge and skills. Risk management knowledge and skills are generally not recruitment criteria for staff and volunteers, except in cases where an internal audit function exists. Based on a survey of employees at different levels within an NPO, Ghani et al. (2019) investigated the impact of employees' understanding of the processes of risk identification, assessment, treatment and monitoring on their risk management knowledge. Their findings show that most employees feel they have insufficient knowledge of risk management. This is attributed to a lack of understanding of the above processes. In addition, boards of directors are not always independent and are not systematically made aware of good risk management practices, which compromises their oversight and therefore accountability role in this area. Based on a sample of over 200 NPOs, Arshad et al. (2016) demonstrate that the efficiency, commitment and leadership of the board are significantly related to the quality of risk disclosures. The lack of a specific guidance on risk management in NPOs may reduce the motivation of some board members in this regard.

The use of external experts – other than chartered accountants, external auditors and public evaluation and control bodies, which are not intended to help the organisation implement ERM – could compensate for the weakness of the second line and the absence of the third line. However, the financial resources of NPOs, especially those of modest size, are limited. Most come from donations and membership fees, and are subject to strict rules of good management. Given that a very large proportion of the funds raised through public appeals must be used to achieve the purpose, and given the reluctance of public authorities to fund NPOs, they would not in all cases enable such experts to be paid.

Provided they have sufficient resources, NPOs appealing to the public's generosity will prefer to voluntarily submit to the controls of an accreditation body, in order to provide the donors with the guarantees they are entitled to expect regarding the use of their donations. Unfortunately, the assessments carried out by these bodies do not focus specifically on the organisation's risk management, and even less on all the components of ERM.

Implementing and maintaining an effective risk management system 37

Furthermore, the establishment of formal structures may not be sufficient to embed risk management at all levels of the organisation (Beasley et al., 2015; Power, 2009; Sheedy & Griffin, 2018). This may be particularly the case for NPOs, which are likely to struggle to achieve organisation-wide buy-in for ERM practices.

The critical role of culture in the adoption and use of risk management

It is increasingly recognised in academic and professional literature that organisational culture, defined by O'Reilly and Chatman (1996, p. 160) as "a system of shared values and norms that define appropriate attitudes and behaviours for organisational members", plays a crucial role in risk management. John et al. (2016) and Sheedy and Griffin (2014, 2018) argue that organisational policies are limited in their ability to determine the behaviour of organisational members and that organisational culture plays a major role in shaping this behaviour.

The decision to implement ERM affects the entire organisation and involves significant organisational change (Paape & Spekle, 2012). Consequently, as a practice imported from the for-profit sector, ERM is likely to be more readily adopted and implemented by NPOs with a greater receptiveness and willingness to change.

Chen et al. (2019) investigated the relationship between NPO culture and the maturity of ERM practices. The results show that the organisational culture factors of "outcome orientation" and "innovation" are associated with ERM maturity in NPOs. Outcome-oriented cultures emphasise performance, results and action as important values (O'Reilly et al., 1991). The authors attest to the important role of organisational culture in the development of ERM practices in NPOs, and the crucial role of leaders in creating and nurturing such a culture. Furthermore, Chen et al. (2019) found that funding uncertainty has a negative impact on ERM maturity. Thus, external conditions may hinder the use of ERM practices by NPOs.

ERM requires a true "risk culture" to be consistently applied at different levels of the organisation (Bromiley et al., 2015). Organisational culture differs from risk culture in that it serves to create the conditions that can lead to a particular risk culture. Sheedy and Griffin (2014, p. 4) support this distinction by arguing that "risk culture is only one aspect of a broader organisational culture". Similarly, Ring et al. (2016, p. 367), while acknowledging the link between the two concepts, suggest that "risk culture is intrinsically part of the fabric of organisational culture, and its nature can be shaped by the organisational culture which a firm strives to adopt". Bui et al. (2018, p. 293) define risk culture as "shares values and beliefs held by a firm's employees (decision makers) toward risk-taking" and place decision-making at the centre of this culture. The term "risk culture" therefore refers neither to a comparative approach to the way risk

38 *Elisabeth Bertin*

is embedded in different cultures, nor to the simple valorisation of deliberate risk-taking, but rather to a way of understanding the world that involves a desire to anticipate (Peretti-Watel, 2005). One of the criteria for the effectiveness of a risk management system is the sharing of a risk culture by all employees of the organisation. This is a key element as it promotes the integration of risk management into the operational functioning of the organisation at the most granular level. Every manager must make it a permanent part of his or her job to identify risks, monitor them, inform his or her superiors and specialist functions and, where necessary, mitigate or control them.

It is clear that there are no empirical studies dealing specifically with risk culture in NPOs. However, the issues raised in research studies analysing the development and impact of risk culture in other types of organisations suggest that their findings may be transferable to NPOs. For example, Pan et al. (2017) suggest that the risk appetite of business leaders develops the risk culture of the organisation. This in turn determines the risk appetite in investment decisions (Li et al., 2013). The work of Osman and Lew (2021) highlights the role of the board and management in driving and formalising processes to embed the right culture in an organisation. The board is responsible for overseeing governance and guiding behaviour, while management is responsible for recruiting the right people, training them and raising their awareness to embed the risk culture. Their results also show the importance of risk culture in minimising risk and creating a shared set of values among employees. In addition, a risk culture serves as a driver for ethical behaviour and strategic decision. According to Sheedy and Griffin (2018), risk culture varies at the business unit, corporate and country levels. Those at the top of the hierarchy tend to have a more positive perception of risk culture than employees in general. A favourable risk culture, combined with effective risk structures, is likely to generate appropriate attitudes and behaviours towards risk.

The above developments suggest that culture can be used to gain wider and deeper acceptance of ERM practices among members of the NPO, and to overcome the difficulty associated with the fact that structural factors alone may not be sufficient to move NPOs towards more mature risk management practices.

The need for a specific risk management framework for NPOs

Given the fundamental differences between for-profit companies and NPOs, and the difficulties in implementing and using a risk management system in NPOs, a new analytical framework is needed that takes into account the management specificities of NPOs in order to help these organisations use this tool.

We propose to move from the ERM model to the NP-RM Diamond, in order to take into account the specific features of NPOs and to promote the appropriation of risk management by these organisations. This new model, adapted to NPOs,

Implementing and maintaining an effective risk management system 39

includes three possible implementation modes, in order to adapt to the diversity of NPOs.

From enterprise risk management (ERM) to the non-profit risk management diamond (NP-RM Diamond)

The above developments lead to the idea that the application and effectiveness of risk management in NPOs rests on the four essential and interdependent pillars shown in Figure 2.1.

The first pillar is *risk governance*. This concept aims to bridge the gap between organisational governance and risk management, highlighting the need for them to complement each other and, where necessary, to overcome their respective shortcomings (Stein et al., 2019). Risk governance refers to the existence of structures and interactions that support risk management and the circulation of information, to the necessary leadership of the governance body in risk management matters, and to the accountability of risk management to stakeholders. Drawing on both ISO 37000:2021 "Governance of organisations", which makes risk governance a facilitating principle of organisational

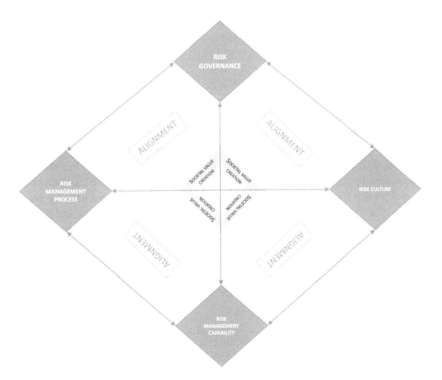

Figure 2.1 The NP-RM Diamond

40   *Elisabeth Bertin*

governance, and the COSO ERM framework, which considers governance as a fundamental component of an ERM system, we can affirm that the governance body of an NPO:

- Sets the tone for the approach to risk management, by developing, in a collaborative or participatory way, a risk management policy – or even charter
- Defines and drives the desired culture
- Defines, in a collaborative or participative way, the organisation of risk management – in particular the articulation between the lines of defence and the compensatory mechanisms put in place in the event of the absence or weakness of one or more lines
- Ensures the ability to manage risks
- Integrates risk analysis into its decision-making processes
- Monitors and understands the risk management activities carried out within the organisation
- Communicates transparently about the nature and extent of risks taken and about the resources and results of risk management, in relation to the creation of societal value

Risk governance is thus more collaborative and cognitive rather than disciplinary, which is consistent with the democratic and transparent governance that characterises NPOs.

The second pillar relates to *risk culture*. This is part of a larger whole, the organisational culture, which implies a necessary compatibility between them. An NPO's culture may vary from one organisation to another, depending on its mission, size, geographical region and membership base. However, it is generally characterised by a deep commitment to a cause or social mission, a strong sense of community and solidarity, and the participatory dimension to decision-making. Outcome orientation does not seem to be a problem, as NPO staff and volunteers are very sensitive to the notion of societal impact. The culture should also allow for innovation, openness to change and ambition, to foster the emergence of a true risk culture. The latter must permeate all activities and all employees. In other words, the link between downside and upside risk management and the fulfilment of the company's social mission must be obvious, to facilitate the implementation of the risk management policy and process.

The third pillar is the *risk management process*. This process, which is essential for all types of organisations, is the very essence of risk management. It consists of five stages:

- Identifying, assessing and prioritising opportunities or risks that may affect the achievement of the NPO's objectives, and in particular the fulfilment of its mission and the creation of societal value
- Selecting a response to manage these events and implementing an action plan

Implementing and maintaining an effective risk management system 41

- Evaluating the effectiveness of risk responses and monitoring of risks and opportunities
- Reporting on risks and opportunities, and on the effectiveness of their management
- Continuous improvement of the system

The fourth pillar is *risk management capacity*, which refers to the adequacy and sufficiency of human, financial, information and material resources, including technology, to implement the other pillars. Recruitment and training of staff and volunteers must take into account an additional criterion related to risk management, be it competence in the field or the ability to promote an appropriate culture. Funders and donors also need to be made aware of the benefits of risk management and accept that a proportion of the funds paid out should be used to implement the risk management system, which requires specific resources. The inclusion of risk management criteria in the frameworks used by certification bodies would help to raise awareness among NPOs of the benefits of adopting this approach.

The arrows in the figure indicate that the four pillars are interdependent, interactive and need to be aligned.

A contingent approach to risk management in NPOs

NPOs are diverse and varied, reflecting a wide range of factors that differentiate them from one another. While mission and scope determine the types of risks the organisation faces, size, complexity, funding model, number of members and level of volunteer involvement influence the organisation's ability to implement NP-RM.

The modalities for implementing NP-RM Diamond need to be adapted. Three levels of NP-RM Diamond integration can be distinguished:

- *Collaboration* is the minimum level of NP-RM integration. If NPOs are unable to implement certain lines and all or part of the process, they can turn to external third parties. In the absence of sufficient financial resources, NPOs can establish partnerships with universities offering risk management programmes, thus creating a "chain of engagement". They can also approach companies which, as part of their CSR policy, agree to allow an NPO to benefit free of charge from the risk management expertise of their staff. The third party(ies) will implement the steps in the risk management process that the organisation cannot. However, the system must be initiated, defined and overseen by the governance body, coordinated internally and be part of an emerging risk culture.
- *Incorporation* refers to the process of including a new practice, in this case risk management, into the day-to-day operations of the organisation. This practice

42 *Elisabeth Bertin*

is added to and works in synergy with existing activities. Every member or department of the organisation is involved in identifying, assessing and managing the risks that affect them. These risk management activities are part of their job. The system is initiated, defined and monitored by the governance body, and coordinated internally, possibly by a specific function.

- *Integration* characterises organisations that have succeeded in making risk management an inseparable part of the organisation's culture and DNA. Integration refers to the process of combining two or more things into one to create a cohesive and unified whole. Risk management is ingrained, so that it is practised, maintained and improved on an ongoing basis, without much effort. The organisation has a risk management or an internal control function and an internal audit department.

Table 2.1 does not necessarily represent a maturity model, which includes a sequence of levels that form an expected, desired and logical path from an initial state to maturity. Many risk management maturity models have been developed by practitioners and researchers. However, the reasoning behind them is not systematically applicable to NPOs. In fact, some features corresponding to the most advanced level, even if it is the one most in line with the COSO ERM model, will never be implemented in most NPOs, due to their size and limited financial resources. Instead, we propose a set of three possible scenarios

Table 2.1 Levels of NP-RM integration

	Collaboration	*Incorporation*	*Integration*
Risk governance	Risk governance is in place and functioning effectively, even if some structures/ functions/lines are outsourced	Risk governance is in place and functioning effectively. The internal audit function is outsourced to third parties	Risk governance is in place and functioning effectively. All risk-related functions are in-house
Risk culture	Risk culture is low or moderate	Risk culture is moderate or high	Risk culture is high
Risk management process	The risk management process is in place and functioning effectively, even if operations are outsourced	The risk management process is in place and functioning effectively on an ongoing basis. The internal audit is carried out periodically	The risk management process is in place and functioning effectively on an ongoing basis. Internal audit is a continuous process
Risk management capability	Risk management capability is low, dependent on third parties	Risk management capability is moderate or high	Risk management capability is high

for implementing the NP-RM Diamond in an NPO. The organisation is free to choose the configuration that best suits its size, risk culture and capability, and to consider whether or not to move to another model.

Conclusion

Everything in an organisation or its environment is in perpetual motion, and nothing is completely predictable. An increasingly uncertain environment, which poses a significant threat to the achievement of objectives, requires the implementation of an appropriate management approach. Risk management is therefore at the heart of the concerns not only of managers but also of stakeholders.

NPOs focus on achieving a social mission as their primary objective, which may lead them to perceive risk management as secondary (Lurtz & Kreutzer, 2017). In addition, the fact that ERM practices are imported from the for-profit sector may lead these organisations to fear a deviation from their welfare and altruistic orientation (Irvine et al., 2009). These concerns may hinder buy-in from across the entire organisation (Maier et al., 2016). However, such an approach to risk management contributes to the creation of societal value. What is needed is an appropriate framework.

The NP-RM Diamond model we propose takes into account the cultural and managerial specificities and diversity of NPOs and aims to provide them with essential guidelines for implementing effective risk management. Risk governance based on a cognitive and participative approach and a risk culture compatible with the NPO culture, i.e. outcome-oriented, focused primarily on societal impact, but also on innovation, openness to change and ambition, then appear as crucial elements for the implementation of a holistic and integrated risk management system in an NPO.

Our work highlights the need for further research and raises questions, such as: What are the key success factors and impacts of the adoption and appropriation of holistic and integrated risk management systems in NPOs? What kind of organisational measures should be taken in NPOs to facilitate the learning of tools in their instrumental and intellectual dimensions?

Note

1 "Pandemic Brought to Light Nonprofits' Lack of Enterprise Risk Management, Experts Say". *Board & Administrator: For Administrators Only.* September 2023, *40*(1), 3–4. https://doi.org/10.1002/ban.31579.

References

Aebi, V., Sabato, G., & Schmid, M. (2012). Risk management, corporate governance, and bank performance in the financial crisis. *Journal of Banking and Finance, 36*(12), 3213–3226. https://doi.org/10.1016/j.jbankfin.2011.10.020

44 Elisabeth Bertin

Al-Amri, K., & Davydov, Y. (2016). Testing the effectiveness of ERM: Evidence from operational losses. *Journal of Economics and Business, 87*(C), 70–82. https://doi.org/10.1016/j.jeconbus.2016.07.002

Anton, S. G., & Nucu, A. E. A. (2020). Enterprise risk management: A literature review and agenda for future research. *Journal of Risk Financial Management, 13*, 281. https://doi.org/10.3390/jrfm13110281

Arnold, V., Benford, T., Canada, J., & Sutton, S. G. (2011). The role of strategic enterprise risk management and organisational flexibility in easing new regulatory compliance. *International Journal of Accounting Information Systems, 12*(3), 171–188. https://doi.org/10.1016/j.accinf.2011.02.002

Arnold, V., Benford, T., Canada, J., & Sutton, S. G. (2015). Leveraging integrated information systems to enhance strategic flexibility and performance: The enabling role of enterprise risk management. *International Journal of Accounting Information Systems, 19*, 1–16. https://doi.org/10.1016/j.accinf.2015.10.001

Arshad, R., Bakar, N. A., & Othman, F. (2016). Board competencies, network ties and risk management disclosure practices in non-profit organisations. *Journal of Applied Business Research (JABR), 32*(5), 1319–1328. https://doi.org/10.19030/jabr.v32i5.9761

Beasley, M. S., Branson, B., & Pagach, D. (2015). An analysis of the maturity and strategic impact of investments in ERM. *Journal of Accounting and Public Policy, 34*, 219–243. https://doi.org/10.1016/j.jaccpubpol.2015.01.001

Beasley, M. S., Clune, R., & Hermanson, D. R. (2005). Enterprise risk management: An empirical analysis of factors associated with the extent of implementation. *Journal of Accounting and Public Policy, 24*(6), 521–531. https://doi.org/10.1016/j.jaccpubpol.2005.10.001

Beasley, M., Pagach, D., & Warr, D. (2008). Information conveyed in hiring announcements of senior executives overseeing enterprise-wide risk management processes. *Journal of Accounting, Auditing and Finance, 23*(3), 311–332. https://doi.org/10.1177/0148558X0802300303

Boatright, J. R. (2011). Risk management and the responsible corporation: How sweeping the invisible hand? *Business and Society Review, 116*(1), 145–170. https://doi.org/10.1111/j.1467-8594.2011.00380

Bromiley, P., McShane, M. K., Nair, A., & Rustambekov, E. (2015). Enterprise risk management: Review, critique, and research directions. *Long Range Planning, 48*(4), 265–276. https://doi.org/0.1016/j.lrp.2014.07.005

Bui, D. G., Fang, Y., & Lin, C. Y. (2018). The influence of risk culture on firm returns in times of crisis. *International Review of Economics & Finance, 57*, 291–306, September. https://doi.org/doi:10.1016/j.iref.2018.01.015

Bundy, J., Pfarrer, M. D., Short, C. E., & Coombs, W. T. (2017). Crises and crisis management integration, interpretation, and research development. *Journal of Management, 43*, 1661–1692. https://doi.org/10.1177/0149206316680030

Chen, J., Jiao, L., & Harrison, G. (2019). Organisational culture and enterprise risk management: The Australian not-for-profit context. *Australian Journal of Public Administration, 78*, 432–48. https://doi.org/10.1111/1467-8500.12382

COSO (2004). *Enterprise risk management: Integrated framework.* Committee of Sponsoring Organisations of the Treadway Commission.

COSO (2017). *Enterprise risk management: Integrating with strategy and performance.* The Committee of Sponsoring Organisations of the Treadway Commission. www.erm.coso.org

Davies, I. A., & Doherty, B. (2019). Balancing a hybrid business model: The search for equilibrium at Cafédirect. *Journal of Business Ethics, 157*, 1043–1066. https://doi.org/10.1007/s10551-018-3960-9

Implementing and maintaining an effective risk management system   45

Eckles, D. L., Hoyt, R. E., & Miller, S. M. (2014). The impact of enterprise risk management on the marginal cost of reducing risk: Evidence from the insurance industry. *Journal of Banking and Finance*, *43*, 247–261. https://doi.org/10.1016/j.jbankfin.2014.02.007

Farrell, M., & Gallagher, R. (2014). The valuation implications of enterprise risk management maturity. *The Journal of Risk and Insurance*, *82*(3), 625–657. https://doi.org/10.1111/jori.12035.

Florio, C., & Leoni, G. (2017). Enterprise risk management and firm performance: The Italian case. *British Accounting Review*, *49*, 56–74. https://doi.org/10.1016/j.bar.2016.08.003

Fraser, J. R. S., & Simkins, B. J. (2016). The challenges of and solutions for implementing enterprise risk management. *Business Horizons*, *59*, 689–698. https://doi.org/10.1016/j.bushor.2016.06.007

Frederiksen, T. (2018). Corporate social responsibility, risk and development in the mining industry. *Resources Policy*, *59*, 495–505. https://doi.org/10.1016/j.resourpol.2018.09.004

Gates, S. (2006). Incorporating strategic risk into enterprise risk management: A survey of current corporate practice. *Journal of Applied Corporate Finance*, *18*(4), 81–90. https://doi.org/10.1111/j.1745-6622.2006.00114.x

Ghani, E. K., Hassin, N. H. N., & Muhammad, K. (2019). Effect of employees' understanding on risk management process on risk: A case study in a non-profit organisation. *International Journal of Financial Research*, *10*(3), 144–152. https://doi.org/10.5430/ijfr.v10n3p144

Golshan, N. M., & Rasid, S. A. (2012). Determinants of enterprise risk management adoption: An empirical analysis of Malaysian public listed firms. *International Journal of Social and Human Sciences*, *6*, 119–126.

Gordon, L. A., Loeb, M. P., & Tseng, C. (2009). Enterprise risk management and firm performance: A contingency perspective. *Journal of Accounting and Public Policy*, *28*, 301–327. https://doi.org/10.1016/j.jaccpubpol.2009.06.006

Grace, M. F., Leverty, J. T., Phillips, R. D., & Shimpi, P. (2015). The value of investing in enterprise risk management. *The Journal of Risk and Insurance*, *82*(2), 289–316. https://doi.org/10.1111/jori.12022

IIA. (2020). *The IIA's three lines model - An update of the three lines of defense*. Altamonte Springs/FI: The Institute of Internal Auditors. https://www.theiia.org/globalassets/documents/resources/the-iias-three-lines-model-an-update-of-the-three-lines-of-defense-july-2020/three-lines-model-updated-english.pdf

Institute of Risk Management. (2002). *IRM: 2002 - A risk management standard*. https://www.theirm.org/media/4709/arms_2002_irm.pdf

Irvine, H., Lazarevski, K., & Dolnicar, S. (2009). Strings attached: New public management, competitive grant funding and social capital. *Financial Accountability & Management*, *25*(2), 225–252. https://doi.org/10.1111/j.1468-0408.2009.00475.x

ISO 31000:2018. (2018). *Management du risque – Lignes directrices.* www.iso.org

John, K., De Masi, S., & Paci, A. (2016). Corporate governance in banks. *Corporate Governance: An International Review*, *24*(3), 303–321. https://doi.org/10.1111/corg.12161

Kleffner, A. E., Lee, R. B., & McGannon, B. (2003). The effect of corporate governance on the use of enterprise risk management: Evidence from Canada. *Risk Management and Insurance Review*, *6*(1), 53–73. https://EconPapers.repec.org/RePEc:bla:rmgtin:v:6:y:2003:i:1:p:53-73

Kummer, T. F., Singh, K., & Best, P. (2014). The effect of fraud on risk management in not-for-profit organisations. *Corporate Ownership & Control*, *12*(1), 641–655. https://doi.org/10.1108/MAJ-08-2014-1083

46 Elisabeth Bertin

Li, Q., Wu, Y., Ojiako, U., Marshall, A., & Chipulu, M. (2014). Enterprise risk management and firm value within China's insurance industry. *Professional Accountant, 14*(1), 1–10. https://actacommercii.co.za/index.php/acta/article/view/198

Li, K., Griffin, D., Yue, H. & Zhao, L. (2013). How does culture influence corporate risk-taking? *Journal of Corporate Finance, 23*, 1–22. https://doi.org/10.1016/j.jcorpfin.2013.07.008

Liebenberg, A. P., & Hoyt, R. E. (2003). The determinants of enterprise risk management: Evidence from the appointment of chief risk officers. *Risk Management and Insurance Review, 6*(1), 37–52. https://doi.org/10.1111/1098-1616.00019

Lu, H., Liu, X., & Falkenberg, L. (2022). Investigating the impact of corporate social responsibility (CSR) on risk management practices. *Business & Society, 61*(2), 496–534. https://doi.org/10.1177/0007650320928981

Lurtz, K., & Kreutzer, K. (2017). Entrepreneurial orientation and social venture creation in nonprofit organisations: The pivotal role of social risk taking and collaboration. *Nonprofit and Voluntary Sector Quarterly, 46*(1), 92–115. https://doi.org/10.1177/0899764016654221

Maier, F., Meyer, M., & Steinbereithner, M. (2016). Nonprofit organisations becoming business-like: A systematic review. *Nonprofit and Voluntary Sector Quarterly, 45*(1), 64–86. https://doi.org/10.1177/0899764014561796

Markowitz, H. M. (1952). Portfolio selection. *The Journal of Finance, 7*(1), 77–91.

McShane, M. K., Nair, A., & Rustambekov, E. (2011). Does enterprise risk management increase firm value? *Journal of Accounting, Auditing and Finance, 26*, 641–658. https://doi.org/10.1177/0148558X11409160

Meidell, A., & Kaarbøe, K. (2017). How the enterprise risk management function influences decision-making in the organization – A field study of a large, global oil and gas company. *The British Accounting Review, 49*(1), 39–55. https://doi.org/10.1016/j.bar.2016.10.005

Naseem, T., Shahzad, F., Asim, G. A., Rehman, I. U., & Nawaz, F. (2020). Corporate social responsibility engagement and firm performance in Asia Pacific: The role of enterprise risk management. *Corporate Social Responsibility and Environmental Management, 27*, 501–513. https://doi.org/10.1002/csr.1815

O'Reilly, C. A., & Chatman, J. A. (1996). Culture as social control: Corporations, cults, and commitment. *Research in Organisational Behavior, 18*, 157–200.

O'Reilly, C. A., Chatman, J., & Caldwell, D. (1991). People and organisational culture: A profile comparison approach to assessing person-organisation fit. *Academy of Management Journal, 34*, 487–516.

Osman, A., & Lew, C. C. (2021). Developing a framework of institutional risk culture for strategic decision-making. *Journal of Risk Research, 24*(9), 1072–1085. https://doi.org/10.1080/13669877.2020.1801806

Paape, L., & Spekle, F. (2012). The adoption and design of enterprise risk management practices: An empirical study. *European Accounting Review, 21*, 533–64. https://doi.org/10.1080/09638180.2012.661937

Pagach, D., & Warr, R. (2011). The characteristics of firms that hire chief risk officers. *Journal of Risk and Insurance, 78*, 185–211. https://doi.org/10.1111/j.1539-6975.2010.01378.x

Pan, Y., Siegel, S., & Wang, T. Y. (2017). Corporate risk culture. *Journal of Financial and Quantitative Analysis, 52*(6), 2327–2367. https://doi.org/10.1017/S0022109017000771

Peretti-Watel, P. (2005). La culture du risque, ses marqueurs sociaux et ses paradoxes: Une exploration empirique. *Revue économique, 56*, 371–392. https://doi.org/10.3917/reco.562.0371

Pérez-Cornejo, C., & de Quevedo-Puente, E. (2023). How corporate social responsibility mediates the relationship between corporate reputation and enterprise risk

Implementing and maintaining an effective risk management system 47

management: Evidence from Spain. *Eurasian Business Review, 13,* 363–383. https://doi.org/10.1007/s40821-022-00223-2

Power, M. (2007). *Organised uncertainty: Designing a world of risk management.* Oxford University.

Power, M. (2009). The risk management of nothing. *Accounting, Organisations and Society, 34*(6–7), 849–855. https://doi.org/10.1016/j.aos.2009.06.001

Quon, T. K., Zeghal, D., & Maingot, M. (2012). Enterprise risk management and firm performance. *Procedia – Social and Behavioral Sciences, 62,* 263–267. https://doi.org/10.1016/j.sbspro.2012.09.042

Ring, P. J., Bryce, C., McKinney, R., & Webb, R. (2016). Taking notice of risk culture – The regulator's approach. *Journal of Risk Research, 19*(3), 364–387. https://doi.org/10.1080/13669877.2014.983944

Sheedy, E., & Griffin, B. (2014). *Empirical analysis of risk culture in financial institutions: Interim report.* Macquarie University.

Sheedy, E., & Griffin, B. (2018). Risk governance, structures, culture, and behavior: A view from the inside. *Corporate Governance: An International Review, 26*(1), 4–22. https://doi.org/10.1111/corg.12200

Silva De Souza, R., Da Silva Gomes, S. M., Leal Bruni, A., Garcia De Oliveira, G., Santos Sampaio, M., & Almeida De Faria, J. (2012). Enterprise risk management and performance improvement: A study with Brazilian nonfinancial firms. In A. Davila, M. J. Epstein, & J.-F. Manzoni (Eds.), *Performance measurement and management control: Global issues (studies in managerial and financial accounting* (Vol. 25, pp. 275–298). Emerald Group Publishing Limited.

Stein, V., Wiedermann, A., & Bouten, C. (2019). Framing risk governance. *Management Research Review, 42*(11), 1224–1242. https://doi.org/10.1108/MRR-01-2019-0042

Viscelli, T. R., Hermanwon, D. R., & Beasley, M. S. (2017). The integration of ERM and strategy: Implications for corporate governance. *Accounting Horizons, 31,* 69–82. https://doi.org/10.2308/acch-51692

3 The role of public actors in the governance of French non-profit organisations

Proposing an integrated governance analysis framework

Eric-Alain Zoukoua

Introduction

The governance of non-profit organisations has mainly been understood in terms of the rules and principles constituting the "best practices" to be followed by the board of directors to ensure its effectiveness (O'Regan & Oster, 2002). The main research topics about governance of non-profit organisations deal with the composition of boards, the relationship between boards and managers or staff, board roles and accountability, board effectiveness and the link between board effectiveness and organisational effectiveness (Cornforth, 2012; Ostrower & Stone, 2006). In broadening of these earlier themes, the research is extended to include topics such as accountability and the relationship with stakeholders, governance structures, and tools for assessing the competences of board members and board performance (Cornforth & Brown, 2014).

These previous studies have mainly focused on the organisational level and have, for the most part, taken gradually account of the role played by key stakeholders such as the public funders in the governance of these organisations (Guo, 2007; Suárez, 2011). In France, as in many Organisation for Economic Co-operation and Development (OECD) countries, the public authorities, made up of the State, its decentralised or specialised services present in the regions and the local authorities rely on non-profit organisations which carry out activities either directly on behalf of these public actors. Areas such as vocational training, social services and health, popular education, sport, leisure, culture, etc. are covered by non-profit organisations that intervene to implement actions of general interest. As such, they are supported by public funding, which makes up a substantial proportion of their resources. Thus, out of a cumulative budget of around 115 billion euros in 2022, direct funding from the French public authorities to non-profit organisations is 44%, to which must be added indirect funding allocated to the users of the organisations' services in the form of allowances, tax credits, etc. so that they can buy the services provided by the organisations (Cottin-Marx & Devetter, 2022). This situation makes public funders the main

DOI: 10.4324/9781003460572-5

providers of financial resources to non-profit organisations. Their actions in the governance of these organisations are legitimised by the organisations' dependence on them for resources (Pfeffer & Salancik, 1978), by the need for transparency in the use of these resources and by the usefulness of the actions financed in terms of covering societal needs for which public funders are responsible. The benefits of relationships with public actors are not only limited to the direct provision of funding but also to access to policymakers and the political process. This enables non-profit organisations to advocate and participate in legislative change (Chavesc et al., 2004). In view of the above, non-profit organisations worldwide are confronted with an increasing demand for accountability and improved financial transparency (Anheier et al., 2013; Verbruggen et al., 2011).

Similarly, the deployment of the principles of new public management (NPM) (Hood, 1991, 1995) in public organisations has had a profound influence on the way they operate and their relations with their various stakeholders, including non-profit organisations. According to Hood (1991, 1995) seminal work, NPM is based on seven principles: the reorganisation of the public sector into "corporatized units" by "product"; the introduction of a logic of public-private competition and even competition between public organisations in calls for tender; an adaptation to the public sector of the "managerial" style borrowed from the private sector; the search for efficiency in the consumption of resources; greater involvement of senior managers; the need for performance and impact measurement standards; more results-oriented performance measurement. Public actors have high expectations in terms of results and performance for the resources allocated. The governance of non-profit organisations which mainly receive public funding is particularly influenced by the actions of public funders. Not taking their action into account in the governance of these organisations gives a fragmented view of this reality. This is all the more true given that the concepts at the heart of good governance of organisations – advocated by the ISO 37000:2021 standard, such as performance, accountability and ethics – are central into the relationship between public actors with all its partners. It is therefore responsible for the good governance of its partners.

While research carried out in France on non-profit organisations highlights the influence of public funding in the life and operation of these, little is known about their role in their governance.

Following up on work that analyses the action of these key stakeholders in the governance of non-profit organisations, our contribution aims to provide some answers to the following question: how does the action of public funders in the context of their cooperation with non-profit organisations shape the governance of these organisations and what analytical framework can be used to analyse this reality?

To shed some light on this issue, we begin by showing how the dissemination of NPM principles, which has transformed the way public organisations operate, is influencing their cooperation with their partners in the non-profit sector

50   *Eric-Alain Zoukoua*

by focusing on performance. We present the mechanisms deployed by public funders. We determine the governance logic underpinning the mechanisms deployed through the perceptions of non-profit organisations heads (board presidents who have voluntary status and hold political positions and executive directors) and public funders of the role and objectives assigned to the governance mechanisms deployed in non-profit organisations. Finally, based on their expectations of the governance mechanisms deployed, we propose an analytical framework that sheds light on the reality of governance in these organisations.

The governance of non-profit organisations with regard to the action of funders: The impact of NPM on the mechanisms deployed

In view of the socio-economic importance of non-profit organisations, their social utility and their role in the deployment of public authority initiatives in local and regional areas, it is important for academics, practitioners and their various stakeholders to have benchmarks against which to measure the reality of their governance. While the frameworks for analysing corporate governance guide our thinking, they need to be supplemented by contextual elements that take into account the full complexity and reality of non-profit organisations. This section presents elements that will help us to understand the evolution of the role of public funding bodies in the governance of these organisations.

The transformation of cooperation between non-profit organisations and public funding bodies under NPM

In order to address the governance of non-profit organisations, the majority of researchers in this field have based their work on corporate governance (O'Regan & Oster, 2002), while adapting it to the realities of these organisations.

The frameworks for analysing corporate governance have been discussed in the literature according to approaches that refer to specific ways of creating value:

- The disciplinary approach of governance or oversight approach: this is the dominant paradigm, based on the predictions of agency theory (Jensen & Meckling, 1976). In this approach, the regulation of management behaviour is the essential lever for a policy of value creation for shareholders (shareholder approach who does not apply to non-profit organisations) and/or for all stakeholders (partnership approach). Disciplining or monitoring managers by means of robust mechanisms makes it possible to reduce their discretionary scope and align their interests on those of the organisation and the providers of resources.
- The cognitive approach of governance: in this approach, value creation is based on the organisation's ability to adapt to its environment and to develop a stock of knowledge. To understand the action of governance as a cognitive

Role of public actors in the governance of French non-profit organisations   51

lever, reference can be made to resource-based theory (Penrose, 2009; Wenerfelt, 1984). It allows for an understanding of the dynamics present in the construction of the cognitive resources of an organisation and the interaction of their construction with strategic development. This approach emphasises the link between the resources and skills contributed by each stakeholder to encourage innovation, which is a source of value creation. From this perspective, governance is seen as the set of mechanisms that enable the greatest potential for value creation through learning and innovation (Bonnet & Wirtz, 2011; Wirtz, 2011). Governance mechanisms should enable management to be informed about how to achieve the objectives assigned to it through control methods designed to coordinate routines and encourage the emergence of new skills that are sources of value creation.

In these two approaches, governance mechanisms do not fulfil the same functions because their role and purpose differ. While these two approaches are those used in the majority of works on governance, a third approach is emerging:

- The integrated approach of governance (Charreaux & Wirtz, 2007; Wirtz, 2006): based on the limitations of the first two approaches in grasping the reality of organisational governance, this approach integrates their contributions in order to grasp all the dimensions underlying the logic of value creation in organisations. The disadvantage of this emerging approach is that few empirical studies have been conducted.

These three logics of governance can be mobilised to determine the framework for understanding the action of public funders in the governance of non-profit organisations. Over the last three decades, the public environment in OECD countries has undergone major changes and reforms initiated by NPM. This paradigm of public action represents a profound change in the nature of public administration. In concrete terms, it involves the implementation in public organisations of a set of ideas and operating methods borrowed from the for-profit private sector. Non-profit organisations have been a shift in much government funding from grants to contracts, accompanied by increased performance monitoring, regulation and inspection. Governments are increasingly relying on arm's-length forms of control through the use of performance management systems, such as top-down target setting, service level agreements and strengthened regulatory, inspection and audit regimes to ensure targets and standards are met.

The rise of NPM principles in public sectors has had an important consequence for non-profit organisations and their governance (Cornforth & Brown, 2014; Salamon & Toepler, 2015).

In France, the principles of NPM were implemented after a number of reforms at State level, with the entry into force of the *French organic public finances law* (Loi Organique relative aux Lois de Finances (LOLF)) in 2002, which introduced

52 Eric-Alain Zoukoua

the obligation of performance through the preparation of an annual performance project backed up by the appendices to the budgets produced by each ministry.

Although the LOLF has not been extended by law to local authorities or other State operators, the performance obligation conveyed by the dissemination of the NPM culture influences the operation of all these public organisations. NPM infuses public organisations with a corporate performance culture by introducing a spending logic that complies with the so-called "3 Es" rule: economy, efficiency and effectiveness (Lewis, 1993).

Because of the impact of their activities on public action, budgetary constraints and the increased demands of citizens, non-profit organisations are being encouraged to take on board concerns relating to the performance orientation of their public funders. Ensuring that the performance of non-profit organisations is assessed is therefore an important part of the control of public policy, of which it is one expression. This leads funders to deploy mechanisms that characterise their actions in the governance of non-profit organisations. Through their actions, public funders influence the non-profit organisations' internal practices. Non-profit organisations are led to integrate the expectations of their funders into their internal governance systems. This is done with a view to increasing their trust and involvement in cooperation. The quality of governance is a factor that encourages non-profit organisations to mobilise resources from public funders (Gazzola et al., 2020). This raises the question of identifying the mechanisms used in the governance of these organisations in French context.

The role of public funders in the governance of non-profit organisations: A desire to establish a culture of performance and accountability

The use of non-profit organisations as operators or instruments for implementing the public policies advocated by the dissemination of NPM principles places their cooperation with public funders in an agency relationship. The public funder takes on the role of principal and the non-profit the role of agent. As agents, based on the predictions of agency theory (Jensen & Meckling, 1976), non-profit organisations are assumed to seek to maximise their utility to the detriment of that of their funders. The risks of adverse selection and moral hazard inherent in this agency relationship legitimise the various governance mechanisms deployed by public funders as part of their cooperation with non-profit organisations. Echoing the research of Pfeffer and Salancik (1978), the situation of resource dependence legitimises the action of funders in the governance of non-profit organisations. The funders will therefore legitimately deploy mechanisms to guarantee that their cooperation with the non-profits runs smoothly. The first mechanisms of this type, in the context of their cooperation with public funders, are agreements. These mechanisms clearly set out the expectations and reciprocal commitments of the parties involved and provide a framework for the relationship between non-profit organisations and public funders. To comply with the agreements, the non-profit organisations are required to produce a series of items of information prior to the agreement, enabling the funders to resolve the risks associated with adverse selection of the non-profit organisations.

When the non-profit organisation receives funding, additional mechanisms are deployed downstream to account for the use of the funds allocated. These take the form of reports on the actions funded, activity reports, financial statements, annual accounts certified by a professional accountant acting as a trusted third party, activity monitoring indicators, management charts and user satisfaction surveys. The analysis of these documents by public funders is one of the central mechanisms for the action of funders in the governance of non-profit organisations.

The governance mechanisms deployed in this way enable funders to strengthen the direct supervision of the organisations in carrying out the actions funded and, ultimately, to ensure that the expected results are achieved (Dubost & Fabre, 2016).

In addition, the institutionalisation of contractual funding initiated with the deployment of NPM principles by public funders has strongly influenced the action of public funders in the governance of non-profit organisations. Projects financed in this way are initiated by the funders, who propose a set of specifications that give rise to a call for projects and competition among non-profit organisations and also with players in the commercial sector. These different forms of contractualisation and the associated methods of allocating resources change profoundly the way in which non-profit organisations and public funders work together. This helps to increase the use of management control systems in the governance of non-profit organisations. For example, non-profits are now required to set up cost accounting systems so that they can report to the nearest euro on the use of the funds allocated, develop cost calculation systems and supply activity monitoring tables that enable funders to monitor their performance.

We find the development of governance mechanisms similar to those used in countries (the USA, the UK, Australia, New Zealand, etc.) where the NPM principles were initially deployed (McMullin, 2021; Salamon & Toepler, 2015; Suárez, 2011). Public funders attach great importance to accounting, financial and organisational controls through audits (Chatelain-Ponroy et al., 2014; Cornforth & Brown, 2014).

By institutionalising a method of allocating resources that is dominated by project-based funding or competitive tendering processes, public funders are moving away from the practices that for a long time surrounded their cooperation with non-profit organisations, which were characterised by "sprinkling" of subsidies through their systematic allocation to all non-profit organisations and their tacit renewal from one year to the next. This new way of allocating resources also influences the way in which non-profit organisations or, more accurately, projects are chosen, because the non-profit organisation as an entity is no longer the focus of their cooperation. It disappears behind the projects or actions that are financed and for which it is in competition with other non-profit and/or

54 *Eric-Alain Zoukoua*

for-profit companies for funding (Hung & Hager, 2019; Paarlberg & Hwang, 2017; Topaloglu et al., 2018). This new approach to intervention by public actors encourages the deployment of a governance approach geared towards oversight, performance and accountability. This is leading some non-profit organisations to respond to more and more calls for projects in order to ensure their survival. This "survival" strategy is seen as destructive to the non-profit's project, as the values underpinning it can in some contexts be relegated to second place as funders take control of them and shape them according to their expectations.

In addition to these contractual mechanisms, the proximity (Boschma, 2005) that exists between non-profit organisations and public funders is an important lever for the deployment of governance mechanisms in non-profits. Geographical proximity, for example, enables public funders to visit non-profit organisations in the field, to take part in some of their activities and to attend meetings of their governing and deliberative bodies (boards of directors and general meetings) at the invitation of the organisations' directors. Formal and informal discussions are then held with the organisation's directors on the basis of questions raised by the documents produced, or relating to the life and operation of the organisation. This fosters the exchange of complex information that enables governance mechanisms to be deployed to assess the results achieved by non-profit organisations and evaluate their impact (Blevins et al., 2022; Chemin & Gilbert, 2010; Zhu et al., 2016). Such mechanisms improve the intelligibility of activity reports and any other documents sent to funders by non-profits.

Through their actions, public funders have established themselves as central players in the governance of these organisations (Cornforth & Brown, 2014; Salamon & Toepler, 2015). With the deployment of the principles of NPM, public funders are demonstrating real activism in their cooperation with non-profits. This activism is reflected in the strengthening of controls on non-profits, the institutionalisation of contractual funding arrangements and the introduction of competition in the choice of a partner.

The search for the best performing partner is thus becoming one of the objectives of public funders in the governance of these organisations and one of the levers for allocating resources to them. This raises the question of the logic of governance underlying the various mechanisms deployed in the governance of non-profit organisations and of the analytical framework capable of accounting for this reality.

The need for an integrated, co-constructed approach to governance to understand the reality of non-profit organisations

The dissemination of the principles of NPM and the underlying focus on the performance of public action are having a profound influence on the governance of non-profit organisations. This raises questions about the governance rationale at work in non-profits as a result of the paradigm shift that has taken place in their

Role of public actors in the governance of French non-profit organisations 55

cooperation with public funders. In order to identify the governance rationale at work in non-profit organisations, we have chosen to compare the perceptions of non-profit board presidents and executive directors of the role played by public funders in their governance, with those of the funders themselves. Few studies have examined the reality of the governance of these organisations through the eyes of the major players in their governance.

The governance logics at work in non-profit organisations: A cross-analysis of the perceptions of non-profit managers and public funders

According to non-profit organisation managers, the oversight function or disciplinary approach of governance dominates the action of public funders in the governance of non-profit organisations.

In their view, two factors justify the use of monitoring mechanisms by public funders. The first is linked to the desire of public funders to reduce the risk of opportunism on the part of non-profit directors and more specifically the risk of embezzlement and other abuses that have marred the operation of many non-profit organisations in France. In the worldwide, the revelation of mismanagement practices by some non-profit organisations has shaken stakeholders' trust.

The second factor that explains the use of monitoring mechanisms borrowed from the business world relates to changes in the institutional and legal environment of public funders, driven by the dissemination of NPM principles.

The combined effect of these two factors justifies the deployment of the funding mechanisms identified above. Transparency, oversight and accountability may be necessary for restoring trust. Non-profit organisations also have strong incentives to demonstrate their competitive advantage by openly reporting on their performance and effectiveness (Charles & Kim, 2016; Fonseca et al., 2021).

While these mechanisms are generally seen as legitimate, they are also criticised. This is particularly the case for non-profits operating in the social services and health sector, where the human factor plays an important role and greatly reduces the relevance of the widespread use of quantitative indicators as tools for monitoring results and allocating resources. Non-profit organisation managers perceive them as ineffective and counter-productive for reporting on the achievement of the organisation's project or even for ensuring the continued existence of their organisations. According to the heads of non-profit organisations, the production of these quantitative indicators strengthens the legitimacy of their organisations in the eyes of funders, but also runs the risk of distancing them from the organisation's project and pulls them into a "self-perpetuating performance game" (Eynaud & Mourey, 2012). The resources mobilised from public authorities can restrict the flexibility and weaken the intervention capacity of non-profit organisations, which, paradoxically, weakens one of the main benefits that public actors derive from their partnership with them (Guo, 2007; O'Regan & Oster, 2002). Public funders' reporting and compliance requirements often limit the

56   *Eric-Alain Zoukoua*

autonomy of non-profit organisations, contribute to bureaucratisation and create accountability conflicts (Hwang & Powell, 2009; Verbruggen et al., 2011).

This situation makes many non-profit managers, mainly politicians, averse to a number of governance mechanisms favoured by funders. One of the most decried mechanisms, and a source of tension, is the audit. The word used by many non-profit organisations managers to describe this mechanism is very revealing of their perception: they speak of "undergoing" an audit. The term "relentless" was also used by many non-profit organisation managers. The contractual and non-permanent funding mechanisms (calls for projects, calls for tenders, etc.) institutionalised with the deployment of the NPM principles are also strongly criticised. They institute a form of cooperation that plunges non-profit organisations into a zone of uncertainty and accentuates the influence of public funders in their governance. These mechanisms favoured by funders in the governance of non-profits generate tensions and, in some situations, inter-organisational conflicts because of their impact on the drop in funding, which threatens the continued operation of the organisations.

The dissemination of NPM principles justifies public funders in taking back control and increasing the standardisation and regulation of the work of non-profit organisations. This approach clashes with the identity and values of these organisations, which find themselves relegated to the status of service providers. By opting for governance mechanisms focused on the use of resources, the implementation of funded initiatives and performance in which the economic and financial dimensions are important, public funders are choosing to make their cooperation with non-profit organisations part of a results-based governance approach. The mechanisms deployed are therefore designed to provide a framework for the managerial latitude of directors in order to promote the achievement of expected results. For non-profit managers, through the mechanisms deployed, public funders adopt behaviour that is similar to that of a majority shareholder expecting a return on its investment. The mechanisms deployed aim to offset any risk of *adverse selection* (choice of a non-performing partner) and *moral hazard* (the risk that the resources allocated will be used for other purposes). This makes their actions part of a disciplinary approach to governance. With regard to the influence of the disciplinary approach of governance and its consequences, many studies recognise that compliance costs not only take up valuable resources but also change the organisation's focus on avoiding sanctions as opposed to pursuing its goals. Thus, one of the most profound governance challenges is to figure out the right type and level of monitoring and enforcement the system should provide. While governance gaps are not desirable (Anheier et al., 2013), the over governance poses a problem as well.

The non-profit managers would therefore like to see the deployment of a governance approach that favours exchange and takes an interest in the organisation's project over the long term. This type of control is more oriented towards advice,

Role of public actors in the governance of French non-profit organisations 57

has an educational purpose and is part of a learning process. The mechanisms expected by statutory directors would place the organisation's project at the heart of the audit and would be part of a more cognitive approach to governance. This approach is perceived as being more in line with the specific characteristics of non-profit organisations and their raison d'être. While this position of both voluntary and salaried non-profit managers remains consistent with the aims of non-profits and their own commitment to the non-profit world, the perception of public funders and the views of some salaried managers lead us to qualify this perception. The deployment of these mechanisms highlights the tensions between the governance approach desired by non-profit managers and rooted in the values and principles of the non-profit world, and the approach adopted by their public funders, which is perceived as oriented towards disciplining non-profit organisations.

In the collective imagination, auditing is seen as a mechanism for uncovering fraud and ensuring the transparency of the entity being audited (Power, 2005). Its implementation, as well as the nature of the controls carried out, are tedious for the members of the audited organisations. However, if we look at the reality of these organisations, the audit fulfils a supervisory role in some cases and an advisory role in others. The "learning or educational" dimensions are not totally absent from audits. An analysis of the audit reports carried out by a local authority on funded non-profit organisations shows that an important place is given to short, medium and long-term recommendations for improving cooperation between the authority and the organisations audited. Similarly, the audit team provides the non-profits with advice on their organisation and processes throughout the audit process. These elements guide the action of the audit mechanism in this dimension of learning and teaching, and then place it in a dimension of cognitive governance. Thus, this mechanism, which *a priori* may be perceived as disciplinary, turns out to be a mechanism that also includes an advisory and support dimension to encourage value creation.

Public funders recognise that, in addition to their monitoring function, in-depth audit-type controls also have an important advisory component. The same is true of the mechanisms fostered by the proximity between the non-profit organisations and the funders, which enable the funders to provide support to non-profits that are in a very fragile financial situation, given their importance to the region. Indeed, through meetings between non-profits and public funders, the latter can support the organisation in shaping its projects, help it to improve its services and provide the necessary financial support. The two logics of disciplinary and cognitive governance are combined in the action of funders. This position is shared by many funders and some salaried managers. The latter appear to be much more pragmatic on these points than the statutory directors of non-profit organisations.

This observation leads us to consider the approach to governance that enables us to better identify the reality of the governance of non-profit organisations.

58   Eric-Alain Zoukoua

The integrated approach as a response to the expectations of stakeholders in the non-profit sector with regard to the governance of non-profit organisations

The paradigm shift brought about by the dissemination of NPM principles amplifies the role of public funding bodies in the governance of non-profit organisations (Dethier et al., 2023).

While the nature of the mechanisms deployed confirms the importance of the logic of disciplinary governance, the reality of cooperation between non-profits and public funders shows that it is only one dimension of the action of public funders. It is not characteristic of all their actions. In fact, public funders state that they take a number of factors into account in their cooperation with the non-profit sector, their knowledge of the local non-profit sector environment, their proximity to the players in the non-profit sector, past actions carried out in conjunction with them, ongoing exchanges with the players in the non-profit sector, etc. – when building their cooperation with these players. In their view, these factors need to qualify the perception of non-profit organisation leaders highlighted above. Public funders claim to deploy numerous governance mechanisms that are not necessarily disciplinary. This is demonstrated by their participation in working meetings on the activities or actions to be carried out by the organisations, exchanges relating to funded projects or aimed at finding solutions to the organisations' financial difficulties, all of which are mechanisms that are not necessarily part of a disciplinary approach to governance. The funders support the integration of exchange, discussion and mentoring, which are all attributes of cognitive governance mechanisms that encourage the emergence of new ideas, the main cognitive lever for enriching the organisation's project and creating value. These mechanisms have a strong cognitive dimension.

In short, the action of public funders in the governance of non-profit organisations does indeed follow a logic of extended governance. These results echo the work of De Andrés-Alonso et al. (2010) in their study of Spanish foundations. Faced with the limitations of the traditional approach based on agency theory in explaining changes in the world of non-profits, these researchers suggest extending the governance approach to a cognitive dimension in order to gain a better understanding of the way in which internal bodies promote the performance of organisations. These authors outline the need to mobilise an integrated approach to governance in NPOs, going beyond the single disciplinary approach in order to account for the reality of governance in these organisations. In the same vein, Salamon and Toepler (2015) advocate moving away from the governance logic of the NPM, which they consider to be more limited and narrow. They suggest a new form of governance based on collaboration and the involvement of partners not only in the implementation of public policy but also in their development and design. Such a stance is in line with the integrated approach to governance based on co-constructed governance proposed in our work.

In the French context, the mechanisms deployed by these actors reflect both the disciplinary logic of governance (risk management mechanisms, mechanisms

Role of public actors in the governance of French non-profit organisations 59

deployed to ensure the proper use of public funds, systems to check that the partner organisation is performing well, control of legality and compliance in the use of funds, etc.) and the cognitive logic (receiving visits from the organisation, helping it to formalise its project, assisting it in responding to calls for tender, finding funding solutions, taking part in events organised by it, attending meetings of its governing bodies, etc.).

Although the NPM movement and the philosophy behind it may lead to such a conclusion, we have to recognise that the reality of the non-profit organisations studied reveals more contrasting situations. They are rooted in a territory, in networks, within communities and have multiple formal or informal interactions with public funders. These elements create proximity. This proximity influences the action of funders in their governance, making it more than just a disciplinary matter. The cognitive dimension of governance is important, given the multiple interactions between non-profit organisations and their funders.

Moreover, the leaders of non-profit organisations and public funders agree on the need to co-construct the governance of these organisations in order to achieve the common goal pursued by the organisations.

The governance of non-profit organisations reveals a variety of realities and can borrow from the disciplinary logic its ability to set up robust control mechanisms capable of providing a framework for the actions of non-profit managers and from the cognitive logic its ability to give meaning and support to the managers' actions through innovation. Our contribution is an invitation to assess the governance of non-profit organisations in the context of an integrated approach to governance (Charreaux & Wirtz, 2007; Wirtz, 2006), which mobilises the contributions of these two disciplinary and cognitive logics to the mobilisation of resources, on the one hand, and the creation of value, on the other.

The tensions that have arisen highlight the organisations' fear of disappearing for lack of support from their funders, and for some of them a desire to move towards new modes of governance. Co-constructed governance, based on an integrated approach to governance, seems to be a solution for non-profit organisations. The mechanisms within this framework would be the fruit of a co-construction based on exchanges between players in the non-profit sector and their public funders through levers enabling the non-profit sector to mobilise the resources necessary for the deployment of their organisational project.

As part of this integrated approach to governance, the mechanisms deployed can be based on control systems built in a concerted and shared manner around the organisation's project and the expectations of public funders. This approach to co-constructed or shared governance would provide non-profit organisations with all the keys they need to examine the relevance of their project and its compliance with institutional developments in its field of operation and to modify their project if necessary. The choice of this type of governance depends on the will of the players involved. The outline of this type of governance has been sketched out by some non-profit leaders and local authority representatives. Their comments lead to the conclusion that this kind of governance can be deployed in non-profit organisations through coordination in time and space between public funders and non-profit organisations. In terms of time, this coordination would be based on jointly developed objectives and multi-year commitments for the allocation of resources. In terms of space, it would involve a one-stop shop for funding body controls and a shift from short-term objective-based control to a real assessment of the impact of funded initiatives (Chemin & Gilbert, 2010; Van Puyvelde et al., 2012).

This approach, which is based on strong collaboration, can take on its essence in a post-NPM perspective through the collaborative NPM movement (Agranoff & McGuire, 2003; McGuire, 2006). This movement emerged in reaction to NPM and advocates greater horizontal collaboration between the State and its non-profit partners, which can take the form of networks, teams or projects (Suquet et al., 2020) and encourage stronger collaborative action. Such collaboration takes place within the framework of a balanced and reciprocal relationship that guarantees the autonomy of the partners rather than encouraging a centralising tendency on the part of public funders, as favoured by the deployment of NPM principles. This co-constructed governance as part of the cooperation between non-profit organisations and their public funders therefore involves collaborative governance (Emerson et al., 2012). Collaborative governance can lead to a new logic in the mobilisation of resources by non-profits, which may prove to be in line with their expectations and enable them to achieve their organisational goals.

Figure 3.1 models the integrated governance framework from a *post-NPM* perspective.

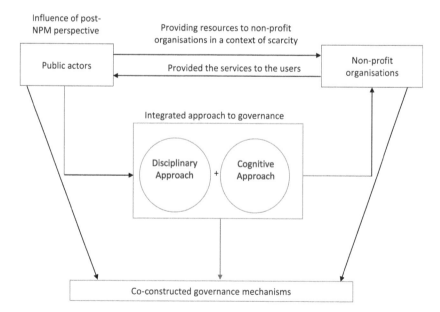

Figure 3.1 Framework for analysing non-profit organisation governance

Conclusion

The aim of this contribution was to analyse the way in which the action of public shapes the governance of non-profit organisations. We analyse through the combined perspective of non-profit managers and public funders, the analytical framework for giving an account of the action of funders in the governance of non-profit organisations. Our results show that public funders play a major role in the governance of non-profits. Through their actions, they guide the life and functioning of these organisations. An analysis of how stakeholders perceive the governance of non-profit organisations shows that, while non-profit managers and public funders have many different expectations, they share a common goal: to provide the best possible response to the users or beneficiaries of non-profit services. While the heads of non-profit organisations seek to ensure the long-term survival of their organisations, public funders seek to ensure a reliable and effective partnership for the deployment of public policies. These two objectives are mutually reinforcing.

The advantage of our contribution is that it takes an in-depth look at the governance practices of non-profit organisations by examining the actions of public funders. We show that this action is dominated by the institutional and budgetary constraints of public funders, on the one hand, but also by the existence of a concerted working framework desired by non-profit managers, on the other. Similarly, our work shows that the "oversight" approach, which stems from a disciplinary logic, cannot fully account for the governance of non-profit organisations. The actions of public funders in non-profit organisations are not limited to monitoring. They include a significant cognitive component which is an important variable in governance. Approaching the governance of non-profit organisations mainly through this logic, which most often reduces it to financial transparency, does not allow us to grasp the full reality and complexity of this phenomenon and the reality of these organisations. Indeed, a non-profit organisation can be perfectly transparent financially without entirely fulfilling its organisational project. In the non-profit sector, the mechanisms and other measures identified as "good" governance practices in the literature represent only one aspect of the issue of governance.

We show that, in order to understand the issue of governance of non-profit organisations, the traditional divide between disciplinary and cognitive approaches widely used in the literature must be overcome. The logics of governance underlying these two approaches are found in varying proportions in the responses given by public funders to the issue of governance of non-profit organisations. Similarly, this issue should not be reduced solely to the actions of internal bodies, which are profoundly influenced by the actions of funders.

Therefore, the issue of governance of non-profit organisations can only be fully addressed from the angle of a broad or integrated approach that enables the contributions of the disciplinary approach and those of the cognitive approach to governance to be mobilised within the same framework for analysing

62   *Eric-Alain Zoukoua*

governance. Such an approach would be based on mechanisms co-constructed by the central actors in governance. While the works of Wirtz (2006) and Charreaux and Wirtz (2007) outline the contours of this broader or integrated approach to governance, it does not address the co-construction of governance mechanisms. By highlighting the importance of an integrated approach to governance based on co-constructed mechanisms in order to grasp all the dimensions of value creation in non-profit organisations and gain a better understanding of the reality of governance in these organisations, our contribution offers a highly interesting framework for analysis.

Our work thus contributes to enriching analyses of the governance of non-profit organisations and helps to build a theory of the governance of these organisations. It also feeds into work on NPM by demonstrating the limitations of applying its provisions in the strict sense. One way of understanding co-constructed governance in non-profit organisations is to consider post-NPM approaches through the contributions of collaborative NPM, which gives an account of the reality of relations between actors in a given territory and underlying the concept of new public governance (Wiesel & Modell, 2014).

References

Agranoff, R., & McGuire, M. (2003). *Collaborative public management: New strategies for local governments*. Georgetown University Press.

Anheier, H. K., Hass, R., & Beller, A. (2013). Accountability and transparency in the German nonprofit sector: A paradox? *International Review of Public Administration, 18*(3), 69–84. https://doi.org/10.1080/12294659.2013.10805264

Blevins, D. P., Ragozzino, R., & Eckardt, R. (2022). "Corporate governance" and performance in nonprofit organizations. *Strategic Organization, 20*(2), 293–317. https://doi.org/10.1177/1476127020921253

Bonnet, C., & Wirtz, P. (2011). Investor type, cognitive governance and performance in young entrepreneurial ventures: A conceptual framework. *Advances in Behavioral Finance & Economics: The Journal of the Academy of Behavioral, 1*(1), 42–62.

Boschma, R. (2005). Proximity and innovation: A critical assessment. *Regional Studies, 39*(1), 61–74. https://doi.org/10.1080/0034340052000320887

Charles, C., & Kim, M. (2016). Do donors care about results? An analysis of nonprofit arts and cultural organizations. *Public Performance & Management Review, 39*(4), 864–884. https://doi.org/10.1080/15309576.2015.1137775

Charreaux, G., & Wirtz, P. (2007). « Discipline ou compétence? L'apport des perspectives cognitives et comportementales à la compréhension des mécanismes de gouvernance d'entreprise ». *Revue française de gouvernance d'entreprise, 1*(1), 211–215.

Chavesc, M., Stephens, L., & Galaskiewicz, J. (2004). Does government funding suppress nonprofits' political activity? *American Sociological Review, 69*(2), 292–316. https://doi.org/10.1177/000312240406900207

Chatelain-Ponroy, S., Eynaud, P., & Sponem, S. (2014). « La gouvernance associative: entre diversité et normalisation ». In A. Burlaud (Ed.), *Comptabilité, Finance et Politique. De la pratique à la théorie: l'art de la conceptualisation* (pp. 219–226). ECS, Mélanges en l'honneur du Professeur Hoarau.

Chemin, C., & Gilbert, P. (2010). L'évaluation de la performance, analyseur de la gouvernance associative. *Politiques et management public, 27*(1), 55–78.

Role of public actors in the governance of French non-profit organisations 63

Cornforth, C. (2012). Challenges and future directions for nonprofit governance research. *Nonprofit and Voluntary Sector Quarterly*, *41*(6), 1117–36. https://doi.org/10.1177/0899764011427959

Cornforth, C., & Brown, W. A. (2014). Nonprofit governance. In *Innovative perspectives and approaches*. Routledge.

Cottin-Marx, S., & Devetter, F.-X. (2023). La puissance publique est responsable du salariat associatif "atypique" – Exemple du secteur de l'aide à la personne. *Les Etudes du Ciriec France*, Economie collective et territoires – Thème 5 – Travail, emploi, formation : penser l'interdépendance, 49–56.

De Andrés-Alonso, P., Azofra-Palenzuela, V., & Romero-Merino, M. E. (2010). Beyond the disciplinary role of governance: How boards add value to Spanish foundations. *British Journal of Management*, *21*(1), 100–114. https://doi.org/10.1111/j.1467-8551.2009.00645.x

Dethier, F., Delcourt, C., & Willems, J. (2023). Transparency of nonprofit organizations: An integrative framework and research agenda. *Journal of Philanthropy and Marketing*, *28*(4), e1725. https://doi.org/10.1002/nvsm.1725

Dubost, N., & Fabre, P. (2016). Des indicateurs pour optimiser l'allocation des ressources? Une enquête exploratoire au sein d'un réseau administré. *Gestion et management public*, *4*(1), 125–142. https://doi.org/10.3917/gmp.043.0125

Emerson, K., Nabatchi, T., & Balogh, S. (2012) An integrative framework for collaborative governance. *Journal of Public Administration Research and Theory*, *22*(1), 1–29. https://doi.org/10.1093/jopart/mur011

Eynaud, P., & Mourey, D. (2012). Professionnalisation et identité des associations du secteur social: chronique d'une mort annoncée? *Politiques et management public*, *29*(4), 671–693.

Fonseca, I., Paço, A., & Figueiredo, V. (2021). Nonprofit organizations, management and marketing strategies for survival: The case of philharmonic bands. *Journal of Philanthropy and Marketing*, *26*(1), e1678. https://doi.org/10.1002/nvsm.1678

Gazzola, P., Amelio, S., Grechi, D., & Papagiannis, F. (2020). NPO funding in Italy: The role and the contribution of corporate governance. *International Journal of Business and Management*, *15*, 12–26. https://dx.doi.org/10.5539/ijbm.v15n12p1

Guo, C. (2007). When government becomes the principal philanthropist: The effects of public funding on patterns of nonprofit governance. *Public Administration Review*, *67*(3), 458–473. https://doi.org/10.1111/j.1540-6210.2007.00729.x

Hood, C. (1991). A public management for all seasons. *Public Administrations*, *69*, 73–76. https://doi.org/10.1111/j.1540-6210.2007.00729.x

Hood, C. (1995). Contemporary public management: A new global paradigm? *Public Policy and Administration*, *10*(2), 104–117. https://doi.org/10.1111/j.1467-9299.1991.tb00779.x

Hung, C., & Hager, M. A. (2019). The impact of revenue diversification on nonprofit financial health: A meta-analysis. *Nonprofit and Voluntary Sector Quarterly*, *48*(1), 5–27. https://doi.org/10.1177/0899764018807080

Hwang, H., & Powell, W. W. (2009). The rationalization of charity: The influences of professionalism in the nonprofit sector. *Administrative Science Quarterly*, *54*(2), 268–298. https://doi.org/10.2189/asqu.2009.54.2.268

Jensen, M. C., & Meckling, W. H. (1976). Theory of the firm managerial behaviour, agency costs and ownership structure. *Journal of Financial Economics*, *3*(4), 305–360.

Lewis, N. (1993). The citizen's charter and next steps: A new way of governing? *The Political Quarterly*, *3*(6), 316–326. https://doi.org/10.1111/j.1467-923X.1993.tb00348.x

McGuire, M. (2006). Collaborative public management: Assessing what we know and how we know it. *Public Administration Review*, *66*(1), 33–43. https://doi.org/10.1111/j.1540-6210.2006.00664.x

64 Eric-Alain Zoukoua

McMullin, C. (2021). Challenging the necessity of new public governance: Co-production by third sector organizations under different models of public management. *Public Administration*, *99*(1), 5–22. https://doi.org/10.1111/padm.12672

O'Regan, K., & Oster, S. (2002). Does government funding alter nonprofit governance? Evidence from New York City nonprofit contractors. *Journal of Policy Analysis and Management: The Journal of the Association for Public Policy Analysis and Management*, *21*(3), 359–379. https://doi.org/10.1002/pam.10050

Ostrower, F., & Stone, M. M. (2006). Governance: Research trends, gaps, and future prospects. *The Nonprofit Sector: A Research Handbook*, *2*, 612–628.

Paarlberg, L. E., & Hwang, H. (2017). The heterogeneity of competitive forces: The impact of competition for resources on united way fundraising. *Nonprofit and Voluntary Sector Quarterly*, *46*(5), 897–921. https://doi.org/10.1177/0899764017713874

Penrose, E. T. (2009). *The theory of the growth of the firm*. Oxford University Press.

Pfeffer, J., & Salancik, G. R. (1978). *The external control of organizations: A resource dependence perspective*. Harper Collins.

Power, M. (2005). *La société de l'audit: l'obsession du contrôle*. Entreprise et Société. La Découverte.

Salamon, L. M., & Toepler, S. (2015). Government–nonprofit cooperation: Anomaly or necessity? *Voluntas: International Journal of Voluntary and Nonprofit Organizations*, *26*, 2155–2177. https://doi.org/10.1007/s11266-015-9651-6

Suárez, D. F. (2011). Collaboration and professionalization: The contours of public sector funding for nonprofit organizations. *Journal of Public Administration Research and Theory*, *21*(2), 307–326. https://doi.org/10.1093/jpart/muq049

Suquet, J., Collard, D., & Raulet-Croset, N. (2020). L'organisation d'un management collaboratif entre acteurs publics et acteurs civils: le rôle d'organisation frontière d'une association d'insertion dans l'emploi pour les jeunes diplômés. *Gestion et management public*, *8*(1), 9–26. https://doi.org/10.3917/gmp.081.0009

Topaloglu, O., McDonald, R. E., & Hunt, S. D. (2018). The theoretical foundations of nonprofit competition: A resource-advantage theory approach. *Journal of Nonprofit & Public Sector Marketing*, *30*(3), 229–250. https://doi.org/10.1080/10495142.2018.1452818

Van Puyvelde, S., Caers, R., Du Bois, C., & Jegers, M. (2012). The governance of nonprofit organizations: Integrating agency theory with stakeholder and stewardship theories. *Nonprofit and Voluntary Sector Quarterly*, *41*(3), 431–451. https://doi.org/10.1177/0899764011409757

Verbruggen, S., Christiaens, J., & Milis, K. (2011). Can resource dependence and coercive isomorphism explain nonprofit organizations' compliance with reporting standards? *Nonprofit and Voluntary Sector Quarterly*, *40*(1), 5–32. https://doi.org/10.1177/0899764009355061

Wernerfelt, B. (1984). A resource-based view of the firm. *Strategic Management Journal*, *5*(2), 171–180.

Wiesel, F., & Modell, S. (2014). From new public management to new public governance? Hybridization and implications for public sector consumerism. *Financial Accountability & Management*, *30*(2), 175–205. https://doi.org/10.1111/faam.12033

Wirtz, P. (2006). Compétences, conflits et création de valeur: vers une approche intégrée de gouvernance. *Finance, Contrôle, Stratégie*, *9*(2), 187–221.

Wirtz, P. (2011). The cognitive dimension of corporate governance in fast growing entrepreneurial firms. *European Management Journal*, *29*(6), 431–447.

Zhu, H., Wang, P., & Bart, C. (2016). Board processes, board strategic involvement, and organizational performance in for-profit and non-profit organizations. *Journal of Business Ethics*, *136*, 311–328. https://doi.org/10.1007/s10551-014-2512-1

Part II

Governance and stakeholders: from regulation to alliances and collaboration

Introduction

Anne Goujon Belghit and Guillaume Plaisance

Governance is often seen as the set of organisational mechanisms that have the effect of delimiting the powers and influencing the decisions of managers, i.e. that regulate their behaviour and define their discretionary scope. This definition has the advantage of bringing together classical approaches, such as the agency perspective, but also integrates partnership, behavioural and cognitive approaches. This definition allows us to understand the overall functioning of the organisation, power relations, regulatory mechanisms and managerial decisions. However, it also seems important to include stakeholders in this definition. According to Freeman (1984), they are defined as actors or groups of actors who influence or can be influenced by organisations.

In order to clearly identify the challenges of this problem, we offer a journey through time and space. To do this, we will follow Charles Ingals from the Little House on the Prairie series, the famous father of a family in the United States at the end of the 19th century, who was skilled in making wooden furniture. This example refers to the work of Chandler (1977), who explained the phenomenon of the replacement of small enterprises by multidimensional organisations. Charles Ingals had to leave the countryside to live in the city in order to support his family. He worked for a shop owner who produced and sold wooden furniture. Charles started work as soon as the customer placed an order, according to the principles of the market coordination mechanism. The activity ended when a large competing company offered a model of mass production of wooden furniture.

This illustration shows the rapid changes of the time. These include the development of technology and socio-economic changes, as the emergence of large organisations changed the expectations of consumers and society. This era also marks a turning point in the governance of organisations and the introduction of

DOI: 10.4324/9781003460572-6

stakeholders in their strategic and operational functioning. Indeed, the emergence of these large organisations has required a rethinking of governance models, leading to a separation between managers and owners who become shareholders.

In for-profit organisations, more complex governance models had to include multiple stakeholders, at least shareholders and managers. In 1932, Berle and Means identified a dilution of ownership, demonstrating the replacement of the power associated with ownership by managerial power, linked to the phenomenon of shareholder dispersion. This dispersion of power, which leads to a weakening of the power of shareholder-owners vis-à-vis managers whom they nevertheless hire, leads to the implementation of mechanisms of regulation and control by shareholders over managers (Jensen & Meckling, 1976). These positive theories of agency are exclusively interested in the mechanisms of power regulation between shareholders and managers. For example, Fama and Jensen (1983) introduced the board of directors between shareholders and managers as a mechanism to reduce agency conflicts.

The interest and originality of non-profit studies lies in the absence of owners. In other words, the governance of non-profit organisations is based on the representation of stakeholders in governance bodies and on the ability of these organisations to understand the interests, hopes, expectations and contributions of stakeholders to the organisation. Non-profit governance is therefore forced to deal with powerful stakeholders, whose demands are sometimes contradictory, but who nevertheless need to be heard. All recent literature on stakeholder governance in the non-profit context therefore agrees that there is a need to gradually move away from the control and agency approach towards a new theorisation of stakeholder governance (Andersson & Renz, 2021). Indeed, a purely normative approach to stakeholders leads non-profit organisations to be faced with far too many stakeholders to be manageable, as well as contradictions between them (Plaisance, 2023). Part II therefore proposes, following on from Part I, to rethink stakeholder governance in the non-profit context by understanding the relational balances to be struck between regulation and collaboration, and the role of stakeholders in defining strategy and also in the fundamental issue of evaluating non-profit organisations.

In Chapter 4, entitled "New rules: how funding and control tools shape the relationship between social actions actors", Pauline Boisselier highlights the specific relationship between non-profit organisations and public funders. In the ISO 37000:2021, managing the quality of relationships with stakeholders, in this case public funders, is crucial to the delivery of the activity: "demonstrating sound and mutually beneficial stakeholder relationships, based on ethical and effective stakeholder engagement behaviours and practices, ensures organisations generate value over time" (p. 24). It seems crucial to remember that non-profit organisations carry out activities that are in line with public activities in a given area. There is a real relationship of interdependence between these stakeholders, with oscillations between instrumentalisation and cooperation.

In Chapter 5, in the case of mergers, Adrien Laurent asks "what strategic processes to meet the challenges of democratic governance?" and underlines that the voluntary actions of non-profit organisations are heavily regulated by public authorities. These organisations are not only based on contracts but also, and sometimes primarily, on solidarity. This specificity increases the importance of the principle of the legitimacy of collective action. This chapter analyses the case of mergers through the mobilisation of actor-network theory. Mergers lead to a redefinition of the internal and external boundaries of non-profit organisations. These forms of cooperation may lead to the disappearance of at least one of the structures, accompanied by a loss of autonomy, or they may generate new arrangements and changes in the identity of the organisation as a result of the integration process. Actor-network theory makes it possible to identify the process of translation in the transformation of a statement to make it comprehensible to other actors. These actors then have to understand and participate in the process by translating their respective interests and objectives through a dynamic and interactive process.

In Chapter 6, Rong Wang examines the "Alliances for outcome evaluation and theory of change to generate impact: integrating network level and organisational level effort via organisational learning", in short, how non-profit organisations use outcome evaluation to serve organisational goals in order to achieve and evaluate their social impact in an area. Indeed, according to ISO 37000:2021, governance members and bodies should "define the organisation's value generation objectives such that they fulfil the organisation's purpose in accordance with the organisational values and the natural environment, social and economic context within which it operates" (p. 11). Based on organisational learning theory and the theory of change, this chapter identifies steps through which non-profit organisations can engage in partnerships. The first step is to identify what to measure and who the audience is. The next step focuses on vertical learning that may exist through network lead organisations or technical assistance organisations. This step can lead non-profits to become more professional. The network is important to build communities of practice and to improve lateral learning. The final step concerns non-profit managers, who should engage in double-loop learning to develop their evaluation capacity and engage in a continuous process. This chapter is also an illustration of the importance of data for decision-making, as already mentioned in ISO 37000:2021.

References

Andersson, F. O., & Renz, D. O. (2021). Who really governs? Non-profit governance, stakeholder theory and the dominant coalition perspective. In *Research handbook on non-profit governance* (pp. 196–219). Edward Elgar Publishing.

Chandler, A. (1977). *The visible hand: The managerial revolution in American business*. Belknap Press.

Fama, E. F., & Jensen, M. C. (1983). Separation of ownership and control. *The Journal of Law and Economics, 26*(2), 301–325.

Freeman, R. E. (1984). *Strategic management: A stakeholder approach.* Pitman Publishing Inc.

Jensen, M. C., & Meckling, W. H. (1976). Theory of the firm: Managerial behavior, agency costs and ownership structure. *Journal of Financial Economics, 3*(4), 305–360.

Plaisance, G. (2023). Governing a union's external stakeholders: A prioritization method based on relationship quality and perceived impact. *Annals of Public and Cooperative Economics, 94*(1), 75–108.

4 New rules: how funding and control tools shape the relationships between social actions actors

Pauline Boisselier

Introduction

This chapter presents an empirical example of the evolution of engagement between two stakeholders. It is part of the French context and concerns non-profit organisations (NPOs) carrying out social actions (fight against poverty and precariousness, employment support, educational support, social support, etc.). We are particularly interested in the relationship between the State and these NPOs, the State being an important financier of social action in France. The State is designated here as all the public interlocutors faced by the NPOs. They must therefore report transparently on the funds they have paid to NPOs. The NPOs, for their part, must account for the proper use of these funds. This relationship is also organised around tools making it possible to measure the performance of the actions that have been financed. The need to establish good governance leads both stakeholders to change their practices. The need for greater transparency and efficiency has led to the use of new tools, one in particular requested by public authorities: the call for projects. However, the evolution of this relationship has an influence on the construction of social action and the management of NPOs. The need for efficiency can have negative consequences on its initial objective. Thus, good governance aimed at aligning the purposes of these organisations with the interests of society can be weakened by excessively high performance objectives. This reflection is based on a study carried out as part of a doctoral thesis (Boisselier, 2023) and takes up certain empirical elements. First of all, we will present contextual elements, allowing us to understand the practices of NPOs in the management of social action but also the relationship they maintain with the State. Then, the second part will address these elements from the point of view of field actors.

Theoretical benchmarks and context of the study

Over time, the voluntary sector has seen different management and evaluation practices imposed on it, such as the use of information systems or standardised

DOI: 10.4324/9781003460572-7

70   *Pauline Boisselier*

forms to communicate with the various public authorities. Even if at first, the NPOs were reluctant, today this managerial model is established in practice. However, this acceptance does not mean the absence of criticism. Management and evaluation tools have direct consequences on the organisation of social action and social workers.

Management tools

Chiapello and Gilbert (2020) describe a management tool across three dimensions. The first is called "functional dimension", the object must serve the performance of the organisation and thus have an organisational purpose. The second, "structural dimension", refers to the nature of the tool, what it is made of and what it will be applied to. Finally, the third dimension, "processual dimension", refers to the technical gesture, that is to say how the tool is used. These three dimensions will take different forms depending on the context. Indeed, organisations will shape their behaviour according to the tools that management offers them. Chiapello and Gilbert (2020) point out that management tools have evolved over time and also their role given to them according to different schools of thought over time. Technological developments and the definition of new standards lead tools to be adapted. They also carry beliefs and values and support managerial thinking.

The study of management tools has been particularly developed in contexts of change and certain studies have focused on specific tools. For example, the role of management control systems has been particularly studied for the implementation of organisational strategy (Bruining et al., 2004; Coller et al., 2018; Henri, 2006; Langfield-Smith, 1997; Nilsson, 2002; Simons, 1990) and particularly in specific situations, such as in the alignment between strategy and strategic investment decision (Slagmulder, 1997) or the implementation of a corporate social responsibility (CSR) strategy (Arjaliès & Mundy, 2013; Gond et al., 2012; Laguir et al., 2019). Management control systems can also have a role in building inter-organisational relationships (Lemaire, 2021). Accounting also plays a role in organisational change processes; particular attention is paid to accounting controls and the resulting impact of responsibilities (Ogden & Anderson, 1999). Accounting is used as a resource by those who hold power in the organisation to impose the definition of the business world they wish to create on other members of the organisation. Farjaudon and Morales (2013) showed that accounting plays a role in building consensus, particularly to enable dominant groups to preserve their interests through what appears to be a compromise. Thus, a powerful actor uses accounting to maintain his position of power in the organisation. Others will go beyond the simple vision of the tool and give accounting a more important role, having a direct societal implication, accounting is thus involved in gender equality (Khalifa & Scarparo, 2021).

Management practices and social action

Social action NPOs have a twofold aspiration: democratic and solidarity. They carry out solidarity actions on the ground but also mobilise citizens on issues that concern them. When the NPO was created, a desire to be part of a solidarity approach was expressed, so the objectives of action, the fields of intervention, the audiences reached were written in the statutes of the NPO. Social action accounts for a significant part of the funds paid to NPOs. These were present in the field of social action before the State and a large part of the management structures are still NPOs today, they are thus qualified as operators. They will cooperate and agree with the State and public authorities in the implementation of social action. The aim of this cooperation is to offer a homogeneous and coherent offer in the various establishments and services. However, NPOs also play the role of mediators, display more or less strong ideologies, appropriate issues and give them meaning by deploying actions to respond to them according to their values.

The NPO must assume these two roles: to satisfy the policy of social action in order to obtain funding and thus ensure its survival, but also to satisfy the needs expressed by society in all their specificities.

As part of the follow-up of actions, the NPOs are regularly inspected by their funders. Fabre (2005), in a study on the evaluation of the performance of NPOs by municipalities, highlighted four main families of control tools:

1 The use of the information produced and provided by the NPO and the link with the legal framework of the municipalities. This includes the study of accounts and activity reports as well as the verification of indicators previously defined between the NPO and the municipality.
2 The use of the community's formalised control systems as a community information system capable of recording, for example, the level of use of a facility.
3 The use of external opinions or information, such as the study of press kits or the use of external experts.
4 Informal and direct monitoring tools, i.e. on-site visits and the exploitation of field feedback.

The allocation of resources to NPOs is a problem for funders, especially when allocating grants. Accounting and management tools make it possible to reduce conflict and achieve a certain homogenisation of objectives. Valéau (2003, p. 9) recalls that management was initially rejected by NPOs, as it was perceived as a potential obstacle to the "natural performance of the informal organisations they liked to cultivate". The 1980s had marked a turning point, competition and the demands of funders had transformed some NPOs into companies. But these companies were criticised for sacrificing activism for efficiency. A more adapted management then became desired, so it was necessary to bring the performance of these two worlds closer together. Valéau (2003, p. 10) derives the following definition: "between what an non-profit organisation 'must' be and what management 'must' be, these organisations 'should' be efficient, 'while' respecting certain values, 'while' devoting themselves to the beneficiaries, 'while' ensuring a more humane management of human resources (HRM), 'while' integrating the requirements of those who finance it". At the end of his study, he comes to emphasise that it is "the trade-offs relating to the production, dissemination and realisation of the project that contribute to defining the heart and contours of the non-profit organisation" (Valéau, 2003, p. 20). This is a finding that is partly shared by Bernet et al. (2016). Indeed, the vision of management leading to the proposal of tools which, allegedly, make it possible to do more with less and to measure the results achieved tends to play an important role in the non-profit sector. However, the authors invite us to reverse this logic and see the NPO as a relevant support for questioning management sciences. This can be done from three perspectives, "social utility in relation to public space, social innovation and democratic governance" (Bernet et al., 2016, p. 220). Even if the criterion of social utility does not belong only to NPOs but has taken its rightful place in the organisations of the Social and Solidarity Economy, it cannot be fully assumed by social entrepreneurs alone. Innovation gives rise to a trade-off in management. The diversity and richness of the non-profit sector have been a source of social innovation for many decades. The professionalisation of the sector as well as the development of calls for tenders and requests for evaluation tend to standardise practices and standardise projects. Innovation must therefore find its place in a necessary but sometimes too important managerial framework. Democratic governance must be specific and distinct from other forms of governance. It can take the form of participatory democracy through elections, but it can also offer open participation systems that are accessible to all.

Strong criticisms are directed at this neoliberal management, Amslem and Gendron (2019) have focused on the adherence of quantitative measures by social workers in a social enterprise. The ethnographic study showed a direct influence on social workers and in particular the relationship they have with the beneficiaries. Information systems make it possible to categorise users and measure their evolution. In this configuration, social work becomes predictable and controllable, leading to decisions being made without knowing the individual. In the case of the integration company, the social worker must lead the user towards employability. Through this system, the social worker focuses on the production of individuals who are able to be employed in the labour market rather than on the development of individuals who are able to cope with and manage psychological and physical pressures. The term used to refer to users is "customer". It is the very identity of social work that is changed. When this system is associated with performance objectives, it may become necessary to select the users who will be most likely to become employable, thus excluding the profiles that are most difficult to support.

The relationship between the State and non-profit organisations

A management tool is a means of materially demonstrating the commitment of an actor. The call for projects is a performance measurement tool at the interface of the relationship between the State and NPOs. It is used from a good governance perspective and is therefore intended to be a source of innovation, transparency and free competition. The call for projects thus makes it possible to set out the various objectives of the State and aims to select the organisations, in this case the NPOs, that will be able to meet them.

The partnership between public authorities and non-profit institutions is based on the public interest. Each of the two partners has advantages in terms of carrying out missions of general interest in the best possible way. Non-profit institutions allow for "more proximity, diversity, flexibility, priority in detecting social need, access to free resources through donations and volunteering, small size that allows for tailor-made services, and finally, the promotion of civic values" (Archambault, 2017, p. 488). As for public authorities, they can generate significant resources, in particular through taxation, and make different types of resources available. They also have the power to regulate and create rights to ensure equality between individuals and territories.

The NPOs work together with the State, which is one of the main funders of the NPOs, particularly with regard to social action. Among the elements that recompose the relationship between the State and NPOs, we note the importance of the way in which public funds are distributed. This is reflected in the increase in calls for projects, funding by users and also the development of sponsorship. Calls for projects make it possible, among other things, to contractualise the relationship between the State and NPOs. The State thus sets the general guidelines and leaves operators free to implement them (Cottin-Marx et al., 2017).

Another important element that strongly binds the State and NPOs is employment. Indeed, the non-profit sector concentrates a large part of the professional integration schemes, in particular with subsidised jobs. NPOs serve as a transitional space for people in difficulty and are thus a variable in the adjustment of employment policy. At the same time, successive reforms and public procurement have contributed to the precariousness of employment in the non-profit sector (Cottin-Marx et al., 2017).

The case of non-profit organisations with social missions

This second part is based on interviews that were carried out with 22 NPOs as part of a thesis. On this occasion, the actors interviewed who were directors of NPOs or presidents evoked their vision of the organisation of social action in France but also that of their relationship with the State. Some elements will be illustrated by excerpts from these interviews.

74   *Pauline Boisselier*

The construction of social action

NPOs have always been an important player in carrying out social actions. Today, they are a real link between users and government services. NPOs are concerned about the quality of the social actions they are able to offer. Despite the various changes they are undergoing, and in particular the reduction in subsidies, they want to maintain the quality of their support. However, NPOs are finding that their mode of operation is bound to change, as well as the very dynamics of social work. The professions of social work are in the process of evolving, for example, they evoke the integration of former people supported by NPOs, as new actors of social work. An actor likely to share his or her career path and to be able to support in turn, either as an employee or as a volunteer. Social action must be thought of differently and the accompaniment of people is thus transformed.

Initially, it is the NPOs that determine the needs to be met, they do so according to the demand of the public and what they observe on the ground. These observations are shared jointly and with partners and institutions: "the actions evolve according to the social and political context, the needs of the members and the inhabitants of the neighbourhood" (NPO#7).

The need is sometimes created by the political context and decisions that are made directly by the government. The role of NPOs is to anticipate this need. For example, the transition to all-digital for many public services has led to a digital divide for a large number of people, so it has been necessary to develop new services to support them, a new mission that has been added to the work of many NPOs.

Funders have confidence in the degree of expertise of the NPOs to identify the need. NPOs are then a source of proposals to carry out actions that meet these needs and funders support them. Since the subprime crisis and the early 2000s, this ratio has tended to reverse in the context of the scarcity of resources. It is the funders who will determine the needs that are priorities and that are likely to evolve according to political orientations: "now, there are guidelines that are wanted by the public authorities that evolve over time according to the needs that are identified by the inhabitants. In any case, we must adapt our proposal to this development" (NPO#6). These guidelines are set out in partnership agreements and go so far as to directly condition the activities of certain NPOs.

Once the need has been assessed, the starting point for NPOs, when they choose to implement an action, is to know whether it will be able to be in line with the purpose of the NPO. The board of directors is then responsible for assessing the conformity of the action with the purpose of the NPO and deciding whether it will be implemented: "then there is the board of directors on each new project who decides, is it the corporate purpose of the non-profit organisation or not, so they allow us to apply when we are in the context of new projects" (NPO#21).

The actions put in place can also come from proposals from people wishing to get involved in the NPO. The NPO then reflects on the adequacy between an observed need and the object of the NPO. Proposals can thus come from several stakeholders, such as volunteers and partners, who recognise the know-how of the associative structure.

As a result of these different choices of action, NPOs may notice a lack of alignment between the objectives of the NPO and the objectives of the funders. A dialogue can then be initiated between the NPO and the funder to readjust the project: "and then, the implementation of certain projects in the field is sometimes a little out of step between expectations and what is achievable, but it doesn't really pose any difficulties, we also readjust as we go along during the different stages of the projects, during the monitoring committees in particular" (NPO#6).

But in other situations, there is an incompatibility between the results of the NPO, which are potentially long term, and those of the funders, which are expected in the short term. Thus, when NPOs no longer feel able to meet the demand and provide the expected results, it can lead to the cessation of the action.

The relationship with the State

The NPOs describe the relationship they have with the State on a basis of trust. Most of the NPOs surveyed have been in existence for many years. For the "youngest", they are generally emanations of old structures that have disappeared or social workers who have become more independent. Thus, there is a relationship of trust between these NPOs, the State and its representatives: "the non-profit organisations that come who have a project, who see a need and who go to see, today we have a legitimacy that is not questionable from the public authorities, to define the public policies to which they want to respond and in such a way as not to fall into the favouritism of this or that non-profit organisation" (NPO#21).

This relationship of trust is possible in particular through the controls that are carried out. NPOs are in demand, they want to show how they use the resources allocated to them: "non-profit organisations that do work with public money must be perfectly supervised and controlled, I don't deny that, here we are very concerned about respecting public policies" (NPO#20).

This close relationship with the State leads to a relationship of dependency for some NPOs. The majority of non-profit funds come from public funding. NPOs depend on funding, but more broadly on the political system: "this evolution will depend a lot on the upcoming elections because inevitably from one municipal team to another there are directions that are taken and others that are a little abandoned. So we are also dependent on the political system in place, unfortunately" (NPO#6).

However, some NPOs choose to be independent and to free themselves from the funding offered by the State. They need to assert this independence in order to be able to best respond to the needs they identify. However, this does not mean that the State is completely disengaged, even if it does not directly finance

76   *Pauline Boisselier*

certain actions, it participates indirectly in the NPO, through a subsidised contract for example. This independence is necessary for some NPOs because they are in opposition to the State in the context of certain public policies. One example is the protection of people's rights in the context of the reception of refugees.

Non-profit organisations: Tools for managing public policies

The State and its local authorities are the main funders of NPOs. Political decisions have a direct impact on NPOs. This is the case, for example, when new calculation methods are used to define a social need. The crisis of the 2000s reversed the exchange relationship between funders and NPOs. Initially, the NPOs were a force for proposals and funding followed. Now, some funding is offered along political lines. The State may have to target certain projects and directly indicate the directions that the NPOs must take, but NPOs try to negotiate these proposals. They also feel that they are losing their status as privileged partners, the State only thinks in terms of specific objectives and the relationship between the State and NPOs becomes more impersonal: "we do not recognise that social and educational action has a cost and that this cost cannot be borne by the beneficiaries, at least in a very minority way. And so this social cost, it is absolutely necessary for the institutions to take it into account, but for the moment, on the contrary, I have the impression that they are playing with us by making us bear the costs and if we drown, they take someone else, that's it, [...]. We are no longer associative in partnership with them, we are private service providers, disposable and interchangeable, so the ideological background of the non-profit organisation does not matter in the end to the institutional" (NPO#5).

Some NPOs thus feel that they are being instrumentalised, whose vocation is only to respond to political wills: "we must all be able to rely on each other because we manage all the difficult issues rather than shooting each other in the legs and we can sometimes be instrumentalized, we have to be careful" (NPO#19).

In some situations, they even become a field of application for social policies. This application is also materialised by a selection that takes place among the public. Indeed, NPOs can be encouraged to choose the people most likely to succeed in social support, thus marginalising the most precarious.

The State is thus sometimes positioned as the sole decision-maker in the application of public policies but also as master of the future of certain NPOs.

One example is a type of action that had been greatly reduced due to a lack of support and which is now once again popular with public policies: holiday stays, formerly known as "holiday camps". Many of the holiday centres hosting camps have disappeared but are now sought after to organise "learning camps" (i.e. a scheme set up by the Ministry of National Education following the crisis caused by COVID-19 in order to strengthen knowledge and skills in a playful setting).

This application of social policy by the State takes the form of the use of specific tools common to all. These tools are complex and require a certain level of expertise, which is therefore only possible for sufficiently structured NPOs. In particular, one tool is increasingly used by the State to implement its public policies: calls for projects. This tendering system is gradually becoming the main means of obtaining public subsidies. Thus, NPOs apply for a project proposed by a local authority for a given period. These calls for projects are offered as part of a "public contract": "it's a mission given to us by the Department that has been transformed into a public market, so today we do public procurement" (NPO#2).

Calls for projects are one of the levers of application of the State in terms of social policy. They allow them to precisely define the need they want to meet. This lever is applicable to all funders, foundations and companies that precisely target the social and societal impact they wish to have. This system puts NPOs in competition with each other and allows funders to select the best possible project according to its objectives: "the problem with calls for tenders is that you enter a system that is very competitive and that is no longer linked to your project but to develop something through, your project through an order, which means that, at one time or another, you are completely dependent on the specifier" (NPO#4).

This system aims to create social innovation but it does not allow NPOs to sustain their activity. Indeed, the recruitment of certain people depends solely on ongoing projects. Some NPOs are constantly looking for new projects and respond to a very large number of calls for projects, sometimes far from their main field of activity, in order to generate financial resources. Some stakeholders consider this system to be inefficient. There is a lack of cooperation between the administrators of the calls for projects and the people on the ground.

This system makes NPOs very dependent on political orientations. The halt of certain projects can be done very abruptly, on criteria that seem subjective. It is a system that is presented as complex and time-consuming, and NPOs respond when they have time to do so. In addition, this type of funding requires a stable financial situation for NPOs because there is a significant time lag between the notification of allocation and the disbursement of funds. Thus, this system of calls for projects is more suitable for large structures that have both in-house skills and financial stability allowing them to manage the financial constraints related to this system.

The power to restructure the non-profit landscape

The State is positioned as the actor who has "the power". It has not only the power to guide public policy but also the power to change the direction of NPOs. This brings us back to the notions of dependence and instrumentalisation mentioned above: "I see more and more, it's the political skill of administrative choices, that is to say that a department director changes and we change direction. As we are enslaved as a service to the public, if not a public service, we have to change hats, change, this is hardly acceptable for an non-profit organisation that would like to be autonomous, in fact we are no longer autonomous" (NPO#5).

78   *Pauline Boisselier*

The State would use two processes to guide the structures: "survival financing" and "financing by public procurement". The first process is to give just enough in terms of funding so that the structure can continue to carry out actions. Public procurement, on the other hand, is a process that has been mentioned above. Today, it is the preferred means of financing social action. There would thus be an intention on the part of the State to transform NPOs, to bring them closer to an entrepreneurial model.

This intention to transform takes the form of incentives for regrouping, i.e. the merging of NPOs with each other: "The public authorities have asked them to grow, to come together, to absorb themselves, to become less interlocutors" (NPO#12).

Even if NPOs try to resist these incentives, they are ready to give in when they have no choice financially and want above all to guarantee the continuation of the shares. This rapprochement therefore leads to the merger of NPOs. There are structures that are absorbed by others. These are the "biggest" NPOs in the sector that have the ability to merge. They are approached to absorb small NPOs that are encountering many difficulties and are at risk of filing for bankruptcy. There are also small NPOs that merge with each other to be able to form a "big" NPO and thus increase their capacity for action and pool their resources and skills in order to be able to compete with other structures.

Ultimately, the non-profit landscape would be made up of small local NPOs, described as "militant" and larger, so-called "professional" NPOs, capable of responding to public orders.

Conclusion

The adoption of new standards leads to organisational changes and the use of new tools. The use of the call for projects is part of a good governance approach, in particular through its desire for transparency, but also with a performance objective. It is a question for the State to define objectives and to ensure that NPOs will be able to meet them. The State must be efficient and transparent in the allocation of resources. However, the relationship between the State and the NPOs has changed. The way in which social action is carried out is being rethought, as illustrated by the call for projects (or public commissions). In the past, NPOs identified needs and proposed projects, and in return received grants to carry them out, so they had a certain flexibility to carry out these projects. With calls for projects, this relationship is reversed, it is the funders who determine a need and request that a project be carried out to meet it. These calls for projects are offered within the framework of a public contract, they allow for the direct application of public policies. Calls for projects make it possible, among other things, to contractualise the relationship between the State and NPOs. The State thus sets the general guidelines and leaves operators free to implement them (Cottin-Marx et al., 2017). By targeting in a precise way, the call for projects can leave little room for negotiation for NPOs. Some, who have been working with the State for many years, feel that they are losing their status as privileged partners. This feeling is all the more accentuated by the increased competition between organisations. However, the NPOs consider that they work in a relationship of trust with the State and call for ever more transparency, they are in demand for evaluation tools to guarantee their work and the proper use of the resources allocated to them. This tool is not reserved for the State, it is used by foundations and companies that are also keen to be able to propose projects according to their values. NPOs must therefore adapt to these guidelines and follow them. The choice to respond to a call for projects or not is supposed to be made according to the conformity with the purpose of the NPO, but this is not always the case.

We can recall that accounting is used as a resource by those who hold power in the organisation to impose the definition of the business world they wish to create on the other members of the organisation. We show that this is also the case for calls for projects, the fact of generalising them allows funders to determine how they want social action to be carried out and how to interact with organisations. Farjaudon and Morales (2013) have shown that accounting plays a role in consensus-building, particularly in enabling dominant groups to preserve their interests through what appears to be a compromise. Our research shows that funders use calls for projects to protect their interests by allowing them to meet specific objectives, thus taking a position of power over the organisation of social action. Indeed, for NPOs that use calls for projects to finance themselves, there are organisational consequences. The more they use it, the more they need to "grow", to structure themselves, this is how NPOs are absorbed and others merge, the non-profit landscape is thus redrawn.

The use of management tools is necessary and accepted by non-profit organisations, as they allow for greater transparency. However, in its performative dimension, it can lead to a redefinition of relationships and have consequences on the functioning of the various stakeholders. The evolution of this relationship has an influence on the construction of social action and the management of NPOs (Figure 4.1). The need for efficiency can have negative consequences on its original purpose.

The call for projects is at the heart of the relationship between stakeholders, particularly the State and non-profit organisations. It is thus part of two logics. On the one hand, governance consists mainly in transparently allocating funds to organisations so that they can produce actions that meet societal needs. On the other hand, performance, which means meeting very specific objectives set by the public authorities through tight budgetary envelopes, to enable more innovation to emerge. The field observations highlighted in this study tend to show that the weight of governance and performance is unbalanced. When the performance dimension of the management tool dominates, the relationship between the State and the non-profit organisations can be weakened. Increased

80 *Pauline Boisselier*

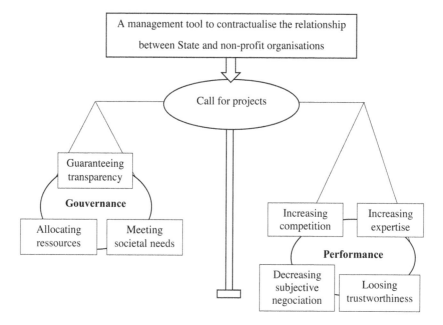

Figure 4.1 (Im)balance between governance and performance

competition, leading to cost wars, the expertise required to put together administrative files and the necessary financial stability, mean that some NPOs are no longer able to access this type of resource allocation. Moreover, overly precise objectives, leaving little room for dialogue, can hinder the development of certain projects previously set up. NPOs that have worked closely with the State for many years find their relationship weakened, as they feel reduced to a mere operator of interchangeable public policies. Thus, governance aimed at aligning the aims of these organisations with the interests of society can be weakened by performance objectives that are too high.

References

Amslem, T., & Gendron, Y. (2019). From emotionality to the cultivation of employability: An ethnography of change in social work expertise following the spread of quantification in a social enterprise. *Management Accounting Research, 42*, 39–55. https://doi.org/10.1016/j.mar.2018.06.001

Archambault, É (2017). Associations et pouvoirs publics : Vers une convergence des modèles en Europe. [Nonprofit organizations and public authorities: Towards a convergence of models in Europe]. *Revue française d'administration publique, 163*(3), 477. https://doi.org/10.3917/rfap.163.0477

Arjaliès, D.-L., & Mundy, J. (2013). The use of management control systems to manage CSR strategy: A levers of control perspective. *Management Accounting Research, 24*(4), 284–300. https://doi.org/10.1016/j.mar.2013.06.003

How funding and control tools shape the relationships   81

Bernet, J., Eynaud, P., Maurel, O., & Vercher-Chaptal, C. (2016). La gestion des associations. [Management of nonprofit organizations]. *VST – Vie sociale et traitements, revue des CEMEA, N°, 131*(3), 51–54.

Boisselier, P. (2023). Évolution d'un secteur. le rôle des outils de gestion dans la construction de l'identité organisationnelle: le cas des associations à but social. [Evolution of a sector. The role of management tools in the construction of organizational identity: The case of social nonprofit organizations]. In *Gestion et management*. Université Côte d'Azur.

Bruining, H., Bonnet, M., & Wright, M. (2004). Management control systems and strategy change in buyouts. *Management Accounting Research, 15*(thèse2), 155–177. https://doi.org/10.1016/j.mar.2004.03.003

Chiapello, È, & Gilbert, P. (2020). *Sociologie des outils de gestion*. La Découverte.

Coller, G., Frigotto, M. L., & Costa, E. (2018). Management control system and strategy: The transforming role of implementation. *Journal of Applied Accounting Research, 19*(1), 141–160. https://doi.org/10.1108/JAAR-01-2016-0002

Cottin-Marx, S., Hély, M., Jeannot, G., & Simonet, M. (2017). La recomposition des relations entre l'État et les associations: Désengagements et réengagements. [The recomposition of relations between the State and nonprofit organizations: Disengagements and re-engagements]. *Revue française d'administration publique, 163*(3), 463. https://doi.org/10.3917/rfap.163.0463

Fabre, P. (2005). L'évaluation de la performance des associations dans les villes françaises, entre proximité et contingence. [The evaluation of the performance of nonprofit organizations in French cities, between proximity and contingency]. *Comptabilité – Contrôle – Audit, 11*(1), 55. https://doi.org/10.3917/cca.111.0055

Farjaudon, A.-L., & Morales, J. (2013). In search of consensus: The role of accounting in the definition and reproduction of dominant interests. *Critical Perspectives on Accounting, 24*(2), 154–171. https://doi.org/10.1016/j.cpa.2012.09.010

Gond, J.-P., Grubnic, S., Herzig, C., & Moon, J. (2012). Configuring management control systems: Theorizing the integration of strategy and sustainability. *Management Accounting Research, 23*(3), 205–223. https://doi.org/10.1016/j.mar.2012.06.003

Henri, J.-F. (2006). Management control systems and strategy: A resource-based perspective. *Accounting, Organizations and Society, 31*(6), 529–558. https://doi.org/10.1016/j.aos.2005.07.001

Khalifa, R., & Scarparo, S. (2021). Gender responsive budgeting: A tool for gender equality. *Critical Perspectives on Accounting, 79*, 102183. https://doi.org/10.1016/j.cpa.2020.102183

Laguir, L., Laguir, I., & Tchemeni, E. (2019). Implementing CSR activities through management control systems: A formal and informal control perspective. *Accounting, Auditing & Accountability Journal*. https://doi.org/10.1108/AAAJ-05-2016-2566

Langfield-Smith, K. (1997). Management control systems and strategy: A critical review. *Accounting, Organizations and Society, 22*(2), 207–232. https://doi.org/10.1016/S0361-3682(95)00040-2

Lemaire, C. (2021). Quand le contrôle de gestion façonne les relations inter-organisationnelles: Le cas de l'introduction d'un tableau de bord dans le médico-social. [When management control shapes inter-organizational relationships: The case of the introduction of a dashboard in the medico-social sector]. *Comptabilité Contrôle Audit, Tome, 27*(3), 7–40. https://doi.org/10.3917/cca.273.0007

Nilsson, F. (2002). Strategy and management control systems: A study of the design and use of management control systems following takeover. *Accounting & Finance, 42*(1), 41–71.

Ogden, S. G., & Anderson, F. (1999). The role of accounting in organisational change: Promoting performance improvements in the privatised uk water industry. *Critical Perspectives on Accounting, 10*(1), 91–124. https://doi.org/10.1006/cpac.1998.0200

82 *Pauline Boisselier*

Simons, R. (1990). The role of management control systems in creating competitive advantage: New perspectives. *Accounting, Organizations and Society, 15*(1), 127–143. https://doi.org/10.1016/0361-3682(90)90018-P

Slagmulder, R. (1997). Using management control systems to achieve alignment between strategic investment decisions and strategy. *Management Accounting Research, 8*(1), 103–139. https://doi.org/10.1006/mare.1996.0035

Valéau, P. (2003). Différentes manières de gérer les associations. [Different ways of managing nonprofit organizations]. *Revue française de gestion, 29*(146), 9–22. https://doi.org/10.3166/rfg.146.9-22

5 What strategic processes to meet the challenges of democratic governance? The case of mergers between non-profit organisations

Adrien Laurent

Introduction

The rules of good governance as defined by the ISO 37000:2021 standard involve first and foremost "that decision-making within the organisation is based on the organisation's ethos, culture, norms, practices, behaviours, structures and processes". The wording of the standard closely links good governance to the maintenance of a clear objective enabling "the expectations of relevant stakeholders" to be integrated. In more detail, the standard identifies strategy as one of the four fundamental principles: "strategy is the pattern of evolving intentions that provide direction for harmonizing and focusing effort to fulfil the organisational purpose, associated value generation objectives and related strategic outcomes".

In this chapter, we attempt to demonstrate that the ISO 37000:2021 standard offers interesting proposals for non-profit organisations (NPOs) given the specific nature of their strategic processes. We clarify the underlying logic of the ISO 37000:2021 standard by shedding both theoretical and empirical light on the strategic practice of NPOs. Our demonstration is based on several stages.

We show that the ISO 37000:2021 standard is to some extent rooted in the "strategy-as-practice" perspective which is particularly interesting for explaining the real and concrete practice of NPO strategy. This approach has emerged in the realm of academic thinking in the recent years with an emphasis on the need to get a better grasp of the reality of organisational strategy by addressing its practical and collective dimension. It encourages a more in-depth exploration of the diversity of players involved in strategic practice, extending beyond the traditional focus on a management elite. As such, it challenges the traditional view of strategy as a functional, planned endeavour. Instead, it underscores the distributed, collective, and day-to-day nature of strategic work.

This perspective gains particular significance when applied to NPOs, which appear specific in two respects. On the one hand, they rely on a vast array of stakeholders, including volunteers (at field and governance level), management staff, employees, and beneficiaries, which introduces unique complexities in understanding their strategic dynamics. On the other hand, they raise the question

DOI: 10.4324/9781003460572-8

84 *Adrien Laurent*

of the democratic nature of their governance and decision-making processes, as well as the social depth of their activity which cannot be reduced to the pursuit of economic or financial performance.

In this chapter, we place particular emphasis on the case of inter-organisational restructuring (IOR) and mergers which, as we show, are a particularly revealing case of the nature of the strategic choices facing NPOs. More specifically, mergers represent a distinct type of restructuring operation, compelling organisations to redefine their internal and external boundaries. We draw from a compelling case study – a French national federation resulting from the merger of two former professional organisations. This merger aimed to create a national network of professionals committed to promoting a new approach to addressing addiction issues. In the course of this merger, the challenge consisted in integrating former members, professionals, and volunteers into a new organisational structure but also defining new missions.

In order to give substance to a "practical" understanding of the strategy of NPOs in the context of a merger operation, we focus on the intricate social dynamics at stake both inside and outside the boundaries of NPOs. To do so, we mobilise the actor-network theory (ANT). This approach offers valuable insights on NPOs' strategy approached as a translation process comprising four steps: problematisation, interessement (or interest-building), enrolment, and mobilisation. This translation process serves as a guide to comprehend the composition and evolution of networks during the merger process. When translation is achieved, participants are enrolled through "associations" in a stabilised and legitimate network (Callon, 1986; Latour, 2006). Having presented the results of our case study and carried out an in-depth conceptual analysis focusing on both the internal and institutional dimensions of the strategic practice of NPOs, we propose a number of recommendations for a practitioner audience.

The need for analytical tools to grasp the social depth of NPOs' strategy

Understanding the practical and collective dimension of strategy

Recent research in strategic management has focused on the need to understand with greater finesse the drivers of strategic practice in organisations. In this approach, strategy is not (only) a property that organisations "have", but more as "something that people do" (Johnson et al., 2007; Whittington, 2006). Interest is focused on the processual and concrete reality of the strategic making: "conventionally, strategy researchers assume that strategy is something *organisations have*. [...] they have strategic planning processes, decision processes and change processes. In this view, strategy is a property of organisations. We take a different perspective: strategy is something that *people do*. Strategy is an activity. [...] What do the people engaged in strategizing actually do and how do they influence strategic outcomes?" (Johnson et al., 2007, p. 3).

This new perspective is linked to the "practical turn" in social sciences (Golsorkhi et al., 2010; Vaara & Whittington, 2012; Whittington, 2006) and its influence on strategic thinking since the 2000s. This implies an interest in three distinct levels of analysis: practices, i.e. "shared routines of behaviour, including traditions, norms and procedures that determine the way we think or act"; practice (or *praxis*), which "corresponds to the activity itself, what people actually do"; and finally, practitioners, i.e. who are "the actors of strategy", the strategists who implement this activity and carry out these practices (Whittington, 2006).

The research agenda defined by the promoters of the "strategy-as-practice" perspective (Allard-Poesi, 2006; Jarzabkowski & Paul Spee, 2009; Seidl et al., 2006; Whittington, 2006) encourages much more detailed investigation of the plurality of players involved in strategic practice. The aim is to identify these practitioners by looking beyond the dominant players, the "elite" (Whittington, 2006), who have hitherto been the exclusive focus of strategy research (Nizet & Pichault, 2015): "strategy practitioners are those who make, model and execute strategies. They are not simply senior managers, whose core business is strategy. Many other actors carry out strategic work" (Whittington, 2006, p. 619).

The study of strategy as practice involves identifying these actors, their resources and skills, and their role in strategic practice. This distances the analyst from a purely functionalist and planning approach to strategy, towards the distributed, collective, and daily strategic work, as confirmed in particular by Beaujolin-Bellet and Schmidt (2012) with regard to the restructuring operations that will be the specific focus of this chapter: "on the one hand, restructurings are not the result of a single, isolated, event-driven decision, but rather the fruit of a tangle of decisions, without it always being easy from the outside to identify the triggering event and the various stages, and without these stages always unfolding in a linear fashion" (Beaujolin-Bellet & Schmidt, 2012, p. 50).

This theoretical perspective is of great interest in highlighting the shortcomings of the existing literature dealing with strategy in NPOs, to which we propose to respond. This literature tends to ignore the processual and distributed dimension of strategy in favour of recommendations about the "content" of strategy. This is problematic in organisations driven by specific missions and by different categories of stakeholders (volunteers at operational and governance levels, management teams and employees with specific motivations, beneficiaries often playing a role in governance, etc.), which this classic perspective on strategy does not allow us to grasp.

However, this "practical turn" in strategy remains somewhat limited in the sense that it does not fully offer operational tools and analytical grids for the researcher or practitioner in order to grasp the complexity of strategic processes and the players involved. To address this, we propose to use an analytical framework rooted in the ANT.

86 *Adrien Laurent*

Strategy as a translation process

ANT, developed in the 1980s by Callon and Latour, challenges traditional views on social phenomena by focusing on objects and their controversies, instead of predetermined social structures. Starting from the objects, we must then: "give an account of the controversies they give rise to and follow the action, *i.e.* the transformations of the world [...] without involving the depth of the structures that escape the awareness of the participants" (Dumez, 2011).

ANT sees all participants, or actants, as entities that attempt to influence their surroundings and create dependencies through translation, a process of making statements comprehensible to others and linking previously unconnected entities (Callon, 1986). This approach emphasises the dynamic nature of relationships and the constant transformation of the world through interactions among actants. Stakeholders, rather than having their existence postulated by the analyst, are therefore defined by the set of relationships they maintain, by their articulation within socio-technical networks.

Translation is central to ANT, involving four stages: problematisation, where issues are identified; interessement, establishing roles and alliances; enrolment, where roles are accepted; and mobilisation of allies, enhancing coordination in the socio-technical network by means of spokespersons who bring together the enlisted actants and reduce the number of voices. Translation is the transformation of a statement to make it comprehensible to another actant. It "makes it possible to link two things that were not previously linked" (Law, 1999), mobilising the actants by translating their respective interests and objectives, in a dynamic process. The translation process itself is riddled with controversy, creating opportunities for negotiation between the various players involved, through the intermediary of spokespersons (Callon, 1986).

This framework offers a novel lens for strategic analysis, viewing problems and stakeholders as emergent from specific contexts rather than pre-existing, and focusing on the negotiation and redefinition of relationships through translation. It does not postulate pre-existing "problems" or even pre-existing players who would be by nature responsible for defining strategic choices. On the contrary, these objects and players are indeterminate and emerge through observation in specific contexts.

In our view, the sociology of translation complements the "practical turn" in strategy by clarifying the processual dimension of strategy (Maisonnasse, 2014) and its complexity. It also provides a more operational framework for researchers and practitioners interested in the strategic practice of NPOs, through a number of concepts and a clear process that can be applied in a wide variety of organisational contexts. We would add that it can make it possible to study collective processes in greater detail by moving away from a heroic vision of the strategist, by focusing on the accidents, controversies, and compromises that run through them. This theoretical approach seems particularly relevant to the study of strategic practice in NPOs and the diversity of those involved in this process: "the approach seems well suited to contexts involving numerous autonomous participants with loose links between them, i.e. where the locus of power is diffuse and objectives divergent and changing. The approach has the advantage of simultaneously targeting the mobilisation of multiple meanings and the links between the many different individuals in a dynamic way" (Denis et al., 2014, p. 892).

Understanding strategy in its institutional context: A tension between isomorphism and the capacity for institutional work

A fundamental aspect of the social dimension of strategy is the institutional nature of strategic practices, especially important in NPOs. Some scholars associate the unique characteristics of NPOs with their institutional context. Durkheim argued long ago that NPOs are founded on solidarity rather than contracts. This underscores the importance of examining the institutional aspects of the organisation, including its purpose, the legitimacy of its collective action, and the consensus on the "rules of the game" that govern relationships and objectives, which encompass both economic and political aspects (Chanial & Laville, 2001).

However, the institutional nature of NPOs extends beyond this collective intent. NPOs emerge from the confluence of individual wills responding to societal needs unmet by the existing institutional framework and revolve around a collective vision and shared beliefs. This collective intent may embody various interpretations of solidarity, from a private, familial approach to one focused on the general interest (Laville & Sainsaulieu, 2013). An institutional logic that considers this collective intent as a public good legitimises the organisation's actions (Haeringer & Traversaz, 2002).

Moreover, this institutional aspect is not solely about collective will. By operating within a specific administrative, social, and economic context, an organisation must validate the legitimacy of its actions (Laville, 2012) and align with external norms. The pressure to conform to the prevailing practices of their environment, deemed legitimate, leads to institutional isomorphism (DiMaggio & Powell, 1983). The institutional setting shapes how actors understand the world and define the structures, actions, and ideologies (Powell & DiMaggio, 1997).

Therefore, voluntary organisations adopt new logics, fostering "new compromises that anchor the NPO in its social mission and empower it with transformative action" (Haeringer & Traversaz, 2002). This dynamic between the foundational and established aspects of the organisation echoes Jürgen Habermas's (1987) notion of a tension between communicative action, which fosters normative orientations in autonomous public spaces, and administrative power, which reframes these orientations for efficiency (Traversaz, 2002). This inherent tension in NPOs reflects a balance between maintaining legitimacy through autonomous public space and fulfilling public policy goals, including how NPOs are utilised by governments to meet their objectives (Traversaz, 2002).

88   *Adrien Laurent*

This insight is crucial for understanding NPO strategy, highlighting the tensions between different institutional logics and goals within the organisation's institutional environment. This is particularly evident in IORs and mergers.

Inter-organisational restructurings and mergers: A typical case of the tensions experienced by NPOs in their strategic practice

Restructurings and mergers in the voluntary sector

Research highlights "grouping movements" within the voluntary sector, indicating a trend towards inter-organisational regrouping characterised by cooperation, pooling, and partnerships (Grenier & Guitton-Philippe, 2011). This structural shift involves various cooperation forms, including mergers, significantly impacting NPO identities and practices. Marival et al. (2015) advocate for a broad interpretation of cooperation, encompassing any form of collaboration for mutual benefit. However, true cooperation implies maintaining legal autonomy, in contrast to mergers, which may result in organisational disappearance and loss of autonomy (Cueille & Devreese, 2012). This study focuses on mergers as specific restructuring forms, redefining organisational boundaries and necessitating a review of internal and external governance (Campbell, 2008; Kohm & La Piana, 2003).

Strategic implications of IOR and mergers

The voluntary sector's recent push towards IOR and mergers is driven by major changes in the institutional environment (regulations, competitive pressures). This has led to a "normalization" of NPOs and a managerial focus threatening organisational identity and collective projects (Busson-Villa & Gallopel-Morvan, 2012). NPOs face pressures to adopt corporate management tools and principles, risking loss of their unique character and mission (Maier et al., 2014). The trend towards grouping, driven by efficiency and competitive adaptation, reflects a broader movement towards organisational concentration (Bastide, 2015).

However, despite the restrictive context, some mergers and cooperations are strategic choices aimed at enhancing collective projects and addressing local needs, demonstrating potential for social innovation and improved socio-political function (Hadj et al., 2015). This study assesses how strategic practices and organisational design in mergers can serve a redefined collective project and contribute to institutional change, advocating for a naturalistic approach to understanding these processes (Kœnig & Meier, 2001).

The reasons why IORs fail

The literature on restructuring and mergers has long emphasised the high proportion of failures among these operations. This is particularly the case in the field of NPOs, which can be explained by reasons that are both common to for-profit organisations and specific to the voluntary sector.

Reasons common to all kind of organisations

Failures often stem from unclear strategic goals, inadequate assessment of targets, incompatibility in size and culture between merging organisations, and ineffective merger management (Benton & Austin, 2010). The simplicity of approaches contrasts with the complexity of restructuring impacts on territories, social dynamics, work groups, individuals, and leadership. Despite restructuring's immediate effects, its long-term and indirect consequences, such as organisational and human dysfunctions, are frequently overlooked. These include information system integration challenges, loss of organisational knowledge, skill gaps, tacit knowledge loss, managerial guilt, employee insecurity, resistance to change, decreased motivation, stifled innovation, and emerging conflicts. The hidden costs are often neglected in favour of immediate benefits such as economies of scale and financial savings, leading to a high failure rate (Bartholdy et al., 2009).

Voluntary sector-specific reasons

Failures in the voluntary sector also arise from decision-making inertia or resistance, often resulting in delayed actions and weakened positions for NPOs (Golensky & DeRuiter, 1999, 2002). The introduction of competitive regulations by public authorities increases divisions within the sector, diminishing NPOs' innovative capacities and leading to a preference for mergers over other restructuring forms. Additionally, the shift towards organisational models focused on economic performance overlooks the importance of the mission, volunteers, and the institutional essence of NPOs. The transition from mission-driven professionals to management-focused leaders, trained in for-profit sectors, creates internal communication barriers and decision-making challenges during restructuring, exacerbating the dilemma between social mission and managerial standardisation amidst new public management pressures from authorities (Avare & Sponem, 2008).

A case study

Our research delves into an important case study – the merger of two federations within the addiction sector in France. This merger led to the creation of the Federation Addiction, aimed at achieving a unified approach to addiction, moving away from the segmented focus on alcoholism and drug addiction. This transformative effort sought to bring together professionals in the fields of care, prevention, and harm reduction, all converging around a cross-disciplinary perspective on addiction.

90 *Adrien Laurent*

Context and comprehensive case overview

Our study centres on the merger that took place in 2011, between two organisations called ANIT(EA) and F3A.

Association Nationale des Intervenants en Toxicomanie (ANIT/*National Association of Drug Practitioners*) was founded in 1980 and responded to the fragmented landscape of drug addiction care. ANIT advocated for a comprehensive understanding of addiction beyond medicalisation or punitive approaches to drug consumption. Simultaneously, the field of alcohology began to take shape in 1975 with the emergence of specialised centres. This culminated in 1994 with the creation of the first federation, which later became the Fédération Française des Acteurs de l'Alcoologie et de l'Addictologie (F3A/*French Federation of Alcohol and Addiction Professionals*) in 2002.

In the early 2000s, the concept of addiction expanded to encompass a wide range of substances, including psychotropic drugs, alcohol, or even food. This shift prompted a re-evaluation of existing compartmentalised approaches to addiction care. Consequently, a new regulation proposed in 2007 led to the establishment of general addiction centres, replacing specialist centres. These new centres could either arise from a change in status or from mergers involving formerly specialised establishments. This transition in the addiction sector occurred alongside broader changes in public funding, marked by budget constraints. In 2010, health policies underwent regionalisation with the establishment of Regional Health Agencies, adding complexity and uncertainty, compelling local organisations to collaborate or merge in response to an uncertain future.

In this context of sweeping reform, ANIT and F3A, the two primary representative organisations in the addiction sector, began to contemplate a strategic convergence, rooted in a unified project.

Results of the case study

Merger as a quest for organisational legitimacy

The motivation behind this merger lay in the evolving landscape of public policy and the challenging environment faced by both associations. It was not simply a response to a managerial reason advocating for merger as a means of organisational efficiency. Instead, it was a response to the imperative of fortifying the legitimacy of organisations whose missions no longer aligned with the changing legal and institutional framework of their sector. F3A, in particular, was a significantly smaller association facing its own set of challenges. In addition to embracing a comprehensive approach to addictions and adapting to ongoing reforms, there was a realisation that the federation might eventually become obsolete. Simultaneously, membership in both ANIT and F3A was on a downward trend.

The merger was a response to deep shifts in public policy and the specific challenges faced by these two associations. From a strategic standpoint, stakeholders

What strategic processes to meet the challenges of democratic governance? 91

within the drug addiction sector needed to reassert their legitimacy in the eyes of institutional partners: "we had to make it clear that we were not in opposition, between the social and the health care sectors, and to do that, there was nothing better than to form an alliance with others whose history, particularly in the field of alcohol, was exactly the opposite" (former chairman of ANIT).

Therefore, the merger between F3A and ANIT became an imperative for restoring organisational legitimacy, not only to the public authorities but also to member organisations and professionals operating within the addiction sector. The merger was formally settled at the beginning of 2011.

Organisational design and enrolment

While the necessity of the merger was evident, the intricate process of organisational design requires a deeper exploration. This process primarily involved translating the varied interests of actants both inside and outside the federation, with the ultimate aim of "enrolling" them. Several key actors emerged and were retained for detailed analysis, including the chairmen of both associations, the managing director (initially of ANIT, which was later renamed ANITEA shortly before the merger, and subsequently of Fédération Addiction), public partners such as the French Ministry of Health and intergovernmental agencies overseeing drugs and addiction, directors, members (whose diversity we'll delve into later), federations' employees, field professionals, and the beneficiaries.

The role of elected chairmen was pivotal in conducting the merger and in initiating a common problem for both federations' actants. Given the profound transformation in public policy, addictology reform, regionalised health policies, and shifts in public funding, an initial challenge was framed as follows: "how can we organise the national representation of addiction professionals to develop shared expertise and influence public policy?".

The initial steps encompassed identifying common problems and intermediaries for bridging the gap between the two associations. Governance bodies saw an exchange of directors between ANITEA and F3A. Additionally, working groups and initiatives addressing common themes were initiated, especially in the context of implementing the "addictions reform". From 2008 onward, efforts concentrated on providing collaborative support to members affected by the merger of centres on the field through written materials, regional meetings, and training on the new system. In more detail, starting in 2009, specific overarching issues that were pertinent to both associations were overseen by joint working committees, bringing together directors and employees from both organisations.

As the process evolved, legitimate spokespersons emerged. Initially, each president represented the members of their respective federation, while the managing director gradually assumed the role of spokesperson for all internal actants, particularly in negotiations with public authorities regarding funding.

92 *Adrien Laurent*

The enrolment of various actants was achieved through diverse interessement mechanisms. The greatest challenge laid in responding to the diversity of the new federation's members. The addiction field boasted a spectrum of players engaged in prevention, harm reduction, or healthcare. These included advocacy groups, organisations managing centres of varying sizes, hospital practitioners, isolated independent professionals (such as general practitioners and pharmacists), education staff, and more. This diversity necessitated a thorough consideration of the new federation's structure, alongside an exploration of the role of beneficiaries in the federation's dynamics.

The formulation of the new federation's project proved to be a pivotal stage in engaging these diverse members, as well as the federation's employees. This project aimed to overcome apprehensions related to the potential loss of identity among F3A members, who were concerned about being absorbed into a politically oriented organisation originating from the "drug addiction" side. Likewise, ANITEA members feared that their project might dilute into a more medicalised approach to addiction that would characterise the former F3A. To address these concerns, the project challenged the dualistic, substance-centric approach. Instead of categorising addiction by substances like alcohol or drugs, it embraced an integrated addictology approach, cantered on the user and grounded in a "medico-psycho-social" perspective. Furthermore, it took a stance against the criminalisation of addictive behaviour, setting the federation apart from other organisations advocating for abstinence and a more prohibitionist stance.

These principles were reflected in several governance mechanisms, enabling active involvement of directors from both associations. It was swiftly decided that the Federation Addiction's board would consist of an equal number of directors from the two pre-existing associations. Consequently, the rules governing representation on the Board of Directors were revised. Initially, former directors of ANITEA and F3A shared equal seats on the Federation's Board of Directors. Additionally, three categories, or "colleges", were created to enhance the representation of members based on their statuses, along with a greater emphasis on regional entities: individuals, representatives of legal entities, and regional delegates. The initial logo of the new federation combined the initials of F3A and ANITEA ("F" and "A"). The F3A magazine retained its original name as a publication within the new Federation Addiction.

A noteworthy transformation within the new entity was the introduction of a participatory approach. This approach aimed to better integrate expert administrators and member professionals in the field, capitalising on existing practices and expertise. Introduced in 2009, in preparation to the effective merger, this approach was intended to develop specific projects, often focused on drafting best practice guidelines and guides for members, alongside other stakeholders and public authorities. Each project featured a working group comprising around 15 members selected based on their expertise and interest in the topic. These groups were led by a two-person team, comprising a lead administrator with recognised expertise in the subject and a federation project manager responsible for technical coordination.

What strategic processes to meet the challenges of democratic governance? 93

This approach helped stabilise the network by enrolling members as contributors of expertise and beneficiaries of the produced content, while also gaining recognition from public authorities for its role in shaping and disseminating common practices within the addiction sector, complementing regulatory measures.

Concomitantly, the federation witnessed growth in terms of size compared to the two pre-existing associations. By 2016, it boasted 571 members, a significant rise from the 340 members it had in 2010 before merging: "we saw members coming back when they were in the process of leaving, and we saw institutions paying like hotcakes, even for membership fees that are quite high ... Now our conferences are attended by 1,000 to 1,200 people, compared to around 200 before" (Managing director).

The extensive restructuring carried out prior to and as part of the merger that gave birth to the Federation Addiction succeeded in enrolling a diverse range of actants through interessement mechanisms. These actants included elected directors, members representing different statuses and regions, and employees. The newly defined project and the accompanying mechanisms fortified the federation's legitimacy among the stakeholders involved in addictions.

The federation's regional structure and local network were strengthened as well. Regional delegates were elected by members in their respective regions and automatically secured seats on the Board of Directors. They played a pivotal role in leading the network of members, disseminating the work of the federation, and fostering collaborative efforts at the regional level on specific themes. Moreover, they facilitated interaction with decentralised public authorities, particularly the regional health agencies responsible for allocating funding through calls for projects.

Lastly, the post-merger phase was characterised by the aim to expand the network beyond its historical members in alcohol and drug addiction care. It aimed to embrace new categories of professionals who, while not necessarily active in decision-making, held crucial roles in addressing addiction issues. This expansion prompted a review of the governance body's architecture, which had historically favoured professionals from the organised addiction system due to the sector's history and the federation's roots. Consequently, a specialised body took shape in the form of a "General Practitioners Addictions" strategic centre, integrated into the federation's board of directors. This entity facilitated the creation of a network of general practitioners engaged in addiction issues and the development of projects specifically relevant to them, particularly in the realm of prevention.

Organisational design as support for institutional work

The multifaceted dimensions of the federation's organisational design, as it emerged through the merger, proved instrumental in engaging the diversity of actants in internal processes. Simultaneously, it increased the federation's capacity to contribute to public policy and advance practices within the sector.

The federation's mission statement explicitly refers to "the desire to form a network at the service of professionals working with users in a medico-psycho-social

94 *Adrien Laurent*

and trans-disciplinary approach to addictions" and explicitly defends an influence on public policy. The overarching objective is to take a cross-disciplinary approach to addictology and create a shared culture among professionals from diverse backgrounds. While the positions adopted by the two merged organisations, especially in interactions with public authorities, were rooted in the expertise of directors, the stated intent was to build expertise within the new federation based on the practices of its members, employing a participatory approach. In other words, strategic and organisational processes were strategically deployed to enrol and mobilise a broad spectrum of actants in the sector, all directed towards the defence of public policy goals: "we're going to finish structuring the new identity of the federation, which is going to be to say: we have both this function of influencing public policy and at the same time supporting changes in the professional practices of our members, we're going to turn towards this dynamic" (Chairman of FA).

More specifically, the Federation Addiction found itself at the forefront of the struggle against two opposing doctrines. On one front, it battled against a repressive response to addictive behaviour, advocating for the decriminalisation of drug use. On the other, it confronted a purely medical perspective on addictology, which viewed addiction as an ailment primarily curable through drug treatment, with abstinence as the ultimate objective. In this context, the federation successfully secured the capacity for representation and dialogue with public entities directly or indirectly involved in addiction-related issues: "we were able, little by little, to set ourselves increasingly complex objectives, the latest being the one we've just achieved by having managed to influence the law on the modernisation of the healthcare system, since there are amendments that we've been able to get MPs to put to the vote" (Director).

Concluding discussion

Towards a detailed understanding of the strategic processes of NPOs

The concept of strategy has evolved from an abstract organisational attribute to a dynamic, collective effort, as highlighted by the "strategy as practice" perspective. This view uncovers the intricate mix of actions, decisions, and interactions that underpin strategic decision-making in NPOs, moving beyond the traditional focus on strategic planning and management elite decision-making. It emphasises the importance of understanding the day-to-day strategic work that involves a wide range of stakeholders, each contributing to the strategic landscape of NPOs in subtle ways. This approach necessitates a framework beyond conventional functionalist and planning models, with ANT providing insight into the network dynamics and composition during strategic processes.

Mergers in NPOs illustrate the deep social implications of strategic decisions, necessitating an understanding of the varied stakeholders involved and the institutional context that shapes these decisions, including the socio-political contributions of NPOs and the external pressures they face. The case study of Fédération Addiction's merger, set in a challenging institutional environment with funding and regulatory changes, showcases the complexity of strategic processes as a translation effort involving a broad spectrum of stakeholders to address common challenges and organisational adjustments.

The chapter concludes by offering an analytical framework for understanding NPO strategic processes. This framework integrates the institutional aspects of strategy – such as the core mission and external institutional pressures – with the local and organisational strategy levels, where the collective and foundational project is translated into accessible terms for various stakeholders (problematisation). Through the lens of ANT, this "socio-technical network" aligns diverse stakeholders with shared problems, employing interessement mechanisms to define and temporarily align the identities, rights, and expectations of all parties involved (Figure 5.1).

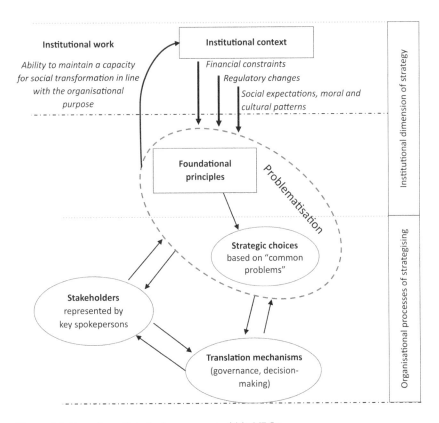

Figure 5.1 Overview of strategic processes within NPOs

96 Adrien Laurent

A perspective consistent with the ISO 37000:2021 standard and its systemic understanding of governance and strategy

To conclude this chapter, we have highlighted the complexity and finesse of the strategic processes that structure NPOs. Our analytical framework summarises the findings. Figure 5.1 illustrates the dual organisational and institutional dimensions of strategy.

Our results and proposals are perfectly aligned with the ISO 37000:2021 governance standard, aiming at maintaining "an organization with a clear purpose that delivers long-term value consistent with the expectations of its relevant stakeholders. The implementation of good governance is based on leadership, values, and a framework of mechanisms, processes and structures that are appropriate for the organization's internal and external context".

In alignment with the recommendations of the ISO 37000:2021 standard, we emphasise that the fundamental aim of strategy is to pursue a purpose by making strategic choices through a process that we describe as translation. By bringing together a variety of interested stakeholders via "common problems" and interessement mechanisms (modes of governance, decision-making processes in particular), this process enables the purpose to be translated into more concrete problems, which is at the heart of strategic practice. As stated in ISO 37000:2021: "an effective strategy functions as a framework for decision-making to enable different components of the organization to align".

At the same time, it is important to include the influence of the institutional framework in the analysis: NPOs are facing increasing pressure from their external environment in various forms, both direct and indirect (regulatory changes, financial pressures, changes in societal expectations, etc.).

A few actionable guidelines for practitioners

As this chapter concludes on strategic practices within NPOs, the section below presents practical recommendations aimed at enhancing the strategic framework of NPOs, ensuring their initiatives are both effective and closely aligned with their foundational goals.

Strategic clarity and articulation

It is imperative for NPOs to articulate a clear strategic vision that resonates with organisational "interested" stakeholders. This entails not merely setting strategic objectives but ensuring that these objectives are collectively and effectively defined, fostering a shared understanding that guides organisational actions and decision-making. Such clarity is foundational in aligning the organisation's activities with its mission, especially in the face of restructuring or mergers. It is also the primary condition for democratic governance.

Stakeholder engagement and inclusivity

An inclusive approach to stakeholder engagement is critical. This involves systematically incorporating insights from a broad spectrum of stakeholders, including staff, volunteers, beneficiaries, and external partners, into the strategic planning process. By doing so, NPOs can harness diverse perspectives, enhancing the robustness and relevance of strategic outcomes. This engagement fosters a sense of ownership and alignment among all parties involved, thereby facilitating smoother implementation of strategic initiatives.

Adaptive responsiveness to external dynamics

NPOs must navigate the delicate balance between adapting to external pressures—such as regulatory changes and shifting societal expectations—and maintaining fidelity to their core mission and values. This adaptive responsiveness necessitates a proactive stance towards environmental pressures and strategic flexibility, allowing NPOs to respond to external challenges without compromising their foundational principles. Such a balance is crucial for sustaining the organisation's relevance, legitimacy, and impact over time.

References

Allard-Poesi, F. (2006). La stratégie comme pratique(s): Ce que faire de la stratégie veut dire [Strategy as practice(s): What it means to do strategy]. In D. Golsorkhi (Ed.), *La fabrique de la stratégie : Une perspective multidimensionnelle* (pp. 27–47). Vuibert.

Avare, P., & Sponem, S. (2008). Le managérialisme et les associations [Managerialism and associations]. In C. Hoarau & J.-L. Laville (Eds.), *La gouvernance des associations : Economie, sociologie, gestion* (pp. 111–129). Érès.

Bartholdy, J., Blunck, B. W., & Poulsen, T. (2009). *What drives private and public merger waves in Europe (SSRN scholarly paper ID 1338347)*. Social Science Research Network.

Bastide, J. (2015). Les mutations institutionnelles du monde associatif. *Mouvements, 81*(1), 26. https://doi.org/10.3917/mouv.081.0026

Beaujolin-Bellet, R., & Schmidt, G. (2012). *Les restructurations d'entreprises [Corporate restructuring]*. La Découverte.

Benton, A. D., & Austin, M. J. (2010). Managing nonprofit mergers: The challenges facing human service organizations. *Administration in Social Work, 34*(5), 458–479. https://doi.org/10.1080/03643107.2010.518537

Busson-Villa, F., & Gallopel-Morvan, K. (2012). La normalisation des associations: Quelle efficacité pour rassurer les parties prenantes ? [Association standardization: How effective is it in reassuring stakeholders?]. *Management & Avenir, 54*(4), 168–190. https://doi.org/10.3917/mav.054.0168

Callon, M. (1986). Eléments pour une sociologie de la traduction. La domestication des coquilles Saint-Jacques et des marins-pêcheurs dans la baie de Saint-Brieuc [Elements for a sociology of translation. The domestication of scallops and fishermen in the Bay of Saint-Brieuc]. *Année Sociologique, 36*, 169–208.

98 *Adrien Laurent*

Campbell, D. A. (2008). Getting to yes ... or no: Nonprofit decision making and inter-organizational restructuring. *Nonprofit Management and Leadership*, *19*(2), 221–241. https://doi.org/10.1002/nml.216

Chanial, P., & Laville, J.-L. (2001). Société civile et associationnisme : Une analyse socio-historique du modèle français d'économie sociale et solidaire [Civil society and asso-ciationism: A socio-historical analysis of the French social economy model]. *Politique et Sociétés*, *20*(2–3), 9.

Cueille, S., & Devreese, E. (2012). Rapprochement sanitaire et médico-social? Une nou-velle donne? Quelques observations théoriques et pratiques à partir d'une expérience en cours en Gironde [Closer ties between healthcare and medical-social services? A new deal? Some theoretical and practical observations based on an ongoing experiment in Gironde]. *Les Cahiers de l'Actif*, 438–439, 95–110.

Denis, J.-L., Langley, A., & Rouleau, L. (2014). Organisations pluralistes [Pluralist or-ganizations]. In F. Tannery, J.-P. Denis, T. Hafsi, & A. C. Martinet (Eds.), *Encyclopédie de la stratégie* (pp. 883–893). Vuibert.

DiMaggio, P. J., & Powell, W. W. (1983). The iron cage revisited : Institutional isomor-phism and collective rationality in organizational fields. *American Sociological Review*, *48*(2), 147.

Dumez, H. (2011). L'Actor-Network-Theory (ANT) comme technologie de la descrip-tion [Actor-Network-Theory (ANT) as a description technology]. *Le Libellio d'Aegis*, *7*(4-Hiver), 27–38.

Golensky, M., & DeRuiter, G. L. (1999). Merger as a strategic response to government contracting pressures. *Nonprofit Management and Leadership*, *10*(2), 137–152.

Golensky, M., & DeRuiter, G. L. (2002). The urge to merge: A multiple-case study. *Nonprofit Management and Leadership*, *13*(2), 169–186.

Golsorkhi, D., Rouleau, L., Seidl, D., & Vaara, E. (2010). *Cambridge handbook of strategy as practice*. Cambridge University Press.

Grenier, C., & Guitton-Philippe, S. (2011). La question des regroupements/mutualisations dans le champ sanitaire et social: L'institutionnalisation d'un mouvement stratégique? [The question of grouping and mutualization in the healthcare and social sector: Is it the institutionalization of a strategic movement?]. *Management & Avenir*, *47*(7), 98. https://doi.org/10.3917/mav.047.0098

Habermas, J. (1987). *Théorie de l'agir communicationnel, tome 1 : Rationnalité de l'action et rationalisation de la société [The Theory of Communicative Action, Volume 1: Reason and the Rationalisation of Society]*. Fayard.

Hadj, S. M. E., Chédotel, F., & Pujol, L. (2015). Construire un projet interorganisation-nel dans l'économie sociale et solidaire [Building an inter-organizational project in the social economy]. *Revue française de gestion*, *1*(246), 159–173.

Haeringer, J., & Traversaz, F. (2002). *Conduire le changement dans les associations d'action sociale et médico-sociale [Managing change in social and medico-social action associations]*. Dunod.

Jarzabkowski, P., & Paul Spee, A. (2009). Strategy-as-practice: A review and future directions for the field. *International Journal of Management Reviews*, *11*(1), 69–95. https://doi.org/10.1111/j.1468-2370.2008.00250.x

Johnson, G., Langley, A., Melin, L., & Whittington, R. (2007). *Strategy as practice: Research directions and resources*. Cambridge University Press.

Kœnig, G., & Meier, O. (2001). Acquisitions de symbiose: Les inconvénients d'une ap-proche rationaliste [Symbiosis acquisitions: The drawbacks of a rationalist approach]. *M@n@gement*, *4*(1), 23. https://doi.org/10.3917/mana.041.0023

Kohm, A., & La Piana, D. (2003). *Strategic restructuring for nonprofit organizations: Mergers, integrations, and alliances*. Praeger.

What strategic processes to meet the challenges of democratic governance? 99

Latour, B. (2006). *Changer de société, refaire de la sociologie [Changing society, rebuilding sociology]*. La Découverte.

Laville, J.-L. (2012). La gestion dans l'économie sociale et solidaire : Propositions théoriques et méthodologiques [Management in the social economy: theoretical and methodological proposals]. *Méthodes & Recherches, 1*, 3–13.

Laville, J.-L., & Sainsaulieu, R. (2013). *L'Association : Sociologie et Economie [The Association: Sociology and Economics]*. Fayard.

Law, J. (1999). After ANT: Complexity, naming and topology. *The Sociological Review, 47*(S1), 1–14.

Maier, F., Meyer, M., & Steinbereithner, M. (2014). Nonprofit organizations becoming business-like: A systematic review. *Nonprofit and Voluntary Sector Quarterly, 45*(1), 64–86. https://doi.org/10.1177/0899764014561796

Maisonnasse, J. (2014). *Construire la coopération au sein des réseaux territoriaux d'organisations: Une analyse à partir de l'Économie de la Proximité et de la Sociologie de la Traduction [Building cooperation within territorial networks of organizations: An analysis based on the economics of proximity and the sociology of translation]*. Aix-Marseille Université; LEST UMR 7317. https://halshs.archives-ouvertes.fr/tel-01095370/document

Marival, C., Petrella, F., & Richez-Battesti, N. (2015). *Associations de solidarité et nouvelles pratiques de coopération sur les territoires : État des lieux, effets et enjeux [Solidarity associations and new cooperation practices in local areas: Current situation, effects and challenges]*. URIOPSS Languedoc-Roussillon. http://www.cresspaca.org/upload/actualites/associations-de-solidarite-et-1067.pdf

Nizet, J., & Pichault, F. (2015). III. Les études critiques dans les différents domaines de la gestion [Critical studies in the various fields of management]. In *Repères* (pp. 55–86). La Découverte. http://www.cairn.info/les-critiques-de-la-gestion–9782707181862-page-55.htm

Powell, W. W., & DiMaggio, P. J. (1997). Le néo-institutionnalisme dans l'analyse des organisations [Neo-institutionalism in organizational analysis]. *Politix, 10*(40), 113–154.

Seidl, D., Balogun, J., & Jarzabkowski, P. (2006). Stratégie comme pratique : Recentrage de la recherche en management stratégique. Remettre l'humain dans la recherche en stratégie [Strategy as practice: refocusing strategic management research. Putting the human back into strategy research]. In D. Golsorkhi (Ed.), *La fabrique de la stratégie: Une perspective multidimensionnelle* (pp. 1–7). Vuibert.

Traversaz, F. (2002). Un retour réflexif sur les pratiques dirigeantes [Reflecting on management practices]. In J. Haeringer & F. Traversaz, *Conduire le changement dans les associations d'action sociale et médico-sociale* (p. VII–XIII). Dunod.

Vaara, E., & Whittington, R. (2012). Strategy-as-practice: Taking social practices seriously. *The Academy of Management Annals, 6*(1), 285–336. https://doi.org/10.5465/19416520.2012.672039

Whittington, R. (2006). Completing the practice turn in strategy research. *Organization Studies, 27*(5), 613–634. https://doi.org/10.1177/0170840606064101

6 Alliances for outcome evaluation and theory of change to generate impact

Integrating network level and organisational level effort via organisational learning

Rong Wang

Introduction

In the past two decades, there has been a shift in the non-profit sector in the US to focus on performance measurement and programme evaluation. This trend was mainly driven by the sector's rapid growth, increased professionalisation, and funding competition (Mitchell & Berlan, 2018). It was also strengthened by the need to demonstrate accountability to stakeholders (MacIndoe & Barman, 2013; Mitchell, 2014). Despite the increasing demand, the effort in data collection and evaluation performance varies significantly within the sector due to resource constraints. In some instances, non-profits do not have a clear agenda on what to monitor or evaluate (Carman, 2007; Carman & Fredericks, 2010). Furthermore, over-collection of data occurs while at the same time there is limited use of evaluation data to inform Organisational decision-making (Carman, 2007; Feldman & March, 1981). Meaningless data collection and reporting can lead to mission drift or goal displacement (Ebrahim, 2005; Lee & Clerkin, 2017; Poole et al., 2001). In other words, effective data collection and use could facilitate value generation through which non-profits coordinate with partner organisations and other stakeholders to ensure the fulfilment of Organisational goals.

This chapter investigates the gap in the literature, i.e., how non-profits may engage in outcome evaluation to serve Organisational goals and achieve social impact. Non-profits are not fighting causes on their own. Relational factors have been shown to influence non-profits' impact, which include frequency of communication, centrality of position, and extent of mutual dependency (Nakashima, 2023). This argument positions non-profits as members of a network initiative. Furthermore, scholars have argued that network members are likely to use performance information in networks where the benefits of developing a shared understanding of network performance outweigh the costs of using it (Nakashima, 2023). However, in most cases, network members tend to overestimate the benefits and underestimate the cost of the collaboration (Shumate & Cooper, 2022).

DOI: 10.4324/9781003460572-9

Alliances for outcome evaluation and theory of change 101

It is still not clear how non-profits can engage in effective data use to generate social change. This issue directly connects to the data and decision issue of the ISO 37000:2021 standard, which emphasises the importance of data as a resource for decision-making. Furthermore, it could offer implications on how non-profits conduct stakeholder engagement to demonstrate accountability and sustainability.

This chapter draws from Organisational learning theory and theory of change (Shumate & Cooper, 2022) to identify steps through which non-profits can engage in partnerships in their data collection effort to inform Organisational decision-making and continuous growth. For each step, case studies are offered based on qualitative interviews and archival data to demonstrate more detail related to how non-profits may engage in evaluation capacity building when participating in networked alliances to tackle a wicked social issue, based on existing resources and communication strategies. Implications are provided on how to integrate network and Organisational level efforts of performance evaluation to generate social impact. The subject of Organisational learning and evaluation capacity building connects to effective non-profit governance in that these issues are instrumental to how non-profits manage their strategic planning and partnership choices. Furthermore, they help non-profits navigate stakeholder relationships in collectively tackling a social issue and continuously improve operational practices (Stephenson et al., 2009).

Organisational learning theory and purpose-oriented networks

A key characteristic of evaluation capacity building is the intentionality of learning (Harnar & Preskill, 2007). Organisational learning theory is a meta-theory that examines how organisations "build, supplement, and organise knowledge and routines around their activities and within their cultures, and adapt and develop Organisational efficiency by improving the use of the broad skills of their workforces" (Dodgson, 1993, p. 377). It emphasises the importance of learning as a means of gaining a competitive advantage, enhancing innovation, and achieving Organisational goals in the long run. Positioned as a process-based perspective, this theory accounts for factors at multilevel (i.e., individual, Organisational, community, macro-environment) to examine what influences an organisation's learning behaviours (Argote & Miron-Spektor, 2011). Organisational learning can be conceptualised as a social and institutional process where learning takes place via leadership, communication, and partnerships (Choi & Woo, 2022; Perkins et al., 2007). Therefore, organisations can learn from other each by recognising the value of new knowledge and practices and applying them to improve performances, known as improving "absorptive capacity" (Lichtenthaler, 2009). Literature has documented that Organisational learning can contribute to value generation in the non-profit sector (Kadyrova & Shapira, 2023).

Scholars have differentiated the single loop versus double loop perspectives in Organisational learning. In the single loop perceptive, organisations

102 *Rong Wang*

evaluate within an existing framework or a set of procedures, detect and correct efforts or areas of improvement without fundamentally questioning or challenging the underlying assumptions or Organisational goals (Argyris & Schön, 1996). This type of learning is focused on solving problems and making incremental improvements to improve performances and outcomes while maintaining the status quo. Single loop learning may result in higher efficiency and effectiveness, but significant transformative changes are rare. An example of single loop learning could be collecting performance data to demonstrate Organisational operation or use of funding. In the double loop learning, organisations challenge themselves by critically evaluating existing goals, assumptions, values, principles, or the system to generate transformative changes and values. It involves a deeper examination of Organisational culture and procedures (Argyris & Schön, 1996; Ebrahim, 2005). Double loop learning can prevent recurring issues by tackling structural causes and facilitating innovation. Examples include the use of evaluation data to revise product or programme design, launch of new programmes or services, and reorganising of governance structure in a non-profit. See Table 6.1 for the summary of the two perspectives of Organisational learning.

The importance of Organisational learning is never understated. The real challenge is how to implement it. Existing literature has captured the following as barriers: a lack of clear and measurable goals, insufficient incentives for participation, and uncertainty related to effective learning processes (Milway & Saxton, 2011). Non-profit scholars have recommended different strategies ranging from receiving technical assistance, mentoring, and coaching, to participating in meetings to share practices and lessons (Preskill & Boyle, 2008). The key is to build evaluation capacity at the Organisational level.

Table 6.1 Two perspectives of Organisational learning

	Single loop	Double loop
Focus	Fixing errors or improving performance based on existing goals and strategies; solving immediate issues	Examining and potentially challenging core values, policies, and strategies based on critical reflection; tackling fundamental issues organisations face
Example	Collecting performance data to demonstrate Organisational operation or use of funding	Collecting evaluation data to improve product design or delivery of a new service; reorganising of governance structure
Pros	Efficiency; stability; low resistance	Facilitating innovation; prevention of recurring issues; strategic alignment with external environment
Cons	Rare to have significant transformative changes; lack of innovation; overlooking root causes	Time-consuming; resistance to change; resource intense; uncertainty and ambiguity

Applying the Organisational learning theory to the non-profit sector, one mechanism to build evaluation capacity is learning from partner organisations within the boundary of purpose-oriented networks. The non-profit sector often forms alliances with other sectors and within its sector to tackle complex social issues. The collaboration among these organisations has been examined via the network perspective, which applies a relational approach to investigate the structures and outcomes of interorganisational partnerships (Bryson et al., 2015). These partnerships can be conceptualised as purpose-oriented networks, where collaborative initiatives are formed by at least three autonomous actors to achieve a common goal (Carboni et al., 2019; Provan et al., 2007). Extensive literature has focused on what organisations are more likely to be a part of these networks and how the partnerships are governed to be effective (Wang et al., 2020). Examples of these networks where non-profits actively participate include cross-sector alliances to reduce education inequality (Shumate et al., 2023), integrated care collaboratives in the health sector (Dessers et al., 2014), and interorganisational collaboration for crime prevention and reduction (Raab et al., 2015).

When being a part of a purpose-oriented network, non-profits are expected to perform certain tasks to demonstrate accountability for both internal and external stakeholders. Stakeholders refer to "any person or group that is able to make a claim on an organisation's attention, resources or output or who may be affected by the organisation" (Lewis, 2005, p. 202). Internal stakeholders for non-profits include entities such as employees, managers, board members, and volunteers; while external stakeholders are funders, beneficiaries, contractors, regulators, community partners, and media organisations (van Puyvelde et al., 2012). With various stakeholders in mind, non-profit accountability can be shown in terms of fulfilling a non-profit's social mission or financial goals, which however demonstrates an institutional tension in non-profit organising (Sanders, 2015). For example, COVID-19 has created significant challenges for the non-profit sector. Many non-profits struggle to balance financial needs and social aims to serve their communities (Herrero & Kraemer, 2022). Literature has suggested that effective stakeholder engagement is needed when assessing how non-profits achieve social or business goals (Koschmann & McDonald, 2015; Lewis, 2005).

The evaluation capacity challenge thus remains in how non-profits engage in Organisational learning to adapt to the constantly changing institutional environment, stay accountable for internal and external stakeholders, and generate and sustain the values they stand for, while being a part of a collective effort. Organisational members of a purports-oriented network may differ in their expectations regarding what to focus on collectively, how to frame the social issue, and how to approach collaborative activities to balance Organisational, network, and community goals (Wang et al., 2020). The literature has also long recognised that networks intended to generate social impact encounter conflicts at multiple levels. As Shumate and Cooper (2022) laid out, micro-level conflicts occur at the interface between individuals (e.g., leaders, managers of organisations that

104 *Rong Wang*

are members of a particular network), meso-level conflicts take place between organisations and networks, and macro-level conflicts arise at the community level. Below the theory of change framework is reviewed to explore how non-profits can navigate these tensions via partnerships and manage their data collection towards social impact.

The theory of change framework

The theory of change provides a framework to examine Organisational design, task division and allocation, and joint actions to unpack the link between what a network does and its outcomes. Five theories of change are proposed to offer various pathways for organisations and their coalitions to adopt: project, learning, policy, catalyst and system alignment (Shumate & Cooper, 2022). Each theory of change can be explained regarding what drives the collective effort, what outcomes are being evaluated, and how to achieve them. The assumption is that social impact results from network activities and can only be assessed at the community or society level. Specific theory of change thus aims to generate improvement a network targets.

Five types of theory of change to generate social impact

Project theory of change is the mechanism by which social changes focus on creating and delivering a new programme or a product. Member organisations in a network engage in joint inputs and joint outputs to generate social impact (Shumate et al., 2023). *Learning theory of change* is a mechanism by which social changes are about improving the quality of the services that member organisations already employ. Networks utilising this theory of change focus on training their members in evidence-based practices and how member organisations learn and adopt these practices influence the outcomes of the network (Shapiro et al., 2015). *Policy theory of change* examines whether governments change policy in response to network efforts in solving a social issue, thus the impact expected is toward entire communities instead of client populations (Shumate et al., 2023). *Catalyst theory of change* applies to networks that intend to disseminate a known solution (e.g., improving 3rd-grade literacy, or enhancing postsecondary completion rate). The key is to catalyse partnerships among member organisations to provide technical assistance and training and share evidence-based practices so similar results or success indicators can be replicated (Shumate & Cooper, 2022). The last theory of change refers to *system alignment*, which captures the mechanism of network members coordinating activities to assess existing programmes and services and explore gaps in services so the network can better service communities (Ferris & Williams, 2010).

The theory of change framework has been utilised in the context of education reform to unpack different pathways for producing better school outcomes

(Shumate et al., 2023). The inquiry has primarily focused on the level of networks and informed network practices. This book chapter applies the framework to a broader context of network alliances to explore how it may offer suggestions for non-profits looking to form strategic partnerships to better engage in performance evaluation towards social impact.

Pathways to integrate network and Organisational level efforts to generate social impact

organisations that aim to build evaluation capacity may engage in three forms of activities to assess their outcomes, based on research on human service non-profits (Lee & Clerkin, 2017). The first is compliance data use which focuses on reporting the efficiency, scope, and effectiveness of their programmes. This type of evaluation capacity is often driven by regulatory requirements from the governments and may simply follow standardised metrics imposed on non-profits. The second is negotiated data use that aims to demonstrate efficiency and effectiveness to stakeholders. The third is professional/anticipatory use in which organisations collect data to inform programmes and services to be more efficient and effective. This activity requires non-profits to be critical of their current operation and identify what needs improvement. Non-profit scholars have argued that the most significant catalyst for social impact is professional/anticipatory data use (Lee & Clerkin, 2017; Shumate & Cooper, 2022). However, the tension arises when networks and organisations may have different preferences and motivations regarding data use and evaluation capacity building.

Institutional pressure underlying Organisational learning

Organisational learning of evaluation capacity building occurs via institutional pressure derived from interorganisational partnerships, in the form of mimetic, coercive, or normative pressure (Lee & Clerkin, 2017). Mimetic pressure takes place when organisations of a similar attribute (for example, from the same sector) mimic each other to obtain legitimacy; coercive pressure occurs when organisations such as government or relevant stakeholder groups (e.g., funders) exert formal or informal pressure; normative pressure refers to mandatory compliance to appear professional (DiMaggio & Powell, 1983). Institutional pressure underlying Organisational behaviours takes place via homogenisation and serial production of standardised or common practices (Wang & Cooper, 2022). In other words, non-profits' data use could take place via following others' (i.e., partners in the same network initiative) existing data practices and continue to implement them over time.

For non-profits that are looking to generate social change by building their evaluation capacity and data use activities, several decisions need to be made at the network level about partnerships and theory of change. At the Organisational

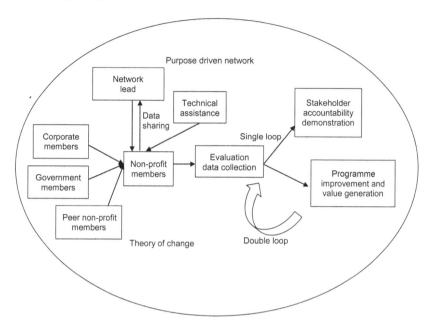

Figure 6.1 Proposed framework: non-profit learning pathways

level, they need to reflect on what to evaluate, for what purpose, using which criteria, and with what evidence and methods (Benjamin et al., 2023). At the network level, what types of partnerships to engage in, who to form partnerships with, and what theory of change to adopt if feasible. It is also important to identify champions of data use from partner organisations in the network and build connections if necessary for evaluation capacity. The following section discusses different steps non-profits may take to build evaluation capacity and generate social impact. See Figure 6.1 for the proposed framework that describes multilevel influences and pathways available.

What to measure as outcomes: Assessing impact indicators for performance evaluation

In the first step, non-profits need to assess what to measure in their data collection for performance evaluation. The term social impact has been defined broadly as the difference made by organisations to make a change in the world. It goes beyond financial metrics and includes positive outcomes or indicators that are measurable (Benjamin et al., 2023). For example, for a non-profit focused on serving homeless people, social impact could mean providing shelters and vocational training, leading to fewer homeless people in a community. Non-profit management literature has differentiated three types of social impact: project-based (i.e., providing physical resources to a community as benefits), service-based (i.e., providing care as benefits), and advocacy-based (i.e., creating regulatory or institutional change) (Agranoff, 2007, 2012; Shumate & Cooper, 2022). Impact assessment helps organisations define, create, deliver, and sustain their goals and values given the resources at hand.

Challenges in what to measure are driven by the inherent dilemma of the non-profit sector, i.e., the tension of financial imperatives and social goals, and thus the balance between financial and social effectiveness. To determine what to measure as social impact, non-profits need to clarify the unit of analysis for evaluation and draw boundaries around what metrics are included and excluded (Benjamin et al., 2023). Relatedly, it clarifies who the audience is or what stakeholders to demonstrate accountability for.

Non-profits can refer to the data use typology proposed by Lee and Clerkin (2017) and also theory of change to identify target stakeholders, what requires changing, and what indicators to track. It is common to observe non-profits collect outcome data for compliance or negotiated use to satisfy regulating requirements or stakeholder expectations (Lee & Clerkin, 2017). However as recent literature in non-profit management has argued, non-profits should engage in professional data use which promotes double loop learning as the organisations reflect on what cultural and operational practices to transform to be more effective (Nordin et al., 2022). The reason is that an organisation can be effective in expanding its client base (compliance use in that they are satisfying pressure from certain social groups) or demonstrating accountability for the board of directors (negotiated use), but it does not necessarily mean existing programmes and services are effective (i.e., professional data use or double loop learning).

Formal learning via normative pressure: Network level influence and role of technical assistance organisations

One way of approaching effective performance evaluation towards social impact is to identify whether it is worth being affiliated with a purpose-oriented network initiative with good data use practices. Due to their collaborative nature, purpose-oriented networks often set rules and practices regarding what metrics to track and how member organisations share data and results from the evaluation (Wolff et al., 2016). Networks with clearly defined metrics to track, a shared database among partners, a strong data team, and frequent communication about data-driven reports are more likely to generate positive social impact (Kania & Kramer, 2011). Through this learning channel, non-profits can revisit the theory of change that is guiding the network and evaluate accordingly what effort they can place to contribute. For example, if the network is guided by the policy theory of change, non-profit members of the initiatives need to think beyond data collection regarding their clients and assess how their performance evaluation could add value to a broader community for positive social change.

The tendency of non-profits to engage in such behaviours can be driven by the network's normative pressure. In other words, they need to conform to collective norms and practices related to data use and sharing protocols that the network invests in (Ofek, 2015).

As non-profits and networks consider the continuum of the theory of change, a series of support can be made available at the network level to offer technical assistance related to data collection and data sharing to ensure all network members are equipped with evaluation capacity. Technical assistance organisations have long been recognised as champions of effective evaluation (Umar & Hassan, 2019). Often, they can be hired by network lead organisations to offer training courses, facilitate retreats, and convene potential supporters (Wolff, 2001). In certain cases, network-lead organisations themselves may also take on the role. The key is to coordinate Organisational-level and network-level efforts for evaluation capacity building, and promote effective data sharing and management (Gibbs et al., 2009; Olson et al., 2020; Umar & Hassan, 2019). The existence of technical assistance organisations could also generate normative pressure for non-profits to engage in data use and performance evaluation so they can remain legitimate in the network and community (Wolff, 2001). Existing literature has demonstrated that technical assistance organisations can strengthen communication among member organisations within a collective initiative and help the network reach a consensus on key metrics (Wolff, 2000).

Creating communities of practices via lateral learning: The influence of peer organisations through partnerships and mimicking

Another pathway for approaching effective professional data use is through network partners, which may be driven by mimetic pressure (Lee & Clerkin, 2017). Partners with good data use practices can be thus viewed as champions of evaluation capacity building. Member organisations affiliated with the same collective initiative are brought together by a common purpose (e.g., tackling a social issue) and interdependence (i.e., their work is interrelated) (Isett et al., 2011). Networks designed to solve a social issue often bring diverse partner organisations to the table, which include non-profits, businesses, and the government sector or public organisations (Wang et al., 2020). Partner organisations tied in a network are thus embedded in an institutional environment where organisations' decisions are subject to the norms and social expectations that are deemed appropriate (AbouAssi et al., 2021; Guo & Acar, 2005). In doing so, organisations may mimic each other's practices that have been accepted by funders, network convenors, or the public (citation). This type of learning can be conceptualised as lateral through which learning takes place via peer organisations (Boyer, 2016).

Two learning mechanisms could be in action: within-sector and cross-sector learning. For non-profits, peer learning that happens within the sector often entails mimicking learning from organisations in the same social issue area or a

Alliances for outcome evaluation and theory of change 109

related area (AbouAssi & Bies, 2018). This type of peer learning can be the most efficient path if partner organisations have agreed upon key metrics and engaged in data sharing. Cross-sector learning in this context refers to non-profits learning from business partners or public organisations when they share a common network affiliation. This learning mechanism can be beneficial when a broader impact is intended at the community or society level (Provan et al., 2004) or when innovation is targeted (Shier & Handy, 2016).

Peer learning differs from vertical learning which is being formally enforced or encouraged by network lead organisations or technical assistance organisations. It takes place through the creation of "communities of practices", in which collective knowledge about data use and performance evaluation can be shared and implemented (Brown & Duguid, 1991; Preskill & Boyle, 2008; Rashman et al., 2009). Peer learning is thus more informal in structure, and partners often gather together to share good practices and help each other improve (Preskill, 2009; Wenger et al., 2002). Lateral communication among patterns is important to ensure dialogues around data use and performance evaluation. Organisations with good data practices contribute to the culture of performance evaluation and learning.

Double loop learning and theory of change

After identifying the main stakeholders to demonstrate accountability for, key metrics to track, and learning mechanisms via network effort or peer organisations, it is also important to note that non-profits should continue to engage in critical thinking and double loop learning. The key in double loop learning is to evaluate whether there is a need to reset Organisational goals, values, or principles to generate social impact (Argyris & Schön, 1996; Ebrahim, 2005). This argument is built upon the assumption that non-profits are open to innovation and change.

Non-profits set their goals differently. Not all non-profits are intended for advocacy or generate policy change. It is also true that the goals of a non-profit may change over time. Partnerships in a networked coalition help to create a culture that motivates non-profits to share knowledge and insights related to data use in programme evaluation (Milway & Saxton, 2011). For continuous growth at the Organisational level, the theory of change framework can be used as a reference. The following section describes how non-profits may navigate their performance evaluation effort bounded in a network initiative, drawing interviews and archival data to illustrate the pathways.

Non-profit learning through project theory of change

In a purpose-oriented network driven by the project theory of change, non-profits as network members may face barriers related to innovation or simply do not have sufficient resources to participate in new programmes or product

110 *Rong Wang*

development and delivery. At the network level, the project theory of change requires professional/anticipatory data use to inform what new programmes or products to focus on. To integrate Organisational and network level efforts in evaluation capacity building, non-profits may engage in learning behaviours by building close collaboration with fewer partners, as joint design and delivery of programme/product requires a lot of effort. Focused partnership building and learning would facilitate the integration of network and Organisational level effort. This chapter argues that both lateral and vertical learning are needed.

One example is Siloam Health, a faith-based non-profit organisation based in Nashville Tennessee whose mission is to serve those in need through health care. Since its founding in 1988, Siloam Health has built its reputation in local communities by serving immigrants and refugees. As a member of a city-wide collaborative network (Welcome Nashville Coalition), Siloam Health has worked with different sectors to identify innovative solutions for refugee resettlement. Their partners include health care providers in the city, metro public schools, local universities, community-based non-profits, and local churches. Through data collection on refugee needs and structural challenges on how to provide equitable health care, Siloam Health invests in joint delivery of products and services to better service the local community. One innovative programme is its community health initiative, in which Siloam-trained health workers serve as ambassadors in their communities to help fellow immigrants navigate health and social service systems. In 2020, this programme helped more than 500 patients improve their health through one-on-one relationships and culturally tailored approaches. The social capital Siloam Health builds through their diverse partnerships, allows the recruiting of capable health workers and also expanding its volunteer base to get work done. Siloam Health's patients and clients come from over 80 homelands and speak more than 50 languages.

Non-profit learning through learning theory of change

When a network is driven by learning theory of change, investment is needed in peer learning to assess what needs to change to improve existing programmes and products. Therefore, Organisational learning is a necessity and is more proactive. Non-profits thus may already have the intention and mindset to continue growing their client bases or expand service areas. Paired with active learning, data collected for evaluation inform improvement areas and how to enhance Organisational effectiveness (professional data use).

One example is GreenHouse17, a non-profit committed to ending intimate partner violence and abuse offers shelter for survivors and victims in rural Kentucky. It also runs a 40-acre farmland to offer nature-based healing and nutritious field-to-table produce to its residents and clients. In addition, the organisation offers employment training to the survivors and victims. What makes

GreenHouse17 unique is that the organisation has a social enterprise branch that has established a sustainable earned revenue model (via sales of flowers and hand-made products by survivors, such as soaps, candles, and bath salts). It is a part of a state-wide social enterprise alliance network in which member organisations gather together regularly to share best practices. The initial focus of the organisation was to function as an agency for providing services to survivors of domestic violence. Since its founding in 2003, the organisation has gone through a series of growth to identify market gaps and how to demonstrate its legitimacy while maintaining financial health. The state-wide social enterprise alliance has a variety of organisations participating, including benefit corporations and advocacy non-profits. Over the past 15 years, GreenHouse17 has continued to launch new services and programmes (e.g., the sales of products to local businesses such as hotels, deli shops). The most important change in the organisation's history is to brand itself as a non-profit that operates as a social enterprise to serve survivors.

Non-profit learning through policy theory of change

Under the guidance of policy theory of change, non-profit partners of a network need to leverage their relationship with public organisations and may work in task groups with peer organisations to tackle what key metrics would be helpful. Often times, non-profits are required to have a strong focus on advocacy and place significant effort in amplifying their work through community engagement and activism (Anheier & Toepler, 2019).

Believing in Forever is a youth non-profit based in Lexington KY, funded by Emmy award winner and hip-hop artist Devine Carama. The organisation's mission is to empower children to become community game changers through art, education, mentoring, and community services. It is a member of OneLex, a government-lead network initiative to reduce gun violence among youth and young adults ages 13–29 in the city of Lexington. With a strong advocacy agenda, OneLex encourages member organisations (ranging from city government, public and private partners, and community-based non-profits) to share knowledge related to how to combat gun violence while simultaneously addressing systematic disparities that are root causes of the issue (e.g., segregated housing, racism). One technical assistance organisation was invited to provide training to member organisations since the founding of the initiative in 2017; however, members reported dissatisfaction. Lateral learning thus became the more dominant mechanism. Believing in Forever has grown in the process with over 100 other non-profits based in local communities, and invested in activities in partnership with the city government for gun violence regulation and other related effort. Their mission now expands to awareness raising and advocacy work targeting the entire community.

112 *Rong Wang*

Non-profit learning through catalyst theory of change

When non-profits participate in a network guided by the catalyst theory of change, both vertical and lateral learning are important. Non-profits need to be more intentional in learning about evidence, and how to replicate effort in their environments. Network members form alliances to learn about existing effective models of solving a particular social issue, assess how best practices may transfer to their network, and map out steps for replication. Technical assistance organisations are often brought in to coordinate learning and collaboration and assist data collection related to performance evaluation.

One example is My Brother's Keeper in Mt. Vernon NY, a non-profit started by six influential community members. The model My Brother's Keeper was championed by President Obama when he was still in office and aims to address persistent challenges faced by boys and young men of colour. The affiliation with the national umbrella organisation allows the non-profit in Mt. Vernon to evaluate if there is enough buy-in at the city level to launch the programmes to help all young people in the community reach their full potential. It also learns through the six milestones the model adheres to: getting a healthy start and entering school ready to learn, reading at grade level by third grade, graduating from high school ready for college and career, completing postsecondary education or training, successfully entering the workforce, and keeping kids on track and giving them second chances. Technical assistance was provided with government funding, and peer learning was also available when alliances in neighbouring cities gathered to share best practices for implementing programmes.

Non-profit learning through alignment theory of change

Under system alignment theory of change, Organisational learning entails identifying effective solutions and how to get there. For non-profit members, it requires a critical review of existing programmes and identifying gaps in their services and operations. Both vertical and lateral learning are essential in assessing how to improve Organisational performance to better serve the community. The Mountain Association is a non-profit investing in people and places in Eastern Kentucky to advance a just transition to a more diverse, equitable, sustainable, and resilient economy. Its services (e.g., providing support for local business owners, ranging from marketing needs, and website development to funding applications) cover 54 counties in the state. The Mountain Association is a member of a network initiative, SPARK (Small non-profit Peer Accelerating Rural eastern Kentucky) non-profit collaborative. The Mountain Association builds its evaluation capacity by conducting Organisational assessment, strategic planning, and participating in peer-to-peer learning forums. The network also has an online learning platform called Basecamp which allows member

Alliances for outcome evaluation and theory of change 113

organisations to access resources related to grant writing, project design, and networking. Furthermore, member organisations of SPARK can apply for a peer learning community scholarship every year and attend a summit for workshops and training sessions on how to improve programme qualities. The Mountain Association has been working closely with local partners for over 50 years in generating impact in Eastern Kentucky. One impact indicator worth mentioning is their focus on the overall reputation of the region, and also how their work can benefit local communities, which moves beyond Organisational level metrics.

Conclusion

This chapter sets out to investigate how to motivate non-profits to engage in Organisational learning toward data use and performance evaluation. It is in response to the challenges of non-profit evaluation, which include lack of data collection or effective use of evaluation data. It encourages non-profits to move beyond mere data collection to report to funders or network leaders and invest in double-loop learning, so evaluation gears towards continuous performance enhancement.

Guided by a network perspective and the theory of change framework, steps of learning are laid out with several viable learning mechanisms, which have practical implications. For non-profit managers, the first step focuses on identifying what to measure and who the audience is. This step serves to demonstrate stakeholder accountability and value generation. The next step focuses on vertical learning that takes place via network lead organisations or technical assistance organisations. It is driven by normative pressure to remain professional. To complement learning, non-profits should also aim to incorporate lateral learning with peer organisations such as partners within the same network. The lateral learning facilitates building communities of practices related to data use. With various learning pathways underway, non-profit managers should also make a deliberate effort to engage in double loop learning where evaluation capacity building is a continuous process.

The proposed pathways move beyond the need to fulfil funder requirement and advocate for a more holistic view of evaluation data collection and use. They aim toward continuous Organisational growth and social impact at the community/society level. However, this chapter only begins to scratch the surface of the complicated process of evaluation capacity building in the non-profit sector by focusing on how to integrate network and Organisational efforts. One thing to note is that Organisational learning towards evaluation capacity building is not a linear process, and non-profits can revisit each step and identify the most feasible learning mechanism based on their existing resources and partnership needs. The final step that involves double loop learning is intended as a reflection point where non-profits can connect evaluation data use and theory of change to assess what Organisational operations or procedures require reform to better serve their clients and the larger community. Future research is needed

114 *Rong Wang*

to empirically test the effect of each learning mechanism and assess how non-profit leadership and network governance can influence the adoption of these learning mechanisms. Furthermore, empirical work should focus on investigating how non-profits can incorporate the guidance of the theory of change framework in their evaluation capacity building activities and manage potential conflicts with the network lead organisation and partner organisations.

References

AbouAssi, K., & Bies, A. (2018). Relationships and resources: The isomorphism of nonprofit organisations' (NPO) self-regulation. *Public Management Review, 20*(11), 1581–1601. https://doi.org/10.1080/14719037.2017.1400583

AbouAssi, K., Wang, R., & Huang, K. (2021). Snuggling together or exploring options? A multilevel analysis of nonprofit partnership formation and evolution in an unstable institutional context. *Nonprofit and Voluntary Sector Quarterly, 50*(1), 143–164. https://doi.org/10.1177/0899764020945800

Agranoff, R. (2007). *Managing within networks: Adding value to public organisations.* Georgetown University Press.

Agranoff, R. (2012). *Collaborating to manage: A primer for the public sector.* Georgetown University Press.

Anheier, H. K., & Toepler, S. (2019, November). Policy neglect: The true challenge to the nonprofit sector. *Nonprofit Policy Forum, 10*(4), De Gruyter. https://doi.org/10.1515/n pf-2019-0041

Argote, L., & Miron-Spektor, E. (2011). Organisational learning: From experience to knowledge. *Organisation Science, 22*(5), 1123–1137. https://doi.org/10.1287/orsc.1100.0621

Argyris, C., & Schön, D. A. (1996). *Organisational learning II: Theory, method, and practice.* Reading, MA: Addison-Wesley. https://doi.org/10.1177/103841119803600112

Benjamin, L. M., Ebrahim, A., & Gugerty, M. K. (2023). Nonprofit organisations and the evaluation of social impact: A research program to advance theory and practice. *Nonprofit and Voluntary Sector Quarterly, 52*(1_suppl), 313S–352S. https://doi.org/10.1177/08997640221123590

Boyer, E. J. (2016). Identifying a knowledge management approach for public-private partnerships. *Public Performance & Management Review, 40*(1), 158–180. https://doi.org/10.1080/15309576.2016.1204928

Brown, J. S., & Duguid, P. (1991). Organisational learning and communities-of-practice: Toward a unified view of working, learning, and innovation. *Organisation Science, 2*(1), 40–57. https://doi.org/10.1287/orsc.2.1.40

Bryson, J. M., Crosby, B. C., & Stone, M. M. (2015). Designing and implementing cross-sector collaborations: Needed and challenging. *Public Administration Review, 75*(5), 647–663. https://doi.org/10.1111/puar.12432

Carboni, J. L., Saz-Carranza, A., Raab, J., & Isett, K. R. (2019). Taking dimensions of purpose-oriented networks seriously. *Perspectives on Public Management and Governance, 2*(3), 187–201. https://doi.org/10.1093/ppmgov/gvz011

Carman, J. G. (2007). Evaluation practice among community-based organisations: Research into the reality. *American Journal of Evaluation, 28*(1), 60–75. https://doi.org/10.1177/1098214006296245

Carman, J. G., & Fredericks, K. A. (2010). Evaluation capacity and nonprofit organisations: Is the glass half-empty or half-full? *American Journal of Evaluation, 31*(1), 84–104. https://doi.org/10.1177/1098214009352361

Choi, Y., & Woo, H. (2022). Understanding diverse types of performance information use: Evidence from an institutional isomorphism perspective. *Public Management Review, 24*(12). https://doi.org/10.1080/14719037.2021.1955953

Dessers, E., Vrijhoef, H. J., Annemans, L., Cambré, B., Dhondt, S., Hellings, J., Hermans, K., Kenis, P., Nys, H., Vandijck, D., & Van Hootegem, G. (2014). Towards a comprehensive research design for studying integrated care. *International Journal of Care Coordination, 17*(3–4), 105–115. https://doi.org/10.1177/2053434514562082

DiMaggio, P. J., & Powell, W. W. (1983). The iron cage revisited: Institutional isomorphism and collective rationality in Organisational fields. *American Sociological Review, 48*(2), 147–160. https://doi.org/10.2307/2095101

Dodgson, M. (1993). Organisational learning: A review of some literatures. *Organisation Studies, 14*(3), 375–394. https://doi.org/10.1177/017084069301400303

Ebrahim, A. (2005). Accountability myopia: Losing sight of Organisational learning. *Nonprofit and Voluntary Sector Quarterly, 34*(1), 56–87. https://doi.org/10.1177/0899764004269430

Feldman, M. S., & March, J. G. (1981). Information in organisations as signal and symbol. *Administrative science Quarterly, 26*(2) 171–186. https://doi.org/10.2307/2392467

Ferris, J. M., & Williams, N. (2010). Foundation strategy for social impact: A system change perspective. *Nonprofit Policy Forum, 1*(1), 1–22. https://doi.org/10.2202/2154-3348.1008

Gibbs, D. A., Hawkins, S. R., Clinton-Sherrod, A. M., & Noonan, R. K. (2009). Empowering programs with evaluation technical assistance. *Health Promotion Practice, 10*(1_suppl), 38S–44S. https://doi.org/10.1177/1524839908316517

Guo, C., & Acar, M. (2005). Understanding collaboration among nonprofit organisations: Combining resource dependency institutional and network perspectives. *Nonprofit and Voluntary Sector Quarterly, 34*(3), 340–361. https://doi.org/10.1177/0899764005275411

Harnar, M., & Preskill, H. (2007). Evaluators' descriptions of process use: An exploratory study. *New Directions for Evaluation, 116*, 27–44. https://doi.org/10.1002/ev.241

Herrero, M., & Kraemer, S. (2022). Beyond survival mode: Organisational resilience capabilities in nonprofit arts and culture fundraising during the Covid-19 pandemic. *Nonprofit Management and Leadership, 33*(2), 279–295. https://doi.org/10.1002/nml.21524

Isett, K. R., Mergel, I. A., LeRoux, K., Mischen, P. A., & Rethemeyer, R. K. (2011). Networks in public administration scholarship: Understanding where we are and where we need to go. *Journal of Public Administration Research and Theory, 21*(suppl 1), i157–i173. https://doi.org/10.1093/jopart/muq061

Kadyrova, A., & Shapira, P. (2023). Microfoundations of dynamic capabilities for social innovations in small non-profit organisations. *Nonprofit and Voluntary Sector Quarterly.* https://doi.org/10.1177/08997640231214738

Kania, J., & Kramer, M. (2011). Collective impact. *Stanford Social Innovation Review. 9*(1), 36–41. https://doi.org/10.48558/5900-kn19

Koschmann, M. A., & McDonald, J. (2015). Organisational rituals, communication, and the question of agency. *Management Communication Quarterly, 29*(2), 229–256. https://doi.org/10.1177/0893318915572386

Lee, C., & Clerkin, R. M. (2017). Exploring the use of outcome measures in human service nonprofits: Combining agency, institutional, and organisational capacity perspectives. *Public Performance & Management Review, 40*(3), 601–624. https://doi.org/10.1080/15309576.2017.1295872

Lewis, L. (2005). The civil society sector: A review of critical issues and research agenda for Organisational communication scholars. *Management Communication Quarterly, 19*(2), 238–267. https://doi.org/10.1177/0893318905279190

116   *Rong Wang*

Lichtenthaler, U. (2009). Absorptive capacity, environmental turbulence, and the complementarity of Organisational learning processes. *Academy of Management Journal, 52*(4), 822–846. https://doi.org/10.1080/00207543.2010.543175

MacIndoe, H., & Barman, E. (2013). How Organisational stakeholders shape performance measurement in nonprofits: Exploring a multidimensional measure. *Nonprofit and Voluntary Sector Quarterly, 42*(4), 716–738. https://doi.org/10.1177/0899764012444351

Milway, K. S., & Saxton, A. (2011). The challenge of organisational learning. *Stanford Social Innovation Review, 9*(3), 44–49. https://doi.org/10.48558/dge6-xz93

Mitchell, G. E., & Berlan, D. (2018). Evaluation in nonprofit organisations: An empirical analysis. *Public Performance & Management Review, 41*(2), 415–437. https://doi.org/10.1080/15309576.2017.1400985

Mitchell, G. E. (2014). Why will we ever learn? Measurement and evaluation in international development NGOs. *Public Performance & Management Review, 37*(4), 605–631. https://doi.org/10.2753/PMR1530-9576370404

Nakashima, M. (2023). Performance information use in a purpose-oriented network: A relational perspective. *Journal of Public Administration Research and Theory, 33*(3), 407–420. https://doi.org/10.1093/jopart/muac039

Nordin, N., Khatibi, A., & Azam, S. F. (2022). Nonprofit capacity and social performance: Mapping the field and future directions. *Management Review Quarterly*, 1–55. https://doi.org/10.1007/s11301-022-00297-2

Ofek, Y. (2015). The missing linkage in evaluating networks: A model for matching evaluation approaches to system dynamics and complexity. *Public Performance & Management Review, 38*(4), 607–631. https://doi.org/10.1080/15309576.2015.1031005

Olson, J. R., Coldiron, J. S., Parigoris, R. M., Zabel, M. D., Matarese, M., & Bruns, E. J. (2020). Developing an evidence-based technical assistance model: A process evaluation of the National Training and Technical Assistance Center for Child, Youth, and Family Mental Health. *The Journal of Behavioral Health Services & Research, 47*(3), 312–330. https://doi.org/10.1007/s11414-020-09686-5

Perkins, D. D., Bess, K. D., Cooper, D. G., Jones, D. L., Armstead, T., & Speer, P. W. (2007). Community Organisational learning: Case studies illustrating a three-dimensional model of levels and orders of change. *Journal of Community Psychology, 35*(3), 303–328. https://doi.org/10.1002/jcop.20150

Poole, D. L., Davis, J. K., Reisman, J., & Nelson, J. E. (2001). Improving the quality of outcome evaluation plans. *Nonprofit Management and Leadership, 11*(4), 405–421. https://doi.org/10.1002/nml.11402

Preskill, H. (2009). Reflections on the dilemmas of conducting environmental evaluations. In M. Birnbaum & P. Mickwitz (Eds.), *Environmental program and policy evaluation: Addressing methodological challenges. New Directions for Evaluation, 122*, 97–103.

Preskill, H., & Boyle, S. (2008). A conceptual model of evaluation capacity building: A multidisciplinary perspective. *American Journal of Evaluation, 29*(4), 443–459. https://doi.org/10.1177/1098214008324182

Provan, K. G., Fish, A., & Sydow, J. (2007). Interorganisational networks at the network level: A review of the empirical literature on whole networks. *Journal of Management, 33*(3), 479–516. https://doi.org/10.1177/0149206307302554

Provan, K. G., Isett, K. R., & Milward, H. B. (2004). Cooperation and compromise: A network response to conflicting institutional pressures in community mental health. *Nonprofit and Voluntary Sector Quarterly, 33*(3), 489–514. https://doi.org/10.1177/0899764004265718

Raab, J., Mannak, R. S., & Cambré, B. (2015). Combining structure, governance, and context: A configurational approach to network effectiveness. *Journal of Public Administration Research and Theory, 25*(2), 479–511. https://doi.org/10.1093/jopart/mut039

Alliances for outcome evaluation and theory of change 117

Rashman, L., Withers, E., & Hartley, J. (2009). Organisational learning and knowledge in public service organisations: A systematic review of the literature. *International Journal of Management Reviews, 11*(4), 463–494. https://doi.org/10.1111/j.1468-2370.2009.00257.x

Sanders, M. L. (2015). Being nonprofit-like in a market economy: Understanding the mission-market tension in nonprofit organizing. *Nonprofit and Voluntary Sector Quarterly, 44*(2), 205–222. https://doi.org/10.1177/0899764013508606

Shapiro, V. B., Hawkins, J. D., & Oesterle, S. (2015). Building local infrastructure for community adoption of science-based prevention: The role of coalition functioning. *Prevention Science, 16*(8), 1136–1146. https://doi.org/10.1007/s11121-015-0562-y

Shier, M. L., & Handy, F. (2016). Cross-sector partnerships: Factors supporting social innovation by nonprofits. *Human Service Organisations: Management, Leadership & Governance, 40*(3), 253–266. https://doi.org/10.1080/23303131.2015.1117556

Shumate, M., & Cooper, K. R. (2022). *Networks for social impact*. Oxford University Press.

Shumate, M., Dougherty, S. M., Miles, J. P., Boyer, A. M., Wang, R., Gibson, Z. M., & Cooper, K. R. (2023). Network effectiveness in context. *Journal of Public Administration Research and Theory.* https://doi.org/10.1093/jopart/muad003

Stephenson, M. O., Schnitzer, M. H., & Arroyave, V. M. (2009). Nonprofit governance, management, and Organisational learning: Exploring the implications of one "megagift". *The American Review of Public Administration, 39*(1), 43–59. https://doi.org/10.1177/0275074007311888

Umar, S., & Hassan, S. (2019). Encouraging the collection of performance data in nonprofit organisations: The importance of Organisational support for learning. *Public Performance & Management Review, 42*(5), 1062–1084. https://doi.org/10.1080/15309576.2018.1481118

van Puyvelde, S., Caers, R., Du Bois, C., & Jegers, M. (2012). The governance of nonprofit organisations: Integrating agency theory with stakeholder and stewardship theories. *Nonprofit and Voluntary Sector Quarterly, 41*(3), 431–451. https://doi.org/10.1177/0899764011409757

Wang, R., Cooper, K. R., & Shumate, M. (2020). The community system solutions framework. *Stanford Social Innovation Review, 18*(1), 34–39.

Wang, R., & Cooper, K. R. (2022). Corporate social responsibility in emerging social issues: (Non)institutionalized practices in response to the global refugee crisis. *Journal of Communication Management, 26*(1), 98–114. https://doi.org/10.1108/JCOM-04-2021-0042

Wenger, E., McDermott, R., & Snyder, W. M. (2002). Seven principles for cultivating communities of practice. *Cultivating Communities of Practice: A Guide to Managing Knowledge, 4*, 1–19.

Wolff, T. (2000). Practitioners' perspectives. In *Handbook of community psychology* (pp. 741–777). Springer US.

Wolff, T. (2001). The future of community coalition building. *American Journal of Community Psychology, 29*(2), 263–268. https://doi.org/10.1023/A:1010330730421

Wolff, T., Minkler, M., Wolfe, S. M., Berkowitz, B., Bowen, L., Butterfoss, F. D., & Lee, K. S. (2016). Collaborating for equity and justice: Moving beyond collective impact. *Nonprofit Quarterly, 9*, 42–53. https://nonprofitquarterly.org/collaborating-equity-justice-moving-beyond-collective-impact/

Part III

Governance and performance: from financial survival to responsibilities

Introduction

Guillaume Plaisance and Anne Goujon Belghit

The link between governance and performance is well known and theoretically recognised in the literature (e.g. Blevins et al., 2022), but sometimes remains uncertain and paradoxical (e.g. Plaisance, 2023). The previous two sections have helped to bring out a different perspective on the governance of non-profit organisations: for example, the need for adaptability and cognitive thinking, or the importance of collaboration. In doing so, they may shed light on the reasons for these paradoxes. In addition, as highlighted in Chapter 6, stakeholder-driven changes in organisational design also disrupt the vision of performance. In a fairly traditional view, the latter is defined as "the demonstrated ability to acquire the resources necessary for organisational survival" (Boateng et al., 2016, p. 60). While this approach avoids focusing on purely financial aspects, it remains narrow in that it does not include essential contemporary dimensions such as social or environmental issues (Coupet & Broussard, 2021; Plaisance, 2023). In its definition of effective performance, already mentioned in the introduction, ISO 37000:2021 proposes a broader approach: the link with the purpose, the adequacy with the organisational requirements, the value created for the stakeholders and, finally, the alignment with the stakeholders' expectations. ISO 37000:2021 also considers that it is the responsibility of governance to ensure the viability and performance of the organisation over time, including sustainable development issues (in particular, operating "without compromising the ability of current and future generations to meet their needs", ISO 37000:2021, p. 34). This broader vision helps to guide organisations' thinking, but it lacks operationalisation. It is therefore possible to consider a multi-dimensional approach based on the

DOI: 10.4324/9781003460572-10

120 *Guillaume Plaisance and Anne Goujon Belghit*

concept of overall performance (extended from Plaisance, 2023):

- Financial dimension: organisations need money and cash flow to manage their daily operations
- Economic dimension: organisations need to build a socio-economic model that will ensure their long-term survival
- Social dimension: organisations need to attract, develop, protect and retain human capital
- Societal dimension: organisations should be in harmony with society
- Environmental dimension: organisations must preserve the natural environment by minimising their negative impacts and maximising their positive impacts
- Operational dimension: organisations are expected to be good at what they do and to strive for quality in their activities

The notion of performance can thus be broadened considerably, and more and more researchers and stakeholders believe that it is the responsibility of non-profit organisations to cover most, if not all, of these pillars. Understanding these new responsibilities and the current conceptual debates is therefore crucial, as the conceptual and semantic puzzle is no longer clear. This is the aim of Part III.

In Chapter 7, Renée A. Irvin wonders about the "Drama-free finance: Structures and strategies for stability and growth in non-profit organisations". The author reminds us that the financial issue remains a major concern for most organisations. Because of the way non-profit organisations operate and the stakeholders they involve, financial survival is often at risk. To move away from this survivalist vision, the author looks at strategies for stabilising and growing organisations, in line with the ISO 37000:2021 proposal: "the governing body should ensure that the organization remains viable, and performs over time, without compromising the ability of current and future generations to meet their needs" (p. 11). The analytical framework proposed by the author thus becomes a veritable virtuous circle for non-profit organisations. It also offers scholars a number of avenues to explore in order to widen this circle and continue the effort to make non-profits more financially secure.

In Chapter 8, Shawn Pope examines "the emergence and evolution of non-profit social responsibility". Indeed, ISO 37000:2021 has proposed a broad definition of the concept: it is "the responsibility of an organisation for the impacts of its decisions and activities on society and the environment, through transparent and ethical behaviour that contributes to sustainable development, including the health and welfare of society; takes into account the expectations of stakeholders; is in compliance with applicable law and consistent with international norms of behaviour; and is integrated throughout the organisation and practised in its relationship" (ISO 37000:2021, p. 4). The author then provides an in-depth perspective on these issues through a history as well as a categorisation of the various responsibilities of non-profit organisations. In doing so, he helps organisations emerge from the fog of multiple requirements and provides researchers in the field with new avenues for exploring the notion of performance.

In Chapter 9, Guillaume Plaisance continues the previous exploration of "social responsibility and sustainability in non-profit organisations", while introducing a "semantic and conceptual precision" that he deems necessary. According to ISO 37000:2021 (p. 4), sustainability is the "state of the global system, including environmental, social and economic aspects, in which the needs of the present are met without compromising the ability of future generations to meet their own needs". In practice, however, the terms sustainability, social responsibility and organisational social responsibility (OSR) are used interchangeably in the literature. Through a review of the literature, the author attempts to overcome the ambiguities and proposes a distinction between these three concepts that has multiple implications for practitioners and researchers. Linking these concepts to the notion of performance also provides a better understanding of the demands placed on non-profit organisations.

References

Blevins, D. P., Ragozzino, R., & Eckardt, R. (2022). "Corporate governance" and performance in nonprofit organizations. *Strategic Organization, 20*(2), 293–317. https://doi.org/10.1177/1476127020921253

Boateng, A., Akamavi, R. K., & Ndoro, G. (2016). Measuring performance of non-profit organisations: Evidence from large charities. *Business Ethics: A European Review, 25*(1), 59–74. https://doi.org/10.1111/beer.12108

Coupet, J., & Broussard, P. (2021). Do donors respond to nonprofit performance? Evidence from housing. *Public Performance & Management Review, 44*(1), 108–135. https://doi.org/10.1080/15309576.2020.1812409

ISO. (2021). *ISO 37000:2021 – Governance of organizations – Guidance.* International Organization for Standardization (ISO), ISO Technical Committee 309.

Plaisance, G. (2024). Accountability in French non-profit organizations: Between paradox and complexity. *Journal of Applied Accounting Research, 25*(3), 420–447. https://doi.org/10.1108/JAAR-01-2023-0006

Plaisance, G. (2023). Which stakeholder matters: Overall performance and contingency in nonprofit organizations. *International Studies of Management & Organization, 53*(3), 125–147. https://doi.org/10.1080/00208825.2023.2237388

7 Drama-free finance: structures and strategies for stability and growth in non-profit organisations

Renée A. Irvin

Financial performance in the context of organisational performance

Successful non-profit performance rests on firm yet flexible structures for governing the finances of the organisation. Without well-designed financial structures and controlling policies to guide acquisition, stewardship, and expenditure of financial resources, a non-profit may lurch from one financial crisis to the next, requiring constant attention to solve frequent financial problems. On the other hand, with sensible governance structures, the organisation is financially stable, expenses are anticipated and paid on time, and its administrators can focus their leadership attention on producing mission-related outcomes. Furthermore, a stable financial structure can enable the organisation to pursue sudden and advantageous opportunities for growth, that is, not only is the non-profit financially stable, but also progressive: It is nimble and innovative in pursuit of its purpose. Finally, a financially robust organisation is more in control of its destiny, achieving organisational actorhood. The chapter explores the role that financial structures play in organisational resilience and performance, illustrating the financial governance role of the ISO 37000 (2021) framework for purpose-driven governance. The main emphasis of the chapter is on providing a step-by-step series of strategies for designing a financial governance structure to pursue the combined goals of stability and growth.

ISO 37000:2021 guides governing bodies in conceptualising purpose-driven organisations, stressing the importance of a "framework of mechanisms, processes, and structures that are appropriate for the organisation's internal and external context," resulting in "improved organisational resilience and performance" even when experiencing disruptions from changing circumstances (ISO, 2021). Duchek (2020) and Plaisance (2022) provide a wholistic conceptualisation of organisational resilience, encompassing the organisation's social resilience, knowledge base, and power. *Financial* resilience – the ability to maintain operations through times of financial exigency and to adroitly adapt to changing resource contexts – is a subset of organisational resilience

DOI: 10.4324/9781003460572-11

This chapter has been made available under a CC-BY-NC-ND 4.0 license.

124 *Renée A. Irvin*

and likewise only a portion of the ISO 37000:2021 framing of organisational performance over time.

Although the chapter locates the financial strategies within the main strategies of financial stabilisation and growth, the end-stage result of a financially healthy organisation is organisational actorhood. Pope et al. (2018) define organisational actorhood in their thoughtful study of non-profit narratives of mission framing and vision. In a *financial* conceptualisation of organisational agency, the organisation effectively charts its own course, seizes valuable opportunities as circumstances change, and delivers long-term value in pursuit of its purpose.

Not only for financial management, but in any area of academic research, single issues are analysed one by one, and, like a physician specialist, the researcher may suggest a treatment regimen for the non-profit patient without taking into account the linked effect of the financial management treatment on other financial management strategies. This chapter is intended to provide a general practitioner view of several intertwined topics in non-profit financial governance. Specifically, key strategies in financial management include stabilisation and risk management of revenue flows; growth strategy; and related concepts of cost control and stewardship of assets. These separate topics have emerged over time as researchers engage deeply with one compelling topic, then move on to another. Thus, this chapter starts with a brief overview of non-profit financial governance topics of interest.

Trends in non-profit finance research

Over time, the non-profit finance literature base has developed gradually, shifting from one topic to another. Assumptions made about best practices may become the intense focus of research for a few years, and sometimes those best practices, once examined under the microscope, are proven either misguided or simply applicable only to a subset of organisations. The heterogeneity of the civil sector makes one-size-fits-all financial governance advice problematic.

Overhead costs

An early concern in the literature was overhead or administrative costs, which are critically characterised as organisational slack (Chang & Tuckman, 1991). Unfortunately, measuring administrative costs compared to "program" costs is an arbitrary procedure at best, easily circumvented with creative classification of costs. A dinner with a prospective donor, for example, which is arguably a fundraising or administrative cost, can be described as public outreach or education about the cause and, thus, a programme cost. Overhead expenses are as vital to a non-profit organisation as they are to any type of enterprise. A research organisation, for example, should not force the laboratory researcher to serve as the front desk receptionist, security guard, IT specialist, HR manager, and so on.

Economist Richard Steinberg was one of the earliest to point out the folly of fixating on fundraising costs (Steinberg, 1986), but journalists could not resist the lure of a percentage and continue to advise the public to avoid donating to organisations with "high" overhead percentages and fundraising ratios. Of course, an organisation with lavish overspending and employee retreats at posh resorts will have high overhead costs, so there is still some utility in the examination of administrative expenses as an indicator of waste. Yet to penalise organisations for having 16% overhead costs instead of 9% (which is probably a misrepresentation of actual overhead costs anyway) is damaging to the organisation.

Resource dependency and mission drift

This strand of literature expresses the power and control of the funding source to influence and even shift the operations of the organisation. Bowman (2007, p. 15) describes non-profits with extreme dependency on funders as "cold" non-profits. He suggests the ameliorating effect of "financial capacity" (such as liquid assets) in combatting excess dependence on key funders:

> Many non-profits are tyrannised by inflexible business models. Cold non-profits easily become locked into program models not fully appropriate to their communities—but favoured by their funders. In other words, financial capacity gives non-profits the flexibility to navigate around restricted funds and to avoid mission distortions that can result from overdependence on grants.

As foundations and governments, for example, may offer funding only for specific programming, the concept of resource dependency is straightforward: It is expected that the non-profit will tailor its programming to fit the funding protocol. Plaisance (2022) provides valuable context with the case of French non-profits: Organisations that were most dependent on their stakeholders were the ones that deteriorated the most during the Covid-19 crisis. This chapter is focused specifically on encouraging non-profits to build their financial resilience, thereby decreasing reliance on external funders, to strengthen resilience and achieve organisational actorhood. Bowman (2007) positions financial capacity or organisational slack as the countervailing force to funder control.

Entrepreneurship vs. fears of marketisation

Early proponents of entrepreneurial ventures at non-profits cited the seemingly unlimited potential of earned revenue, which might allow the non-profit to rely less on donor revenue and restricted grants. Although this produced a spirited debate in the academic community (e.g. Dees et al., 2001; Eikenberry & Kluver, 2004), the actual reliance on earned income at non-profits appears to have not

126   *Renée A. Irvin*

changed over time and may simply be a matter of mission relevance, as discussed by Wilsker and Young (2010) and described as "benefits theory."

Revenue diversification and risk minimisation

It seems sensible to assume that adding revenue sources would be stabilising to overall non-profit revenues, in that the loss of one source may be ameliorated by a gain in another source. Research testing this assumption has yielded little support, with two recent meta-studies concluding that adding additional revenue sources may not add more stability and may not enhance growth either (Hager & Hung, 2019; Lu et al., 2019). A more useful and nuanced concept of revenue choices focuses on the revenue portfolio mix. If a new revenue source does not correlate with business cycle fluctuations of the existing revenue sources, the addition of that new source could help minimise financial risk by stabilising the organisation's total revenue volatility (Kingma, 1993; Qu, 2019).

Designing the organisation's revenue portfolio mix to minimise correlation across revenue sources sounds reassuring, but non-profit revenue sources are not stocks in a portfolio that one simply owns: Each non-profit revenue source requires different management skillsets, and the addition of a new source (requiring new administrative tasks and talents) may be destabilising and costly for the organisation. Wilsker and Young's (2010) benefits theory is relevant for this discussion of portfolio mix; e.g., the shelter for women seeking refuge from domestic violence is not going to rely on the same types of revenue sources as the kids' sports club. In economic terms, we would expect each organisation to pursue the revenue sources that yield the greatest long-term profit. Thus, while it is an admirable goal to minimise revenue volatility, the more compelling objective for the organisation is economic performance (profitability) over time. Non-profit organisations thus tolerate revenue source volatility in order to achieve a stronger economic performance in the long run, within the contexts of their mission activities. Finally, revenue portfolio design is not the only way to stabilise non-profit finances: The financial capacity of the organisation – specifically the amount of liquid, unrestricted net assets compared to the annual budget – matters more.

Optimal reserves

Regardless of the composition of the revenue portfolio, holding adequate reserves to be able to ride through financial tempests is an important risk management strategy. The professional and academic literature tended to cite the best practice advice of "three months" of operating budget as a good reserves fund target, but this advice was found to be overly generous in a few pockets of the non-profit sector and dangerously low for other organisations (Irvin & Furneaux, 2022). The interaction with revenue portfolio design makes reserves targeting fascinating: One can, in theory, select the revenue portfolio that maximises profit

Structures and strategies for stability and growth 127

(not necessarily minimising risk) over time, allowing the organisation to grow faster than others, on average. The reserves can temper the destabilising effect of high volatility from the high-risk, high-return revenue portfolio.

Stabilisation and growth

In this chapter, we pivot from the existing non-profit literature to a new topic that is conceptually more global: What is the collection of financial management strategies to enhance both stability *and* growth in non-profit organisations? The following sections progress sequentially deliberately: First, an organisation must establish practices that can tame and harness the volatility of revenue and expense streams. Reserves strategies are fundamental, but other financial stability tactics are enumerated. Then, assuming an organisation has fundamental stability structures in place, a following section illustrates how an organisation can pursue growth and efficacy strategies that lead to fundamental changes in their role in society.

Financial stabilisation in practice: Cash, reserves, and endowment

Before exploring the methodology of achieving financial stabilisation, we start with a description of a stable, boring non-profit organisation. Good non-profit finance is invisible. Ideally, the organisation sets its goals, charts its course, and utilises financial resources to obtain those goals. The ebb and flow of revenue and any volatility in costs are anticipated and mitigated with existing and internal resources so that the financial fluctuations inherent to any non-profit are unseen, unremarkable, and do not disrupt programming. Executive leadership concentrates on the mission. There is and always will be the imperative to develop and earn revenue, but the fluctuation in finances both seasonally and over the years is *anticipated* and dealt with in a way that protects the mission-related programmes from abrupt changes. Our first goal is to create that stable, boring non-profit organisation.

Financial stabilisation in the non-profit context starts with three important strategies; cash flow management, emergency reserves, and endowment (see Bowman et al., 2007; Irvin & Furneaux, 2022). Each performs a unique and critical revenue stabilisation function. Note that financial stabilisation is not simply the product of designing a revenue portfolio mix that produces a steady flow of revenue over the months and years. Instead, the revenue portfolio decision is enveloped within a larger strategy of revenue growth and asset stewardship. We will explore growth decisions later, but first must define three forms of stabilisation funds and illustrate how they create financial stability.

Cash reserves help the organisation plan for and respond to normal seasonal fluctuation in revenue and expenses. These are precise levels of cash (including

128   *Renée A. Irvin*

cash equivalents such as savings and checking) kept on hand to respond to *anticipated* shortfalls during the year or planning cycle.

Targeting the correct amount of cash reserves to keep on hand is straightforward if the organisation has a general pattern of revenue and expenses throughout the year. For example, in Table 7.1 we see the revenues and expenses anticipated for the first part of the year for a small non-profit sports organisation.

Table 7.1 shows that the organisation, if it begins with a cash balance of €0 in January, will be €9,100 in deficit by the end of the month, plus additional deficits building in February through April. After that, the city contract, grant, and tournament-related revenues arrive to cover the expenses. The organisation must pay for its expenses January through April, so it should set aside enough cash at the beginning of the year to be solvent. The recommended amount in this case would be the sum of the deficits through April, or €53,700. One might recommend €60,000 in cash to hold on January 1, for good measure.

What if the organisation borrows from a credit line to fund the monthly deficits? This can be done, but the organisation must pay interest on that debt, making simply holding cash or very liquid investments the more attractive option. In practice, the opposite tactic – holding too much in cash and savings – appears to be quite common. Non-profit organisations sometimes hold enormous amounts of cash, savings, and checking accounts, which suggests a loss of potential investment

Table 7.1 Monthly cash forecast (€)

GenkiKids Sports Centre, Inc. Annual Budget

	January	February	March	April	May	June	July
Revenue							
City contract	0	0	0	0	80,000	0	0
Foundation grant	0	0	18,500	0	0	0	0
Donations	500	500	500	500	500	500	500
Tournament admissions	0	0	0	0	0	22,900	37,500
Merchandise	0	0	0	0	0	4,300	8,100
Tournament fees	0	0	0	0	900	1,200	600
Total revenue	500	500	19,000	500	81,400	28,900	46,700
Expenses							
Salaries	4,600	4,600	4,600	4,600	4,600	4,600	4,600
Payroll taxes	300	300	800	800	800	800	800
Other labour costs	800	800	1,300	1,300	1,300	1,300	1,300
Utilities	500	500	400	400	300	200	200
Lease	2,400	2,400	2,400	2,400	2,400	2,400	2,400
Supplies	1,000	1,000	1,000	1,000	1,000	1,000	1,000
Contract employees	0	0	17,000	17,000	17,000	17,000	17,000
Total expenses	9,600	9,600	27,500	27,500	27,400	27,300	27,300
Monthly surplus (deficit)	(9,100)	(9,100)	(8,500)	(27,000)	54,000	1,600	19,400

Structures and strategies for stability and growth   129

earnings. It is recommended that any cash beyond what is reasonably required to cover anticipated seasonal financial patterns be placed in emergency reserves or endowment, where it can be invested to produce income or appreciate in value over time.

Emergency (or "operating") reserves function as a savings account for years in which *unanticipated* financial shocks occur. They are separate from the cash kept on hand to cover anticipated seasonal fluctuation in revenue or expenses, described above. Revenue falls during a recession, for example, and expenses may spike as well during a recession or other adverse event. Such financial shocks are irregular and do not occur annually yet can be severe in magnitude. Reserves can help an organisation maintain its programming through these adverse periods. Organisations pay into the emergency reserves fund in good financial years and may invest at least some of the reserves fund to help grow the fund.

How much to hold in reserves is a perennial question. As noted above, the "three months" commonly cited in the lay literature appears to be ill-advised for most non-profit organisations. The revenue volatility experienced by organisations determines how much reserves are needed to weather a severe financial shock. Smaller organisations, especially those with total annual revenue of €200,000 or less, have more much volatile revenue patterns, and thus need more reserves; the Irvin and Furneaux (2022) results suggest that having emergency reserves equivalent to almost one year of expenses is prudent for these smaller organisations. As a general rule, larger organisations have steadier, more established revenue sources, and thus experience less revenue volatility. For the largest organisations with annual budgets of €750,000 or more, emergency reserves as low as three months of expenses are often adequate to weather unexpected fiscal shocks.

While not as impactful on revenue volatility as size, the mission itself can have a critical effect on revenue patterns. Grant-making foundations have the most revenue fluctuation because their revenue depends on both variable investment earnings (which can be negative) and on receipt of bequests and other lumpy donations in a given year. Research organisations may last several years on one large grant, so their revenue is also highly volatile.

Emergency reserves can be at least partially invested, to help grow the fund to the preferred level. A reserve fund policy should clearly instruct board members and staff on how the fund is built (how much to pay in, using what types of sources); what the target level of reserves should be; what portion of the reserves should be invested; and rules for payout. Particularly important are rules defining what a financial emergency is. For example, a total revenue drop of 10% or more in a given year may trigger the permission to withdraw from emergency reserves, subject to a majority or super-majority of the governing body. It is not recommended that an executive director has sole authority to withdraw from the reserves without governing body oversight and approval.

130 *Renée A. Irvin*

Emergency reserves might also be used for another important purpose: To react strategically to advantageous opportunities that could increase future revenue of the organisation or reduce future costs. Having reserves can allow the organisation to respond quickly to these unique and often entrepreneurial opportunities. Again, use of emergency reserves for strategic growth purposes should not be a choice made in isolation by the executive director, but should be subject to approval by the board or governing body.

Endowment funds are a special form of reserves or savings that are designed to provide steady annual operating support, often for a restricted, specific purpose. For example, a school may have an endowment fund that provides ongoing funding for scholarships. Many non-profit organisations choose 4% or 5% of an endowment's balance as an annual payout (withdrawal). In essence, endowment funds are invested in financial assets that appreciate in value over time or pay out income in the form of dividends or interest. The annual payout can provide a dependable source of annual revenue for the organisation.

Depending on the legal requirements of the organisation's home country, the use of the endowment funds may be limited to only earnings or appreciated assets, and the historic gift value that the donor donated may be held intact. Thus, if the original donation was €1,000,000, when the fund grows to €1,400,000, the organisation may spend as much as €400,000. Endowment funds can function as both a source of fairly steady revenue paid out over time, as well as a second source for emergency reserves.

Aside from holding assets in the three main stabilising funds described above, certain policies and practices can also help to stabilise the organisation's financial operations.

Windfall policy

Bequests are often directed automatically by non-profit organisations to endowment funds, suggesting that the legacy of a deceased donor is honoured by stewarding and using the funds into perpetuity. Placing bequests, large donations, and other windfalls into endowment funds for slow and steady use over time can have a remarkably stabilising effect on financing of programming.

Moving average payout from endowment

The simple technique of using a moving average payout (instead of a flat 5%, for example) from the endowment further stabilises non-profit overall revenue. Table 7.2 illustrates how, with the sharp increases and decreases of investment returns in any given year, the endowment total balance fluctuates quite a bit, creating a 5% payout that likewise rises and falls with investment fluctuations. Note that the fluctuation in the payout with a simple 5% annual calculation yields a payout that ranges from €64,725 in a market downturn year to €83,671 in a

Structures and strategies for stability and growth 131

Table 7.2 Stabilising endowment payout with a moving average payout (€)

Year	2021	2022	2023	2024	2025	2026
Total endowment balance						
Beginning of year	1,344,944	1,193,208	1,374,226	1,673,420	1,294,500	1,545,973
Annual payout method						
5%			68,711	83,671	64,725	77,299
3-year average 5%			65,206	70,681	72,369	75,232

year with favourable market returns. In contrast, when the organisation uses the past three years to compute an *average* endowment balance and then withdraws 5% of that average, the fluctuation in the annual payout is almost halved. Here, the moving average payout fluctuates within the narrower range of €65,206 to €75,232. An even more stabilising and conservative payout would be a five-year payout. Finally, some organisations utilise a guardrail payout approach, removing outlier years and calculating the payout from a narrower range of past year balances or incorporating inflation into the calculation.

Capital projects budgeting

A fourth type of savings recognises the rare and very expensive costs of building new buildings or purchasing land and equipment as the organisation grows. Organisations may approach saving for these capital projects in a number of ways – by approaching major donors (who respond favourably to impressive and tangible buildings), setting aside savings in a capital projects budget, taking out loans, or issuing bonds. Regardless of the funding strategy, the common element here is planning ahead for the inevitable upgrades needed for the organisation's physical facilities.

Internal control

The above three main reserves strategies – cash reserves, emergency reserves, and endowment – centre on building, maintaining, and using saving to ensure that revenue is accessible for funding programming despite revenue's inherent variability. Once the funds are in place, systems must be in place to protect them. Internal control ensures that the funds are spent for the right purpose and neither squandered, wasted, nor embezzled. In addition, internal controls prevent the kind of events that damage an organisation's reputation and lead to a decline in donated revenue. For example, a purchasing policy will commonly specify a range of approvals needed: Little to no extra approval for very small purchases, approval of a supervisory staff member for larger expenses, and finally, board majority approval and even competitive bid review for the largest purchases. Prior chapters in this volume cover these important internal control techniques

132   Renée A. Irvin

to protect the organisation's reputation and detect and prevent fraudulent or simply incompetent use of funds.

The collection of stabilisation methods described here will have beneficial effects on the organisation, including allowing non-profit leaders to focus more on mission activity and less on meeting each financial crisis as it occurs. Non-profit financial managers, once focused on stability, will no doubt add to this list of organisational tactics to enhance financial stability. Here, however, is a sharp warning for the reader: Stability is not the end goal. After all, to reduce financial risk to zero, one can place savings in a vault, but savings kept in a vault will neither earn interest or dividends, nor appreciate in value, nor be used in new programming. Stability is the platform upon which financial and organisational growth can occur. The next section, therefore, identifies how to use a stable financial base to innovate, accept risk, and grow in new directions.

Financial growth in practice

Stabilising finances is a key administrative strategy for non-profit organisations, allowing steady support for the organisation's programming dependably over time. Just as important, however, is growth. First, the organisation must increase its total revenue annually to cover inflationary increases in expenses. In other words, to maintain programming at the same level over time, the organisation must be growing by at least the rate of inflation. Furthermore, growth must accommodate staff pay increases as they gain experience and remain with the organisation. This necessitates a total rate of growth exceeding the annual rate of inflation. The non-profit sector, primarily providing services, not products, pays a large amount of its expenses for labour, so the annual revenue increase needed to accommodate salary increases may be substantial. Finally, it would be the rare non-profit that is satisfied with its current level of programming and dedication of resources to meet mission objectives. Any expansion of its programmatic reach requires growth in revenue. The following stresses how savings and investment are tightly linked to growth strategies.

Saving, paying off debt, and growing unrestricted net assets

The simple act of allowing a surplus to occur in a given year adds to the organisation's assets or, if specifically used to pay down debt, reduces liabilities. As a result of either action, the organisation's net worth increases for the year. The choice to increase savings or to pay down debt is not necessarily a light decision. If one pays extra principal on a debt balance, such as a building's mortgage, the organisation will retire its debt sooner, leading to a larger expendable budget as less of the budget must go towards debt repayment. The interest rate on the debt (say, 5% annually) suggests that any extra payment on that debt to reduce the principal balance "returns" 5% as a fairly risk-free investment.

Structures and strategies for stability and growth 133

However attractive it is to pay off debt early to eliminate debt payments from future budgets, putting savings into paying off debt means that the funds are now tied up in the ownership of the fixed asset (often a building) and no longer available for short-term needs or a recession. The organisation should not pay off debt too aggressively unless it has sufficient cash reserves and operating reserves as described above. An art museum, for example, will not want to be forced to sell its building or its collections to remain in operation during a financial downturn.

Deficit spending to grow operations

Although the organisation should target a rate of growth that implies a surplus amounting to somewhat more than the rate of inflation, it is not catastrophic to incur a budget deficit in any given year. A deficit may be the result of an internal investment in capacity. For example, an organisation hiring a major gift officer to join its development team will be paying salary for that individual long before the major gifts and bequests materialise. The purchase of an important piece of equipment or vehicle in a deficit year may result in reduced rental or maintenance costs in subsequent years.

The cost of incurring a deficit is small if the organisation's cash reserves are drawn down that year, as cash does not provide any return. Perhaps, however, the organisation has dipped into some invested funds from a reserves account to pay for some operating expenses. In that case, the opportunity cost of incurring the deficit is the foregone earnings on those invested funds. Similarly, if the organisation chooses to borrow money to pay operating expenses, the increased debt will require interest payments until the debt is paid off. Thus, every decision to incur a deficit implies a loss of interest earnings or reduced earnings on potential investments.

Planning to save

Savings does not necessarily materialise in the form of a budget surplus year after year. Employees and governing body members, dedicated as they are to the non-profit's mission, will want to employ all possible resources toward that purpose. Thus, a mid-year budget variance report showing a growing surplus in a good year may evaporate into a budget deficit by year's end as earnest staff members adapt to the good news by spending more on programming. For this reason, a dedicated effort to grow reserves funds or simply increase the organisation's net assets might be best approached by putting a savings contribution directly into the next year's budget as a line item. This is analogous to an individual saving for retirement with a monthly contribution into a retirement account. Further, an organisation's allocation to savings may be strengthened with policies regarding what percentage of the budget to devote to savings, what reserve fund size the organisation is targeting, and what limited circumstances would justify a temporary break from the saving that had been in the planned budget. Aside from a budget line item contribution to savings, the organisation may direct windfalls or certain sources of revenue towards savings, as noted above.

Investing financial assets

Here, the organisational investment choices mirror choices made by individuals. Holding financial assets in the form of cash is prudent if the cash is likely to be needed within a short time period (for example, within three years). Many common investments, such as stock index funds, are liquid and obtainable within a day or two if needed. Others, such as investments in private equity or long-term certificates of deposit, are not available or impose a penalty for early withdrawal. In general, with so many practically liquid financial investments available, illiquidity may only rarely be a concern. Any discussion of invested financial assets for non-profit organisations should be guided by the mission. That is, most non-profits would not want their invested assets to finance activity that contradicts the organisation's purpose.

Portfolio asset class policy

The organisation should have a portfolio asset class policy for both the emergency reserves funds (including some cash) and endowment funds (with minimal cash). An example for an emergency reserve fund might be: 30% cash, 20% bonds, 50% equities. Likewise, an example for an endowment fund might be: 20% cash, 20% bonds, 60% equities. At regular intervals, such as annually, the portfolio percentages should be reviewed and the assets rebalanced to meet the policy percentage specifications. Portfolio rebalancing in this manner nudges the organisation to sell overpriced assets in times when the market is more likely to drop and buy underpriced assets in times when the market has fallen and is more likely to recover or surge.

Reducing costs

If the non-profit is suffering sharp losses and does not have reserves to maintain its operations fully, a review of operational expenses is certainly warranted. As a growth strategy, however, cutting costs will not yield future growth unless the cost savings is put to work in creating new revenue opportunities. At worst, reducing costs leads to what some describe as the non-profit starvation cycle (Lecy & Searing, 2015), where continual underinvestment in overhead costs dampens the ability to raise revenue for future programming. Hung et al. (2023) provide a more comprehensive model of the starvation cycle and how it may or may not influence donor preference for low overhead expenses. Note that the academic scrutiny of overzealous cost reduction centres on the annual revenue and expense cycle of the organisation, with little context of how a robust reserve strategy affects the organisation's financial behaviour. An organisation with limited reserves may indeed shrink unsustainably if it reduces administrative and fundraising expenses in a cost-cutting effort. On the other hand, an organisation with robust reserves may have the option to drastically reduce costs in one area in order to invest more strategically in another area that will yield benefits farther out in the future.

Strategic investment internal grants

An organisation with multiple programmes and departments may set aside some funds as an internal grant programme, to allow programme managers to suggest strategic investments and pursue growth opportunities. This internal grants process requires the organisation to hold a portion of its budget unbudgeted in order to fund the winning proposed initiatives. The advantage of the strategic investment process is that it provides a mechanism for programme managers to identify new opportunities and bring their ideas forward to upper management decision-makers, who may lack valuable frontline perspective.

Seizing rare, advantageous opportunities

An organisation with a robust emergency reserves fund, adequate cash flow, and an endowment that helps pay a portion of the annual budget may have enough financial capacity to fund sudden opportunities that arise. For example, a building that would be perfect for the organisation may come on the market with a favourable price. Having reserves enables the organisation to move quickly and pursue a growth strategy without resorting to the much slower process of selling the idea to stakeholders (donors and grantmakers), that is, the organisation's agency and agile progressivity arise from the organisation's stability and financial capacity.

Borrowing, growing, and paying off debt over time

Compared to simply using reserves, a riskier strategy is to borrow funding for expansion. Presumably, the expansion results in enhanced future revenue, which will allow the organisation to pay off the debt. There are natural limits on this strategy, as debt payments could become onerous and even the cost of debt would increase as further debt is incurred (as creditors charge higher rates on loans, the higher the existing loan burden). Donors and foundations are not attracted to solicitations or grant applications framed as "help us pay off our debt," Thus, while some borrowing exists in the third sector, it is generally eschewed as a growth tactic and debt levels in the sector are far lower than in governments or for-profit enterprises.

136 *Renée A. Irvin*

With a toolkit of stability and growth-enhancing tactics now established, it is worthwhile to stop and take a broader view to examine the bigger questions. Given an organisation that is financially stable and able to pursue growth opportunities, how do these new qualities shape leadership decision-making? What sort of opportunities can an organisation pursue, and how do mission methods and outcomes change? The next section argues that a stable non-profit organisation is fundamentally different from a financially unstable non-profit. Stability enables innovation and growth, which has exciting implications for governance, as introduced below.

Performance, from stability to growth

This chapter provided a blueprint for financial planning and structures that enable an organisation to perform with a level of efficacy that provides an invisible but solid framework for the vital work of the organisation to occur. Within this framework, "stability" does not imply a complacent, stalled organisation. On the contrary, financial stability provides the freedom for leaders and managers to concentrate on the mission (rather than dramatic financial swings), achieve decision-making independence from single sources of revenue, pursue innovative projects that may entail some risk, and grow in new, purpose-driven ways. Table 7.3 illustrates the sequential nature of non-profit financial sophistication.

Earlier in this chapter it was noted that the non-profit finance literature, though helpful in viewing facets of financial management, has drawn insight from for-profit, government, and personal finance contexts that are not necessarily analogous to the non-profit context. There are uniquely non-profit organisational financial challenges, such as multiple forms of revenue, and opportunities, such as the freedom to accumulate savings without fear of being purchased by another firm, that compel non-profit researchers to calibrate our research specifically for this unique sector. Furthermore, non-profit financial management

Table 7.3 Financial stability and growth over time

Stability strategies lay the groundwork for growth strategies

◊ Establishing reserves: Cash reserves, emergency reserves, endowment
　◊ Establishing policies and procedures to create and protect financial stability
　　◊ Avoiding cost reductions that threaten long-term sustainability
　　　◊ Seizing sudden opportunities requiring investment
　　　　◊ Pursuing new revenue strategies with long-run payoffs

Resulting in a virtuous cycle of organisational strength and efficacy
◊ Independence from single revenue sources
　◊ Innovating, accepting and accommodating risk as part of the innovation process
　　◊ Anticipating and leading mission growth and change over time
　　　◊ Organisational actorhood

---

textbooks often do not mention stabilisation strategies, even though revenue and cost swings are hallmarks of the non-profit organisational experience.

Table 7.3 illustrates a sequence of financial strategies ideally resulting in robust organisational financial strength. Research is welcomed and particularly needed precisely to guide practitioners, to answer questions such as: How much cash is optimal, given the annual variability of revenue? If financial growth is valued as much as capital preservation, how large should emergency reserves be and how should emergency reserves and endowment be invested? Beyond the practical questions to guide individual organisations in determining their strategy, research is needed from an external perspective on organisational leadership and financial health. Does a financially robust and stable organisation really result in more innovative, risk-taking, and generation-spanning planning, as this chapter posits? Or does a financially stable, robust organisation become hidebound, complacent, and risk-adverse?

Thus, the non-profit-specific research base needs considerable strengthening at two levels: First, practical strategies for financial stabilisation and financial growth (as *combined* topics, not separate) need more study and illustration for non-profits to follow, including in non-profit management textbooks. This chapter provides a solid start for non-profits to operationalise their stabilisation strategy. Second, financial stabilisation policy is promoted in this chapter as foundational to good governance, yielding an ideal future of organisational independence, effective decision-making, and mission leadership in the sector. An ideal model is only useful, however, if it withstands the test of time and rigorous analysis. The tenets of this chapter provide motivation to research a broad array of fundamental questions whose answers will ultimately serve the non-profit sector well.

References

Bowman, W. (2007). Organizational slack (or goldilocks and the three budgets). *Nonprofit Quarterly*, *14*(1), 14–22.

Bowman, W., Keating, E., & Hager, M. A. (2007). Investment income. In D. Young (Ed.), *Financing nonprofits: Putting theory into practice* (pp. 157–181). Altamira Press.

Chang, C., & Tuckman, H. (1991). Financial vulnerability and attrition as measures of nonprofit performance. *Annals of Public and Cooperative Economics*, *62*(4), 655–672. https://doi.org/10.1111/j.1467-8292.1991.tb01372.x

Dees, J. G., Emerson, J., & Economy, P. (2001). *Enterprising nonprofits: A toolkit for social entrepreneurs*. John Wiley & Sons.

Duchek, S. (2020). Organizational resilience: A capability-based conceptualization. *Business Research*, *13*, 215–246. https://doi.org/10.1007/S40685-019-0085-7

Eikenberry, A. M., & Kluver, J. D. (2004). The marketization of the nonprofit sector: Civil society at risk? *Public Administration Review*, *64*(2), 132–140. https://doi.org/ 10.1111/j.1540-6210.2004.00355.x

Hager, M. A., & Hung, C. (2019). Is diversification of revenue good for nonprofit financial health? *Nonprofit Quarterly*, *26*(1), 57–60.

138 *Renée A. Irvin*

Hung, C., Hager, M. A., & Tian, Y. (2023). Do donors penalize nonprofits with higher non-program costs? A meta-analysis of donor overhead aversion. *Nonprofit and Voluntary Sector Quarterly, 52*(6), 1587–1608. https://doi.org/10.1177/08997640221138260

Irvin, R. A., & Furneaux, C. (2022). Surviving the black swan event: How much reserves should nonprofit organizations hold? *Nonprofit and Voluntary Sector Quarterly, 51*(5), 943–966. https://doi.org/10.1177/08997640211057405

International Organization for Standardization (ISO). (2021). ISO 37000:2021. Governance of organizations – Guidance. https://www.iso.org/standard/65036.html

Kingma, B. R. (1993). Portfolio theory and non-profit financial stability. *Nonprofit and Voluntary Sector Quarterly, 22*(2), 105–119. https://doi.org/10.1177/089976409302200202

Lecy, J., & Searing, E. (2015). Anatomy of the nonprofit starvation cycle: An analysis of falling overhead ratios in the nonprofit sector. *Nonprofit & Voluntary Sector Quarterly, 44*(3), 539–563. https://doi.org/10.1177/0899764014527175

Lu, J., Lin, W., & Wang, Q. (2019). Does a more diversified revenue structure lead to greater financial capacity and less vulnerability in nonprofit organizations? A bibliometric and meta-analysis. *VOLUNTAS: International Journal of Voluntary and Nonprofit Organizations, 30*, 593–609. https://doi.org/10.1007/s11266-019-00093-9

Plaisance, G. (2022). French non-profit organizations after one year of Covid-19: Insights into organizational resilience. *Journal of General Management (Online First)*. https://doi.org/10.1177/03063070221140725

Pope, S., Bromley, P., Lim, A., & Meyer, J. W. (2018). The pyramid of nonprofit responsibility: The institutionalization of organizational responsibility across sectors. *VOLUNTAS: International Journal of Voluntary and Nonprofit Organizations, 29*(6), 1300–1314. https://doi.org/10.1007/s112666-018-0038-3

Qu, H. (2019). Risk and diversification of nonprofit revenue portfolios: Applying modern portfolio theory to nonprofit revenue management. *Nonprofit Management and Leadership, 30*(2), 193–212. https://doi.org/10.1002/nml.21385

Steinberg, R. (1986). Should donors care about fundraising? In S. Rose-Ackerman (Ed.), *The economics of nonprofit institutions: Studies in structure and policy* (pp. 347–366). Oxford University Press.

Wilsker, A. L., & Young, D. R. (2010). How does program composition affect the revenues of nonprofit organizations? Investigating a benefits theory of nonprofit finance. *Public Finance Review, 38*(2), 193–210. https://doi.org/10.1177/1091142110369238

8 Double or tandem movement? The emergence and evolution of non-profit social responsibility

Shawn Pope

Introduction

A development that is surely surprising to many observers is that, in recent decades, a movement for social responsibility has swept the non-profit sector. The movement has been remarkable for the diversity of its practices and the depth of its commitment from participants. Indeed, it is now almost a taken-for-granted assumption that a contemporary non-profit, especially one that is large and well known, will devote considerable effort to championing social responsibility – which can be defined in general as "transparent decision making aligned with broader societal expectations" (International Standards Organization, 2024). More specifically, non-profits are now demonstrating this new commitment by instituting systems to support accountability to donors and regular reporting to local communities. Many also have adopted purpose statements, codes of conduct, statements of core values, and a medley of sustainability initiatives that they are actively pursuing.

This is a surprising development because, in the public imagination, non-profits are *already* responsible actors – by virtue of their missions. The very purpose of non-profits, certainly the ones that readily come to mind as emblematic of the sector, is to improve society in some significant area, be it youth employment, homelessness, or cultural preservation. It seems unnecessary, therefore, for the same non-profits to also champion social responsibility, especially since it may distract from their primary callings. Why would Habitat for Humanity, the World Wildlife Fund, or Doctors without Borders, which have operated so selflessly for so long, and which always seem to be budget-constrained, spend any resources to explicitly, comprehensively, and vocally espouse social responsibilities that are tangential to the task of building houses, saving species, or curing the sick?

Indeed, even as it has been coming into plain view, the movement for non-profit responsibility has remained poorly understood. It has been wholly ignored, however. Academics, at least, have already fixed their gaze on narrow dimensions of the movement. There are developed discourses, for example, on non-profit accountability (Williams & Taylor, 2013), ethics (Bromley & Orchard, 2016), transparency (Gandía, 2011), citizenship (Clemens, 2017), and sustainability

DOI: 10.4324/9781003460572-12

140   *Shawn Pope*

(Weerawardena et al., 2010). What has remained overlooked, though, is the contemporaneous emergence of these various discourses, as well as their coherence as part of a larger movement (Pope et al., 2018).

More to the point, this chapter examines the emergence of non-profit responsibility. To the extent they have studied it, academics have explained the arrival of non-profit responsibility as a natural reaction to the scandals that rocked the non-profit sector in the 1990s and to the growing reach, power, and influence of these organisations in the same period (Pope & Bromley, 2023). Certainly, this explanation is plausible. In fact, there were many major scandals at that time and, indeed, it was around then that many non-profits became so large that external checks controls on their power seemed warranted. Yet, the explanation is incomplete. When one looks beyond the non-profit sector, one appreciates that a similar movement emerged simultaneously for businesses, that is, the movement for "corporate social responsibility." This chapter considers both as tandem movements that stem from a similar set of background trends.

Another challenge to the standard account is the manner in which the movement has evolved. If the movement were simply a reaction to non-profits' growing power or all-too-common lapses in oversight, it would have continued to operate by a logic of external control. In other words, it would have continued to be animated by efforts (that are presumably resisted by non-profits) to oversee, audit, and certify them from the outside, so as to squelch any potential for misbehaviour. Yet today's movement is an enthusiastic affair in which non-profits, by all accounts, are fully and voluntarily seeking to identify and embrace their social responsibilities as an expression of their own values and self-identities.

In telling the story of this evolution, the chapter loosely follows Figure 8.1's roadmap. At its centre are arrows with decade-by-decade themes in the discourse on non-profit responsibilities. These arrows are stacked to indicate that earlier themes have been carried forward to today. For instance, non-profits are *still* expected to have impactful missions and be lawful, even as there are newer emphases on citizenship, stakeholders, and core values. As a final note, the arrows are outlined with dashed lines to indicate the permeability of the movement to larger trends, some of which are macrosociological (i.e., globalisation), some of which are sectoral (the background growth of non-profits), and some of which have provenance in the business world (e.g., the practice of sustainability reporting first emerged there).

The "double movement": The standard account of the emergence of non-profit responsibility

In the standard account, non-profit responsibility emerged in the 1990s as a kind of double movement. The double movement was coined by Karl Polanyi, an Austro-Hungarian anthropologist, to refer to aftermath of the 19th-century transformation of economies around the world towards free markets (Polanyi, 1957).

Emergence and evolution of non-profit social responsibility 141

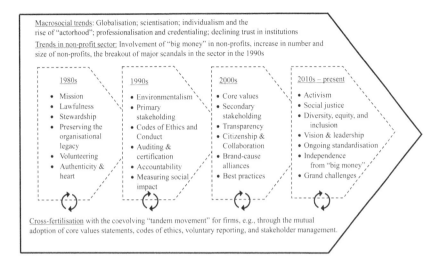

Figure 8.1 Changing emphases in the development of the movement for non-profit social responsibility

As economies became dis-embedded from traditional institutions, Polanyi observed a concomitant push for social protections, as evidenced in the Labour Movement of the 19th century and the "New Deal" programmes in the 1930s in the United States.

Similarly, the growing power of non-profits over the last century began to outstrip the control of local communities. As background, while some of today's well-known non-profits were founded in the 1800s (e.g., the Salvation Army in 1865) and the American Red Cross in 1881), it was not until the post-war period of the 1940s that non-profits took off as a major constituent of civil society (Hammack, 2001). This proliferation is reflected in Part 1 of Figure 8.2, which shows the increasing incidence over the last century of "non-profit" in a large corpus of English text.

By the 1980s, the non-profits from the first wave of creation were becoming several generations removed from the direct control of their founders. Rather, many had transitioned into "going concerns" under new leadership who were not so much visionaries as professional managers. Meanwhile, many non-profits were becoming gargantuan, including the United Way, which recorded $1 billion in revenues in 1989. This size brought more potential to do good, but also warranted more oversight. Concurrently, non-profits were going global, filling the ranks of a growing class of "international nongovernmental organisations" (Boli & Thomas, 1997). Doctors without Borders, for example, was created in 1980 to deliver medical aid in the wake of conflict, epidemics, and natural disasters. Such organisations no longer operated within local communities, but on a global stage with a much weaker and fragmented regulatory regime.

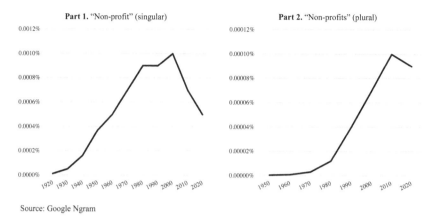

Source: Google Ngram

Figure 8.2 The appearance of "Non-profit" and "Non-profits" in a large corpus of English text

At the same time, the compensation of the leaders of non-profits skyrocketed. As one example, Klaus Schwab, the founder of the World Economic Forum (est. 1971), made a reported $400k in annual salary by the 1990s (Goodman, 2022). These sums, although common in the corporate world, struck many observers as unbecoming for a sector long animated by an ethos of self-less volunteering in pursuit of charitable, rather than pecuniary goals. Nevertheless, "big money" continued to arrive throughout the 1990s. Today, over 200 billionaires have taken the "giving pledge," vowing to give away at least half their fortunes while alive or at death. As the super-rich became more involved, suspicions arose that many non-profits were being controlled from the outside by powerful individuals, whose influence on organisational affairs dwarfed those of traditional stakeholders such as workers and served communities.

The growth in non-profit ranks, size, globality, and resources were tinder for a social responsibility movement to ignite in the 1990s in the aftermath of several major scandals. These scandals engulfed some of the biggest names. In 1992, for example, the United Way was discovered to have misrepresented its spending practices, leading to the firing and imprisonment of its CEO. In 1995, as another example, the CEO of the Hale House Foundation, which provided shelter and services to homeless families, was found to have embezzled money from the organisation to fund a lavish lifestyle. As the decade wore on, other non-profits were exposed to various forms of fraud, deception, and wonton ineffectiveness. The scandals were picked up and amplified by cable news, a new form of media, which provided close and penetrating coverage of the events, oftentimes by packaging them into narratives of pervasive abuse in the sector.

In the wake of the scandals, new initiatives were created to restore public trust. These included initiatives that verified the existence of non-profits (e.g., Candid,

Emergence and evolution of non-profit social responsibility 143

est. 2016, formerly GuideStar, est. 1994), evaluated their resource efficiency (Charity Navigator, est. 2001), and monitored them for wrongdoing (Charity-Watch, est. 1992). Frameworks also emerged to promote best practices for governance (Board Source, est. 1988), accredit non-profits as meeting standards of excellence (Non-profits First, est. 2005), and offer a code of conduct that any non-profit could adopt regardless of its field of work (World Association of Non-governmental Organisations, est. 2000). As this infrastructure fell into place, the power of the non-profits came to be checked from the outside by initiatives that no longer assumed that a particular non-profit was necessarily honest or inherently beneficial to society.

"The Tandem Movement": A fuller account of the emergence of non-profit responsibility

While the imagery of a "double movement" is helpful and not necessarily wrong, it can only go so far in explaining the emergence of non-profit responsibility. Tightly focused on the sector, it gives a myopic view of precipitating events. A fuller account would also consider the contemporaneous movement for social responsibility in the business realm. Viewed from this wider vantage, non-profit responsibility is part of a "tandem movement" (discussed in this section) that itself reflects a host of macro-sociological trends (discussed later).

Below, we give this fuller account in four parts – with a brief history of the firm-directed movement; a discussion of the roles that non-profits played in that movement; an account of the more recent evolution of both movements through the (apparently voluntary) adoption of a set of highly progressive practices; and an illustration of the ways that the two movements have fully converged in recent years through a host of social responsibility initiatives that members can join –regardless of organisational sector.

Firms were undergoing a similar movement for social responsibility

A significant fact overlooked in most accounts of the emergence of non-profit responsibility is that a highly similar movement was occurring at the same time in the for-profit sector. Generally called "corporate social responsibility" or "CSR," this latter movement has so many parallels with non-profit responsibility that it would be grievous mistake to consider them separately. Indeed, not only did CSR emerge in earnest around the same time (the 1990s), when it did so, it was generally attributed to analogous causes (e.g., the need to check the growing power of multinational firms).

As brief history, while discussions about CSR began in earnest in the 1950s, they did not go anywhere for decades. As a sign of the zeitgeist, Howard Bowen published a seminal book in 1953, *The Social Responsibilities of the Businessmen*, that was considered so fringe that, in the year before publication,

144 Shawn Pope

Bowen had to resign from his professorship at University of Illinois because his views led him to be cast as a communist sympathiser. In the 1970s, discussions about CSR flared up again, but met with stiff resistance. Most famously, Milton Friedman – no marginal figure given that he would win a Nobel Prize six years later – decried the notion that companies have social responsibilities in a *New York Times* article provocatively titled "The Social Responsibility of Business Is to Increase Its Profits" (Friedman, 1970).

Only in the 1980s did CSR gain traction. It did so, however, by jiving more with dominant ideology. More specifically, CSR was recast as a sound component of traditional business strategy. In particular, Edward R. Freeman became foundational figure in CSR discourse by popularising the idea of stakeholders – any group or individual who can impact or be impacted by an organisation. Freeman's key pivot was the argument that companies would be more successful if they considered the interests, needs, and power of other groups beyond their owners. It should be underscored (since it is often overlooked) that Friedman viewed his stakeholder theory as a pathway to better strategy and, hence, more profits. This is hinted by the prominence of "strategic management" in the title of his celebrated book, *Strategic Management: A Stakeholder Approach*. It is also indicated by what followed the publication of Freeman's book – a several-decade quest by academics to establish a link between CSR and profitability, i.e., to show that the two concepts are not necessarily at odds (Margolis & Walsh, 2003).

As with the parallel movement in the non-profit sector, it was not until the 1990s that CSR really took hold in the United States and, thereafter, went global in the early 2000s. In those decades, CSR began to impact nearly every aspect of business, from sourcing to production, marketing, and hiring. Given the stiff resistance of years prior, few would have guessed, for example, that Harvard Business School graduates would create their own pledge in 2008 to run their future enterprises responsibly (i.e., The MBA Oath). It would have been hard to imagine, as well, that oil majors such as Exxon and Total, which contribute so heavily to environmental degradation, would include the language of social responsibility in their mission statements, thereby portraying it as one of their existential concerns.

As for why the long-dormant CSR movement came to life at that moment in history, the standard account mirrors the imagery of a double movement, that is, CSR was *needed* in response to the increasingly apparent dislocations from global capitalism. The list of social strains that made a CSR seem timely is long and varied – the deregulation of the 1980s, the rise of the massive multinational firm, the concentration of power in many industries through mergers and acquisitions, the elaboration of supply chains into countries without strong labour protections, the continual eruption of business scandals, the plundering of communist countries as they transitioned to market economics, and a set of dire environmental problems that is simply too long to list.

Non-profits were the chief supporters of the for-profit social responsibility movement

A wider vantage onto the movement for non-profit responsibility, which takes into account the contemporaneous movement in the business realm, reveals another significant correspondence between the two: It was primarily non-profits that created the infrastructure for businesses to identify and practise their social responsibilities. Indeed, as displayed in Table 8.1, they played many roles in the CSR movement as administrators, agenda setters, certifiers, consultants, representatives, and watchdogs.

These roles fell to non-profits as the exact type of contributions that these organisations are known for making in society, since they involve important, painstaking, and generally unprofitable social work at the intersection of multiple societal constituencies. These same roles, it should be mentioned, were played by non-profits in the creation and safeguarding of their own social responsibility movement. In other words, a larger vantage onto both movements suggests that non-profits are the engine of social responsibility wherever it appears and that these organisations are the providers of much-needed private regulation wherever public governance is deemed insufficient.

As background on the emergence of this private governance, non-profits began to change their engagement strategy in the 1990s. Rather than seeking to educate the public, lobby governments for change, or just remediate the externalities of capitalism after the fact, they started working directly with companies to address the problems at their source. This change was necessary for two reasons. On the one hand, the problems were increasingly recognised as urgent (e.g., "tipping points" from unchecked climate change were increasingly recognised as looming in the not-so-distant future). In other words, non-profits could not afford to wait for governments to pass laws through slow-moving democratic processes that would, at any rate, ultimately be worked out in the courts.

On the other hand, it was recognised that governments were susceptible to capture by corporations, which could donate large sums of money to American political campaigns and influence congressmen after elections through lobbyists such as the United States Chamber of Commerce. Moreover, governments were unreliable partners due to the coming and going of new cabinets every few years. At the international level, there were also intractable difficulties in getting countries at very different levels of development to agree to common standards on such things as pollution emissions and labour protections.

Indeed, many of the previous efforts at the global level failed miserably. The United Nations Centre on Transnational Corporations, for example, which was intended to create a more robust system of cross-border business regulation was found in 1975 but ultimately abolished in 1992 – without much to show for its efforts. Meanwhile, similar initiatives such as the OECD Guidelines on Multinational Enterprises struck observers as lacking the teeth to enforce any violations of principles that were, at any rate, so abstract as to be

Table 8.1 The roles of non-profits in supporting the firm-directed CSR movement

Role and description	Organisational examples
Administrators. Non-profits serve as conduits for firms to practise their charitable programmes. The relationships with firms may be one-time, semi-permanent partnerships, or through established foundations	TotalEnergies Foundation, which receives the bulk of its funding from TotalEnergies SE, a for-profit company, uses that funding to promote road safety, youth inclusion and education, environmentalism, and cultural dialogue and heritage
Agenda setters. Non-profits give direction to the CSR movement by orienting its actors around a set of especially important issues. Here, non-profits introduce new ideas to businesses, oftentimes through the convocation of conferences, the maintenance of expert networks, or the publication of original research	The World Economic convenes an annual mega-conference in January in Davos, Switzerland that brings together hundreds of heads of state, executives of multinational firms, prominent academics, leaders of civil society, and artists and cultural figures to foster awareness and spear collective action on pressing social and environmental issues
Certifiers. Non-profits create and administer initiatives that define, promulgate, and assure the standards by which companies can practise CSR. As corporate members of these initiatives may display special logos on their products, non-profits can be instrumental in channelling reputational and branding benefits to strong CSR performers	The Marine Stewardship Council, established in 1997, has created standards through multi-stakeholder dialogue by which members commit to manage fish stocks in a sustainable, lawful way that minimises damage to the larger ecosystem and does not jeopardise the long-term vitality of populations of commercial species such as tuna and salmon
Consultants. Non-profits provide firms with expertise to help them identify and practise their social responsibilities. Here, non-profits assess firms current state of affairs, offer strategies for improvement, and help companies to communicate their efforts to stakeholders	San Francisco-based "Business for Social Responsibility" operates much like traditional consultant, charging a fee to share advice and skills with company leaders as they develop strategies to tackle their social responsibilities in areas such as sustainability, philanthropy, and diversity
Representatives. Non-profits that serve as representatives ensure that the interests of their served communities or other non-profits are voiced in the halls of power. In this way, non-profits guide policymakers and the CSR movement practices that are beneficial to a wide set of stakeholders	The Forest Stewardship Council creates its guidelines for timber management based on the votes of an assembly of disparate stakeholders, including non-profits such as the Sierra Club, as well as academics and industry representatives
Watchdogs. Non-profits monitor companies for breaches of public trust and name and shame offenders. The ability of non-profits to threaten companies with negative publicity has been amplified by the emergence of social media, which has decentralised the publication of news, democratised the decision as to which new stories are most important, and made it possible for shocking stories to spread faster	Greenpeace has developed new tactics for shining a harsh light on problematic corporate practices. For example, several years ago its members boarded and occupied an oil rig in the North Sea to stop BP from drilling there. Members also sought to draw attention to the burning of the Amazon and the resulting destruction to wildlife by dressing as spider monkeys during a protest outside the headquarters of Burger King in the United Kingdom

Emergence and evolution of non-profit social responsibility 147

almost meaningless. Against this backdrop of failure, direct engagement with companies, although likely to be resisted by them and even to open non-profits to accusations of being co-opted, was nonetheless recognised to be increasingly needed.

As this engagement became normalised, non-profits began to play the roles in Table 8.1. They came to *administer* the social work of companies by taking their funds and, for example, selecting grantees for worthy causes (e.g., Ford Foundation). They *set the agenda* for CSR through mega-conferences (World Economic Forum) and by pushing specific issues in corporate proxy votes (Interfaith Centre on Corporate Social Responsibility). They *certified* company practices as meeting sustainability guidelines through a host of newly created industry standards (e.g., Rain Forest Alliance). Lastly, they worked as *consultants* to help companies identify and practise their social responsibilities (Business for Social Responsibility), as *representatives* on city and state councils to direct governments towards economic policies that would benefit the most stakeholders (New York Council of Non-profits), and as *watchdogs* to monitor companies for breaches of public trust and to name and shame offenders (Charity Watch). Through these roles, non-profits developed an infrastructure for the CSR movement, in the process creating and legitimating new directives that could be enforced with new sources of social sanctioning.

Both movements continued to evolve towards more progressive practices

Another benefit of viewing the non-profit and for-profit movements together is the ability to see their coevolution. In other words, not only did these movements *emerge* from similar circumstances, they also *developed* in similar ways. Appreciating this development reveals another shortcoming of the imagery of the double movement: Whereas the double movement suggests a push to restore social control, the more recent wave of social responsibility is towards practices that, by all accounts, are voluntarily and enthusiastically adopted (see the practices in the final column of Table 8.1 and Figure 8.2).

For example, many non-profits whose work is not centrally involved with social justice have nonetheless promoted it as a core value – without any apparent compulsion from the outside. This includes the National Council of Non-profits, whose website touts its commitment to "centering equity in all that we do," "embedding diversity, equity, and inclusion throughout the organisation," and "focusing first on racial equity, because systemic racism impacts all individuals and communities." Similarly, although the Sierra Club is, at first pass, an environmental group, it clearly sees itself as much more: Its website champions its involvement on many social fronts, from immigration to women's rights and community policing.

This enthusiastic, self-driven nature of the contemporary movement is missed by many observers. Rather, when looking at the for-profit movement, the view is still dominant that companies have to be *forced* to be socially

148 *Shawn Pope*

responsible – that they simply cannot be trusted to do anything that contravenes their primary profit motive. Another common view is that, while companies may do CSR voluntarily, it is only because it is ultimately profitable, for example, by allowing companies to reach new customers, reduce costs, or curry favour with regulators.

And yet, while those motivations are plausible, a recent study has not found them to be highly prevalent. (Lim & Pope, 2021) gathered and analysed over 100 surveys of self-reported CSR motivations from business leaders in dozens of countries and industries over the past two decades. They found that the most common motivations, by far, were normative ones, which portray CSR as being "ethical," the "right thing to do," or a "reflection of the company's own values." The dominance of these motivations across time, industries, and countries suggests that CSR, at this stage in its development, is not merely a business trend but is a profound cultural one. Stated otherwise, the movement that we have today has changed the ideas that business leaders are expected to hold and profess.

Both movements increasingly overlap through ecumenical frameworks

Another benefit of putting the non-profit and for-profit movements in the same analytic lens is the ability to see their convergence through frameworks that have participation from both companies and non-profits. It is an underappreciated fact that several major responsibility frameworks – which are nearly always discussed from the perspective of firms – also have membership from non-profits. At the international level, non-profits can ratify the principles of the United Nations Global Compact, produce sustainability reports by the standards of the Global Reporting Initiative, or commit to the CSR principles of the International Standards Organisation. As far as these frameworks are concerned, both non-profits and firms are simply "organisations," with only secondary consideration for the type, whether schools or the firms that supply them with pencils. In other words, for these frameworks, the "c" in CSR refers to *corporate entities* of all stripes, not strictly to for-profit corporations.

This development, of course, is understandable given that the various types of "organisations" are, indeed, fundamentally similar (Bromley & Meyer, 2017). Among the host of likenesses, both non-profits and firms are overseen by boards of directors, which can be structured appropriately to avoid conflicts of interest and to have a gender balance. Both employ workers that can be adequately compensated, fairly treated, and provided with a workplace free of bullying and harassment. Both have buildings that use energy and produce waste. Both have suppliers that can be paid a fair wage and that can source sustainability; funders that expect their contributions to be used for intended purposes in a transparent manner; and surrounding communities that expect little noise, pollution, and traffic. Given these likenesses, it is not surprising that frameworks would evolve with no interest in limiting membership to a single organisational type.

Emergence and evolution of non-profit social responsibility   149

Perhaps the fullest realisation of the increasing convergence of non-profits and businesses is the creation of a new organisational form that lies at the intersection of each organisational type. More specifically, throughout the 2010s in the United States, many states began to allow organisations to structure themselves as "benefit corporations." Unlike the traditional "C type" corporations, these organisations expressly do not have profits as their only motive. Rather, they are also allowed to pursue (and be legally protected in doing so) positive social impacts. With this change, social responsibility was no longer bolted onto organisations through the adoption of practices, but built into the very definition of a new organisational form.

The tandem movement in macrosociological context

A final benefit of viewing non-profit responsibility in tandem with for-profit responsibility is that it invites a look at the broader causes of both movements. This section raises three of these causes: The rise of discourses of actorhood, the scientisation and rationalisation of organisational life, and globalisation.

In recent decades, it is not only individuals who have been construed as "social actors," but also the organisations that they create (Bromley & Sharkey, 2017). For example, in the United States, courts have affirmed corporations as having many of the same rights as natural persons, from political voice to the ability to hold property and to sue others and be sued by them. Academics, as well, have increasingly portrayed non-profits, governments, and even cities as social actors, a conceptualisation that serves to emphasise the boundedness of these organisations and their ability to enact strategic change, leadership, and vision. The rise of empowered organisational actorhood is a precipitating condition for social responsibility, given that actorhood, wherever it appears, needs to be coupled with education, humility, and broader social control. From this perspective, it is no surprise that the social responsibility movement was adopted the earliest and most stridently in the United States, given that this country, perhaps more than any other, is steeped in the notion of individualism.

Another background condition is the rise of the cultural authority of science and reason. This trajectory was appreciated as far back as Max Weber's depiction of modernity as an "iron cage" – a sphere of abstract, deracinated knowledge that is independent of local circumstances (i.e., theories). In the case of the social responsibility movement, scientisation took off in the 1980s as non-profits were increasingly treated as objects of study. It was then that many academic journals were created to analyse these organisations, masters' programmes were instituted to train their leaders in the latest social-scientific knowledge, and "best practices" were devised to guide non-profits towards practices that were construed as potentially beneficial for all. Reflecting this worldview, as displayed in Part 2 of Figure 8.2, it was only in the 1980s that writers started

150 *Shawn Pope*

commonly referring to "non-profits" in the plural, suggesting that they increasingly thought that some things could be said about all of them.

The final background trend is globalisation, the increasing interconnectedness of the world through a common culture and the increasing movement of people and goods across national borders. Globalisation, of course, feeds into the scientisation of the world, given that the latter movement places the highest value on knowledge that is "universal." The global realm differs from domestic contexts in having no hegemon to create and enforce hard laws. Instead, the global domain has nearly 200 nations that are equally sovereign and that are envisioned to interact with one another on the basis of mutual respect. Because these nations have quite different laws, the global realm presents non-profits with reputational risks, for example, from setting up shops in countries that are, for example, "pollution havens." The vacuum of public regulation at the global level is naturally filled with private regulation, including the many initiatives for organisational social responsibility that have emerged in recent decades.

Discussion

While the movement for social responsibility that has swept the non-profit sector in recent decades is surprising – given that the organisations in this sector have been doing so much good for so long – perhaps it is not entirely unexpected. The movement that has arisen, spreading through a multiplicity of platforms and advancing a plethora of values, from accountability to transparency, seems to be a tandem movement with the one for firms. Although the latter movement is more appreciated, heralded, and critiqued, it is not so different in its basic nature and fundamental practices. Indeed, these movements have converged recently through a host of new frameworks that have participation from both types of organisations. At the intersection of the movements is also the creation of hybrid forms, particularly the "benefit company," through which the driving motivation for non-profits (social impact) can be married with that for firms (profits).

A wider vantage onto both movements also reveals them to be products of their time, reflections of the institutional conditions at the moments of their birth. These conditions are acute (i.e., scandals) and diffuse (the rise of empowered actorhood). As such, even as these movements claim to be (and actually have been) transformational, they are themselves an outgrowth of larger trends that are continuing to have effects at all levels of society, both the individual and organisational. These trends serve to remake practices, but more importantly they change ideas, which are the ultimate drivers of the practices that diffuse.

In presenting the movement for non-profit responsibility, this chapter offered two frameworks. The first was a loose timeline of the themes that have characterised the movement over recent decades (Figure 8.1). The second was a listing and illustration of the responsibilities that non-profits are increasingly expected to practise (Table 8.2). In offering these frameworks, the intention was to approach

Table 8.2 Examples of the dimensions of non-profit social responsibility

Responsibility	Description	Link to social responsibility	Example practices
Mission	Ensuring that the non-profit pursues a fundamental purpose that advances a worthy social cause	Society benefits when non-profits supply goods that are underprovided by governments and firms	Statements of mission, vision, and purpose that are centred around a core area of social work
Efficiency	Using non-profit resources in a way that maximises positive social impact	Efficiency strengthens non-profits' ability to fulfil their primary social obligation – positive impact	Benchmarking, measurement, key performance indicators, training, and professionalisation
Governance	Encouraging sound management through by the appropriate rules, processes, and structures	Good governance promotes leadership that is legitimate, accountable, and professional	Board elections, board independence, board compensation, and board structure
Transparency and accountability	Supplying non-profit constituents with enough information to evaluate and understand the non-profit's affairs	Transparency fosters accountability allows for external oversight by empowering stakeholders with critical information	Voluntary reporting; establishing formal channels for feedback and engagement
Stakeholder management	Considering and involving a wide range of non-profit constituents in decisions that affect them	It promotes awareness of a non-profit's social impacts and gives rise to strategies for improving them	Stakeholder inventories, analysis, and communication
Citizenship	Fulfilling voluntaristic obligations to the larger non-profit community	Citizenship is a baseline obligation by which non-profits foster a vibrant and collaborative field of enterprise	Serving on non-profit councils; attending multistakeholder conferences and colloquia
Ethics	Following standards of right and wrong that are widely held in a culture, industry, or other setting	Ethical prescriptions are baseline social responsibilities that are expected of all non-profits	Codes of conduct, for example, on the treatment of whistleblowers and donor confidentiality
Core values	Formalising the non-profit's beliefs as to which ideals are most important for practice	Core values foster a culture and decisions that promote desirable ends for the non-profit and its constituents	Statements of core values and values-based hiring and promotion
Environmentalism	Using resources sustainably and minimising negative impacts on the natural world	It fulfils the profound ethical obligation of the non-profit to be a good steward of the planet	The adoption of clean technology; recycling programmes; teleworking; going paperless
Activism	Advancing social causes that are tangential to the mission and not yet consensus-based	Activism remakes the socio-political field along lines that non-profits find inherently more responsible.	Becoming party to an amicus brief; promoting causes such as Black Lives Matter and MeToo

152 *Shawn Pope*

the movement analytically rather than descriptively, to draw out its essential characteristics at a slightly lower level of analysis. As such, these frameworks may give practitioners some orientation as they try to understand and navigate a new dimension of complexity in their sector, including a more grounded understanding of the junctures in history that have led to the current epoch.

In closing, it should be emphasised that none of the discussion in this chapter is to endorse the movement for non-profit responsibility or assess its ability to improve society. While there have been many positive changes, one should not judge the movement in itself, but in relation to other movements that could have happened but did not, in fact, occur. It should be clear, for example, that private regulation is not a perfect substitute for public regulation. Private regulation lacks the authority to force all companies to get onboard. It also tends to be associated with a medley of initiatives that have perverse incentives to lower their own standards to remain competitive. To understand why the counterfactual of a more mandatory, enforceable, and standardised movement did not actually occur, one must put the movement that did occur in its proper sociological context, as this chapter has attempted to do.

References

Boli, J., & Thomas, G. M. (1997). World culture in the world polity: A century of international non-governmental organization. *American Sociological Review, 62*(2), 171–190. https://doi.org/10.2307/2657298

Bromley, P., & Orchard, C. D. (2016). Managed morality: The rise of professional codes of conduct in the U.S. Nonprofit sector. *Nonprofit and Voluntary Sector Quarterly, 45*(2), 351–374. https://doi.org/10.1177/0899764015584062

Bromley, P., & Meyer, J. W. (2017). "They are all organizations": The cultural roots of blurring between the nonprofit, business, and government sectors. *Administration & Society, 49*(7), 939–966. https://doi.org/10.1177/0095399714548268

Bromley, P., & Sharkey, A. (2017). Casting call: The expanding nature of actorhood in U.S. Firms, 1960–2010. *Accounting, Organizations and Society, 59*(May), 3–20. https://doi.org/10.1016/j.aos.2017.06.001

Clemens, E. S. (2017). The constitution of citizens: Political theories of nonprofit organizations. In W. W. Powell & R. Steinberg (Eds.), *The nonprofit sector* (2nd ed., pp. 207–220). Yale University Press. https://doi.org/10.12987/9780300153439-012

Friedman, M. (1970). A Friedman doctrine: The social responsibility of business is to increase its profits. *The New York Times Magazine, 13*, 32–33.

Gandía, J. L. (2011). Internet disclosure by nonprofit organizations : Empirical evidence of nongovernmental organizations for development in Spain. *Nonprofit and Voluntary Sector Quarterly, 40*(1), 57–78 https://doi.org/10.1177/0899764009343782

Goodman, P. S. (2022, January 18). *"He has an incredible knack to smell the next fad": How Klaus Schwab built a billionaire circus at Davos*. Vanity Fair. https://www.vanityfair.com/news/2022/01/how-klaus-schwab-built-a-billionaire-circus-at-davos

Hammack, D. C. (2001). Introduction: Growth, transformation, and quiet revolution in the nonprofit sector over two centuries. *Nonprofit and Voluntary Sector Quarterly, 30*(2), 157–173. https://doi.org/10.1177/0899764001302001

International Standards Organization. (2024). *ISO 37000 – the first ever international benchmark for good governance*. https://committee.iso.org/ISO_37000_Governance

Lim, A., & Pope, S. (2021). What drives them to do good? A global meta-study of business Leaders' CSR motivations. *Corporate Social Responsibility and Environmental Management, 29*, 233–255. https://doi.org/10.12987/9780300153439-012

Margolis, J. D., & Walsh, J. P. (2003). Misery loves companies: Rethinking social initiatives by business. *Administrative Science Quarterly, 48*(2), 268–305. https://doi.org/10.2307/3556659

Polanyi, K. (1957). *The great transformation: The political and economic origins of our time*. Beacon Press.

Pope, S., & Bromley, P. (2023). The movement for nonprofit social responsibility: From doing good to being good. *Stanford Social Innovation Review, Summer, 21*(3), 48–54. https://doi.org/10.48558/C3FS-EM31

Pope, S., Bromley, P., Lim, A., & Meyer, J. W. (2018). The pyramid of nonprofit responsibility: The institutionalization of organizational responsibility across sectors. *VOLUNTAS: International Journal of Voluntary and Nonprofit Organizations, 29*, 1300–1314. https://doi.org/10.1007/s11266-018-0038-3

Weerawardena, J., McDonald, R. E., & Mort, G. S. (2010). Sustainability of nonprofit organizations: An empirical investigation. *Journal of World Business, 45*(4), 346–356. https://doi.org/10.1016/j.jwb.2009.08.004

Williams, A. P., & Taylor, J. A. (2013). Resolving accountability ambiguity in nonprofit organizations. *Voluntas, 24*(3). https://doi.org/10.1007/s11266-012-9266-0

9 Social responsibility and sustainability in non-profit organisations

Towards a semantic and conceptual precision

Guillaume Plaisance

Introduction

Recent disruptions (whether due to the pandemic or to more structural crises) have led to various responses from organisations. Companies (i.e., for-profit organisations, FPOs) have introduced corporate social responsibility (CSR) initiatives, while non-profit organisations (NPOs) ostensibly already played a strong societal role. Simply maintaining their activity is an important outcome for society, in particular, minimising the effects of the crises. In this context, society expects companies to develop specific initiatives, often through CSR, while an NPOs' mission is generally considered sufficient.

This distinction between FPOs and NPOs is based on an observation previously noted by Andreini et al. (2014, p. 128): "It is easy to believe that non-profit equates to socially responsible". The authors indicate that this evidence is only apparent and superficial, however, since there is some confusion between organisational responsibility and more specific initiatives.

Consequently, Andreini et al. (2014), followed by Zeimers et al. (2019), pointed to the lack of clarity in the concept of social responsibility in NPOs, as well as its interchangeability with the concepts of sustainability and organisational social responsibility (OSR) in research. While they are related and similar, the present chapter, like Zeimers et al. (2019) and the International Organization for Standardization (ISO, 2012), considers that clarifying and distinguishing the two is essential, including in the context of NPOs.

In addition to the theoretical importance of such a distinction, the current situation also poses problems for organisations. Filho et al. (2019, p. 153) recently summarised it as follows: "the lack of a consensus about what social responsibility means, or how (or whether) it should be differentiated from related concepts remains a major weakness for practice development", with the concepts related to social responsibility being sustainability and OSR.

In order to develop the conceptual and semantic precision required, the chapter is structured as follows. The first section defines the three concepts and then outlines the current challenges and debates surrounding them. This is followed

DOI: 10.4324/9781003460572-13

This chapter has been made available under a CC-BY-NC-ND 4.0 license.

Social responsibility and sustainability in non-profit organisations   155

by an explanation regarding the interchangeability of the concepts, although this is not sufficient to justify the situation. A strict distinction between OSR (I use this acronym, although the original authors used CSR), social responsibility, and sustainability is thus proposed. The implications for theory and practice are then discussed based on the distinction made.

OSR in NPOs: Definitions and current challenges and debate

Waters and Ott (2014, p. 1) took a somewhat broad approach to put forward a synthesis of the definitions of OSR, concluding that it covers "the voluntary actions a company or organisation implements to pursue goals, with a responsibility to its stakeholders". Bivona (2010) identified the common point shared by the majority of definitions, namely, that it remains voluntary and goes beyond the economic sphere and the scope of the organisation. In short, non-financial and non-economic aspects such as social welfare or environmental protection are included in the concept. In addition, its targets are stakeholders and society in general.

In other words, NPOs are recognised for their holistic influence over the economic, social, and ecological environments. They play an increasingly social and economic role, and their political action is also significant due to their involvement in civil society and their key function of advocacy. In addition, NPOs seek to perpetuate their positive action in society as long as possible (Neesham et al., 2017), i.e., to preserve their organisational sustainability and that of their actions (Weerawardena et al., 2010). In order to deal with the holistic impact of NPOs on their communities, the literature sometimes uses the term sustainability, sometimes social responsibility, and sometimes OSR.

The concepts, as defined by the Cambridge Dictionary,[1] are closely interconnected:

1 OSR is "the idea that [an organisation] should be interested in and willing to help society and the environment as well as be concerned about the products and profits it makes".
2 Social responsibility refers to "the practice of producing goods and services in a way that is not harmful to society or the environment".
3 Sustainability is defined as "the idea that goods and services should be produced in ways that do not use resources that cannot be replaced and that do not damage the environment".

In this, OSR and the mission of NPOs have the same goal, namely, the well-being of society and their stakeholders. This is illustrated by putting the purpose of NPOs into perspective with the definition of OSR adopted by the European Commission (as the organisations' responsibility for the impact they have on society), whereas "the goal for the NPOs is to make an impact on society" (Kelly & Lewis, 2009, p. 375).

156 *Guillaume Plaisance*

The literature highlights the convergence between the goal of OSR and the mission of NPOs. NPOs defend "noble causes" (Dhanani & Connolly, 2012, p. 1144) and the "dimensions of [organisational] social responsibility are closely aligned with the goals of many NPOs that function primarily to serve the public interest through the distribution of goods and services" (Waters & Ott, 2014, p. 2). For some researchers, OSR in NPOs is therefore intrinsic. In this, the notion of OSR would appear obvious (and therefore irrelevant?) for such organisations (e.g., Lin-Hi et al., 2015).

However, both researchers and NPO stakeholders are interested in the concepts and even have new requirements for them. Recently, Zeimers et al. (2019) also noted the confusion surrounding OSR and NPOs, but rejected the notion and called for studies of the concept within NPOs (in line with Chell et al., 2016). Empirical research has illustrated this position for many years. For instance, an increasing number of NPOs now publish OSR (Casey, 2018; Gazzola et al., 2017) or sustainability (Veltri & Bronzetti, 2014) reports with the help, for example, of standardisers who adapt their principles to the non-profit sector (e.g., the *Global Reporting Initiative*). Another example is Cornelius et al. (2008) who noted that working conditions of employees in NPOs were no better, or were sometimes even worse, than those of FPOs.

These findings led Bivona (2010, p. 2) to explain that "although NPOs embody in their mission – by definition – [OSR] intentions, in some fields intense commercial competition may erode the 'moral high ground' of the organisation and transform NPOs into 'shadow businesses'". Chelladurai (2016, p. 7) even went so far as to write: "one could argue that the concept of [OSR] is more important in the non-profit sector than in the profit sector". Finally, for Gazzola et al. (2017, p. 356), the issue of social responsibility has become an "ethical obligation" for NPOs.

The conflict between the empirical literature and the practices of NPOs and their stakeholders, on the one hand, and the conceptual literature, on the other hand, can be explained by the conceptual and semantic confusion identified in the introduction. Despite the use of similar words, authors do not necessarily refer to the same practices and concepts. For this reason, semantic and conceptual clarification is essential. This observation is corroborated by other scholars who have also called for such clarification.

Zeimers et al. (2019, p. 955), for instance, explain that "scholars have referred to CSR, non-profit responsibility or sustainability" in order to address social responsibility in NPOs. Some authors, such as Langergaard, combine the three concepts and use "sustainability" as an umbrella word since, while "sustainability (…) is still an underdeveloped, ambiguous and often vague concept" (Langergaard, 2019, p. 457), it is indissociable from NPOs. In short, the literature on these concepts uses them as if they were interchangeable (Palakshappa & Grant, 2018).

Nevertheless, they are "similar but not the same" as Bansal and Song (2017) noted. The ISO highlighted this point as early as 2012: "they are different concepts and thus not interchangeable" (ISO, 2012, p. 3). This chapter is thus in line

Social responsibility and sustainability in non-profit organisations 157

with the literature already published on the subject. Filho et al. (2019, p. 153), for instance, explained that "sustainability is linked with social responsibility and sustainable development and is concerned with equitably balancing the interconnected needs of the environment, the economy and society, both in the present and into the future, and both locally and globally". In addition, Chelladurai (2016, p. 12) considered that "the social responsibilities of any organisation (whether profit or non-profit) must be distinguished from the discretionary socially oriented initiatives of that organisation". Finally, Andreini et al. (2014, p. 129) explained that "because of this social value, and thus the absence of monetary gain, all OSR activities promoted by an NPO could be interpreted as 'socially responsible'. However, this seems to be a rather superficial interpretation".

In short, Zeimers et al. (2019, p. 956) "contend the need for differentiated research and a distinctive approach to non-profit social responsibility" compared to OSR. I thus developed the following remarks.

Understanding the interchangeability of concepts to better distinguish them in the future

A comprehensive review of the conceptual links of the three concepts: Explaining their interchangeability

First of all, it is interesting to understand why management scholars have been led to frequently interchange concepts. The concepts of OSR, social responsibility, and sustainability are widely associated in the literature, as mentioned above. For Dixit (2020, p. 268), for instance, the social responsibility of a hospital, defined as "its moral obligation to deliver quality healthcare which is patients' fundamental right", is linked to its sustainability. More generally, the concepts of OSR and sustainability are related in many studies (Chung et al., 2019; Nevárez & Féliz, 2019).

While many publications establish a link between OSR and sustainability (Filho et al., 2019; Montiel, 2008; van Marrewijk, 2003), Lin-Hi et al. (2015) incorporate sustainability into OSR. Idowu (2008, p. 264) also assimilated the two, specifying that "entities (…) which aspire to be perceived by their stakeholders as being socially responsible must be interested in sustainability and sustainable development".

This assimilation can be explained by their common underpinning (Chelladurai, 2016; Lin-Hi et al., 2015; Moldavanova & Goerdel, 2018; Nevárez & Féliz, 2019; Unerman & O'Dwyer, 2010; Weerawardena et al., 2010) around the *triple bottom line* (Elkington, 1998), with the three issues synthesised under the acronym *Profit – People – Planet*.

Moldavanova and Wright (2020) introduced a twist to this triptych, suggesting that culture could be included as a fourth dimension of sustainability. While this notion may appear recent, in fact the concept of "culturally sustainable

158 *Guillaume Plaisance*

development" first appeared at the end of the 20th century (Throsby, 1995). Moldavanova and Wright thus showed that sustainable development can draw together worlds that are often disparate and heterogeneous, namely the economy and culture, but also and above all, that NPOs played a massive part in this development.

An analysis of the theories underlying work on OSR in NPOs also confirms the role of theoretical anchoring to explain the links between concepts. In addition to Elkington (1998)'s theoretical framework, Carroll's work (e.g., Carroll, 1979) is also highly recurrent. The pyramidal argument regarding economic, legal, ethical, and philanthropic responsibilities sheds further light on the subject of OSR in NPOs (Chelladurai, 2016; Palakshappa & Grant, 2018; Smith, 2011), with discussions focusing on the "required", "expected", and "desired" dimensions, as well as their hierarchy.

Thus, researchers who assimilate and use the concepts studied here interchangeably generally rely on a triple bottom line approach. However, this theoretical underpinning alone cannot justify the assimilation of such broad concepts. The authors of these approaches note the complexity of the concepts studied and call for the adaptation of their theoretical frameworks to the different organisations. Moreover, the approaches are theoretical and not necessarily in line with actual organisational practices (explaining the conflict between the conceptual and empirical literatures). Finally, since both Elkington's and Carroll's approaches are normative, the two authors call for renewed thinking in order to address contemporary issues. The semantic and conceptual clarification proposed here is in line with the desire for a fresh take on the responsibility of organisations.

Towards a strict distinction between OSR, social responsibility, and sustainability in NPOs

The different definitions of OSR illustrate the plurality of the concept (Table 9.1). OSR is moral, incorporating notions of responsibility (Chung et al., 2019), but it is also a strategy (Olaya Garcerá et al., 2020) and, above all, a commitment and a series of social initiatives towards society and the community (Andreini et al., 2014; Chung et al., 2019; Palakshappa & Grant, 2018), endorsing social, environmental, and economic issues (Lin-Hi et al., 2015).

Social responsibility includes the actions and initiatives seen for OSR. However, it puts them into perspective with the values of NPOs (Chelladurai, 2016; Păceşilă & Colesca, 2020). From this angle, NPOs also have social, economic, and environmental commitments (Dixit, 2020), but they are viewed through the filter of social and societal objectives specific to the organisation (Chelladurai, 2016; Moldavanova & Goerdel, 2018), its *raison d'être* (Andreini et al., 2014) and its mission (Andreini et al., 2014; Pope et al., 2018). Social responsibility is thus translated into several governance mechanisms, including ethics, accountability, compliance, etc. (Dixit, 2020; Pope et al., 2018).

Social responsibility and sustainability in non-profit organisations 159

Table 9.1 Definitions of organisational social responsibility, social responsibility, and sustainability in NPOs

Authors	Definitions in NPOs
Organisational social responsibility	
Olaya Garcerá et al. (2020)	"a university management strategy, seeking to maintain a holistic approach to the university organisation itself, and devising interdisciplinary (synergy between university faculties and departments) and inter-institutional (association of various functions of the institutional structure) initiatives"
Chung et al. (2019)	"a company's voluntary responsibility to the societal good, beyond its legal obligations"
Palakshappa and Grant (2018)	a "vehicle, promoting sustainable practice within business, and bridging sectors through the development of community/ business collaborations and partnerships"
Lin-Hi et al. (2015)	Respecting the triple bottom line, "doing good" and "avoiding bad"
Andreini et al. (2014)	"an organisation's contribution to both generating and solving social and environmental problems"
Social responsibility	
Dixit (2020), in the case of public hospitals	"(a) creation of value and efficiency for the stakeholders; (b) protection of the interests and investment of all stakeholders (including the government); (c) protection of the environment; (d) recognition of the human rights of the patients and the participants in the clinical trials; (e) ethical business practices; (f) public accountability of business decisions; (g) compliance with the law and regulations; and (h) protection of animal interests in scientific research"
Păceşilă and Colesca (2020)	"all the behaviours and actions of organisations which engage in the community according to their values and objectives"
Moldavanova and Goerdel (2018), defining "socially responsible organisation"	"an organisation that engages in internally and externally sustainable organisational practices, such as shared leadership, strategic orientation, and being proactive in achieving societal goals, such as the advancement of social equity across generations"
Pope et al. (2018), about "organisational responsibility"	1 "leadership (model innovative practices); 2 citizenship (advance the collective movement); 3 ethics (respect community norms); 4 accountability (be transparent and efficient); 5 lawfulness (follow the lax); 6 mission (make a positive social impact)"
Chelladurai (2016)	Organisational responsibility: "the fundamental responsibility of any organisations (profit or non-profit) is to achieve its stated goals" Social responsibility: "to serve society by attaining their stated goals within the rules and regulations set by society"

(Continued)

160 *Guillaume Plaisance*

Table 9.1 (Continued)

Authors	Definitions in NPOs
Andreini et al. (2014)	1 "the ability to fulfil the institutional mission that provides the NPO's *raison d'être* and the main attraction for stakeholders (members, volunteers, donors, states and local governments, etc.)"
	2 "the way in which the mission is achieved, and to the NPO's ability to respond to other wide-ranging social and environmental issues (…). Examples include the environmental impact of the NPO's actions, the working conditions of its employees, partners and volunteers, and its relationships with donors"
Sustainability	
Dadić and Ribarić (2021), defining "financial sustainability"	"a comparison between earned income and other sources of income" "organisations that have a larger share of income from self-funding relative to income from grants and donations"
Yekini and Yekini (2020)	"providing for society, and everybody has the opportunity to enjoy it for the public good, which is dignifying to them in their own society"
Langergaard (2019), explaining the various dimensions of "social sustainability"	1 Social cohesion 2 Social interaction 3 Social justice or equity 4 Sustainability of community 5 Participation and local democracy
Moldavanova and Goerdel (2018)	"a sustainable organisation is understood here as an organisation that is capable of 'deliver[ing] social value via the pursuit of its social mission' (Weerawardena et al., 2010, p. 347), thus serving the needs of both current and future generations"
Ceptureanu et al. (2017)	"a sustainable NPO is an organisation that can continue to fulfil its mission and satisfy the key stakeholders' requirements, regardless of difficulties encountered"
Lee (2017)	"closely related to organisational success and failure"
Manfred et al. (2017)	a "should relate to corporate responsibility but offer something that goes well beyond ethics-based considerations; b should integrate and embrace economic concerns, instead of opposing them; c should take into consideration the dependence of economic concerns on societal and environmental interests and impacts; d should allow negotiations between different stakeholder groups about conflicts, trade-offs, and contradictions that have scope for application beyond academic debates; e should be understandable and transferrable across different contexts and cultures; and f should provide a basis upon which corporate sustainability can be assessed, measured, reported, and improved"
Jones and Mucha (2014)	1 "living within the world's natural limits; 2 understanding the interconnections among economy, society, and environment; 3 equitable distribution of resources and opportunities"

(Continued)

Social responsibility and sustainability in non-profit organisations 161

Table 9.1 (Continued)

Authors	Definitions in NPOs
Omura and Forster (2014)	"how to ensure their continuity of services to community"
Besel et al. (2011), defining financial sustainability	"the ability of non-profits to diversify their funding base and subsequently grow their operating budget over a five-year period"
Weerawardena et al. (2010)	For an NPO: "being able to survive so that it can continue to serve its constituency"
	Non-profit sustainability: "the organisation will be able to fulfil its commitments to its clients, its patrons, and the community in which it operates. These stakeholder groups depend on the non-profit to service a need and to deliver on the promise of its mission. Sustainability in this context means stakeholders can place their trust in that commitment"
	For the non-profit sector: "important societal needs will be met"

In contrast, sustainability in NPOs is divided into several streams. First, some research reduces sustainability to a financial issue of survival (Besel et al., 2011; Dadić & Ribarić, 2021; Lee, 2017). Second, internal sustainability is studied, with the view that the NPO must be able to maintain itself over time and to continue its action (Moldavanova & Goerdel, 2018; Omura & Forster, 2014; Weerawardena et al., 2010). Third, external sustainability means acting on behalf of society and meeting societal objectives within the context of the NPO's mission and actions (Langergaard, 2019; Weerawardena et al., 2010; Yekini & Yekini, 2020). The last two types of sustainability often intersect in the literature, with the idea of maintaining the activity that serves the interests of stakeholders and the community (Ceptureanu et al., 2017; Manfred et al., 2017; Moldavanova & Goerdel, 2018; Weerawardena et al., 2010). Again, sustainability encompasses economic, social, and environmental issues (Jones & Mucha, 2014; Manfred et al., 2017). Finally, Moldavanova and Goerdel (2018, p. 56) explain that "sustainability should be properly distinguished from OSR, since sustainability is concerned with the long term and meeting the needs of future generations, rather than merely balancing the interests of present-day stakeholders".

In analysing the definitions, differences begin to emerge between the three concepts, adding further support to the need to distinguish them clearly:

1 OSR concerns the relationship that the NPO has with its environment, both philosophically (its responsibility, Chung et al., 2019) and operationally (its actions in favour of economic, social, and environmental issues, Lin-Hi et al., 2015). The horizon is relatively short term (Hogan, 2010), strategic (Olaya Garcerá et al., 2020), and focused on generic actions for the protection of the

environment and in favour of society (Andreini et al., 2014; Chung et al., 2019; Palakshappa & Grant, 2018).

2 Social responsibility integrates social, societal, environmental, and economic issues in the NPOs' mission and purpose (Andreini et al., 2014; Pope et al., 2018). The actions taken are no longer general, but are specific and in line with the NPO's values (Chelladurai, 2016; Păceșilă & Colesca, 2020). The horizon thus appears to be medium to long term.

3 The sustainability of NPOs is focused on both daily life (i.e., viability) and on a long-term horizon, addressing organisational survival (e.g., Lee, 2017) and the NPOs' ability to act over time (e.g., Moldavanova & Goerdel, 2018) and to adapt to the demands and needs of stakeholders and society over the long term (e.g., Weerawardena et al., 2010). For Arhin et al. (2018, p. 351), sustainability is "an ongoing process rather than an end in itself; and as a multidimensional construct comprising elements such as financial, social, operational and identity forms of sustainability".

Figure 9.1 illustrates the distinction between OSR and social responsibility, taking different time horizons into account (i.e., the time target for the actions undertaken) and whether or not issues are integrated into the mission. Sustainability is permanent and cross-cutting and is represented in line with the suggestion by Arhin et al. (2018).

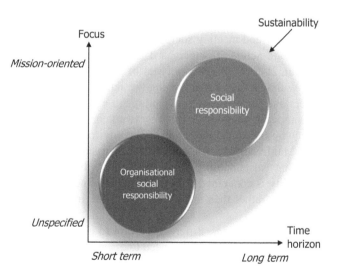

Figure 9.1 An illustration of the distinction between OSR, social responsibility, and sustainability in NPOs according to their link with the mission and the targeted time horizon

Reading: Sustainability does not include OSR and SR but covers all the dimensions proposed by the typology. The figure should be considered in 3D.

Implications of this distinction for theory and practitioners

Revisiting the theoretical underpinnings of the concepts of responsibility and sustainability

The previous section highlighted the importance of differentiated concepts of OSR, social responsibility, and sustainability in NPOs. This section explores classical theoretical anchors through the filter of the proposed distinction.

One of the characteristics of NPOs remains stakeholder pressure and perceptions. Scholars (Chung et al., 2019; Lin-Hi et al., 2015; Veltri & Bronzetti, 2014) insist on the reputational dimension of OSR initiatives: the image that stakeholders have of NPOs' initiatives and of the organisation is sometimes more important than the action itself. As a result, theories that integrate stakeholders make it possible to analyse the OSR of NPOs (initiatives vary depending on the expectations and hopes of stakeholders) as well as their social responsibility (stakeholders take part in defining the NPO's mission). Some of the theories found in the literature include attribution, expectancy violations, institutional, neo-institutional, resource dependency, and stakeholder theories. In contrast, theories that focus solely on the NPOs' mission, such as corporate citizenship and social capital theories, appear appropriate for analysing their social responsibility. At the same time, organisational ecology and resource-based approaches are linked to the NPOs' sustainability as a survival issue.

Furthermore, the proposed distinction allows for an analysis of the conflict between theoretical studies that make OSR an intrinsic principle of NPOs and empirical studies. Thanks to the nuance between OSR and social responsibility, it is assumed that only the latter is intrinsic to NPOs, while OSR initiatives are viewed as necessary.

However, the concepts discussed in this chapter are also surrounded by a galaxy of notions used in the literature. The taxonomies of OSR, social responsibility, and sustainability were thus examined, resulting in two main findings. First, OSR has been studied in NPOs in order to determine its effects on performance: on the perceived quality of activities (Andreini et al., 2014; Chung et al., 2019), on image and reputation (Chung et al., 2019), and on social capital (Degli Antoni & Portale, 2011). Second, scholars highlight the proximity of OSR to governance and accountability (Alali et al., 2019; Alonso-Cañadas et al., 2019; Besel et al., 2011; Cho et al., 2021; Degli Antoni & Portale, 2011; Jones & Mucha, 2014; Manetti & Toccafondi, 2014; Nardo & Siboni, 2018; Weidenbaum, 2009).

In light of the distinction proposed in Figure 9.1, the taxonomies would benefit from a certain readjustment. Thus, while the link between OSR and overall performance seems logical since OSR is concerned with unspecified initiatives, future studies should also focus on the link between social responsibility and overall performance. The latter also focuses on the mission. In this regard, since only social responsibility is concerned with the mission, future research needs to link it (and not OSR) to governance, the gatekeeper of NPO values and mission.

164   *Guillaume Plaisance*

The implications of this distinction for practitioners

Clarification of the concepts of OSR, social responsibility, and sustainability in the context of NPOs allows these organisations to clarify the vocabulary they use. The aim is also to eliminate the potential discomfort (Waters & Ott, 2014) that some NPOs may have with a concept that originates in part from FPOs.

Moreover, findings tend to distinguish between mission-related and non-specific actions. NPOs are socially responsible *de facto*, but OSR actions are not intrinsic to NPOs. In short, these organisations are inevitably concerned with sustainability and OSR (Unerman & O'Dwyer, 2010), while their social responsibility is linked to their mission. Moldavanova and Wright (2020) use a metaphor for NPOs as a "vehicle". While NPOs tend to have a positive social impact because of their nature (i.e., their social responsibility), their mere existence is not enough. In metaphorical terms, the vehicle must run and be propelled (thanks to OSR and sustainability initiatives). In short, NPOs' commitment is essential (Moldavanova & Goerdel, 2018) and this chapter calls for NPOs to engage in the process.

The recent literature has also helped to hone the analysis. Mathras et al. (2023) introduced the concept of core and non-core activity OSR activity. In other words, OSR initiatives can be implemented directly through the flow of activities, within day-to-day operations (e.g., ensuring the recycling of waste produced by the activity) or they can be unrelated to the activity and mission (e.g., protecting biodiversity around a site by planting shrubs and setting up beehives).

The notion of social responsibility is different because it focuses on *how* the mission, in other words, the societal purpose, is achieved and not just on its actual achievement. In other words, it is the classic distinction between the ends and means, while the emphasis is often placed on the purpose and accomplishments (Riddel, 1999). When designing actions, addressing stakeholders, or building a team, NPOs must be socially responsible. While the time horizon may be long term, the social responsibility of an NPO is in fact conceived and mobilised in the very short term from the outset. This distinction between a targeted time horizon (see Figure 9.1) and mobilisation of an issue (see Figure 9.2) is therefore crucial.

More generally, the chapter sheds light on the situation of NPOs when confronted with a crisis (e.g., Covid-19 or an identity or socio-economic crisis). NPOs are often dependent on CSR from FPOs, funding from public authorities, or contributions from individuals. NPOs' OSR is therefore a specific means for the organisations to demonstrate their impact on society and their stakeholders. The congruence between mission and social responsibility is an asset that provides more effective and, *a priori*, fuller accountability, and thus more resource attractiveness. In addition, the distinction between OSR in NPOs and CSR helps to counter the identity concerns of NPOs. The isomorphisms observed by the literature (Weerawardena et al., 2010) in order to ensure organisational sustainability should therefore be avoided: NPOs can be inspired by and adapt practices from other sectors, but should not adopt them *per se*. Given the current crisis

Social responsibility and sustainability in non-profit organisations 165

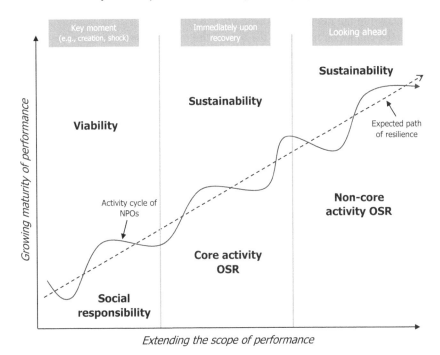

Figure 9.2 Articulation of the concepts of social responsibility, OSR, and sustainability with those of performance and resilience in NPOs

regarding the availability of resources, this chapter reminds us that the survival of NPOs is continually threatened by "financial vulnerability", the risk of interruption to their activities, and challenges to "critical" organisational characteristics, such as human and social capital (Ceptureanu et al., 2017, p. 973). The place of OSR in times of crisis is therefore non-negotiable for NPOs, in order to protect their human resources and preserve their partnerships. Social responsibility and OSR are thus levers of resilience, while short-term sustainability (viability) is, by definition, intimately linked to resilience.

In order to visualise the interweaving of these different concepts, Figure 9.2 assumes that each key moment for an NPO (a new project, a shock, its creation) is the starting point for thinking about its performance. In other words, the scenario offered by Figure 9.2 is not uniform and unique, but exists at every key stage of an NPO's life, for every project, and for every process. The scope of the concepts is therefore discussed internally within each NPO. Following each key moment, performance broadens over time. For example, expectations placed on an NPO during a crisis are low, but over time, stakeholders become more demanding. The more time passes, the more the scope grows, and the more mature the NPO's performance. The two axes in Figure 9.2 relate only to the two

166 *Guillaume Plaisance*

curves, while the keywords in bold are used to characterise performance. Performance cannot be mature at the outset: the main requirement is to be viable, to survive, and to be responsible with regard to the activities proposed. Later, when the shock or key event has passed, performance will gain in maturity and will be extended. NPOs need to begin by aiming for sustainability (especially internal sustainability) and should implement OSR actions linked to the activity. With regard to longevity, an NPO needs to be mature. Its sustainability must be guaranteed by cultivating its external sustainability in particular. Its OSR activities are then expanded beyond its core activity. In this process, resilience (the dotted arrow) increases as OSR, social responsibility, and sustainability milestones are reached, but there are always variations (expressed by the curve). Figure 9.2 also serves as a reminder of the difference between the targeted time horizon (see Figure 9.1) and the expected implementation date. Schematically speaking, we can consider OSR to be short term, since it is potentially devised on an annual basis, whereas social responsibility is long term, since it aims for an ideal in line with its values. However, a social responsibility mindset is the primary goal, since values are the basis of all strategic thinking.

Conclusion

This chapter proposed a theoretical essay to counteract the interchangeability of the concepts of OSR, social responsibility, and sustainability in the non-profit sector. The analysis of the definitions of the three concepts offers a clearer distinction in accordance with the focus (mission-oriented or not) and the time horizon. OSR is short term and unspecified, social responsibility is mission-oriented and relatively long term, while sustainability covers all four dimensions (both mission-oriented and non-mission-oriented, short term and long term). Thus, the present chapter answers the call for new research on OSR in NPOs (e.g., Chelladurai, 2016; Waters & Ott, 2014; Zeimers et al., 2019).

Affirming this serves as a reminder of the relevance of OSR in NPOs as non-specific actions, but also that NPOs are inherently socially responsible. These issues concern all organisations (Chelladurai, 2016; Idowu, 2008), but in light of the core values and identity (*raison d'être*) of NPOs (Păceşilă & Colesca, 2020), the various sectors need to be distinguished (Smith, 2011).

The literature has long merged the concepts in order to simplify while the research field was emerging. OSR has been used as an "umbrella" term for sustainability and social responsibility (Goodpaster, 2013, p. 598; Palakshappa & Grant, 2018, p. 606). Now that it is more mature, it is crucial not to confuse different realities. While the link between OSR and sustainability exists (Palakshappa & Grant, 2018), the concepts are nonetheless quite different.

Although the literature cited in this chapter was identified by systematised means (through a close analysis of the Scopus database), I do not claim to be exhaustive and bibliometric analyses could complement our work. Research perspectives may also complement the contributions. Many other links between

Social responsibility and sustainability in non-profit organisations 167

OSR, sustainability, performance, mission success, or governance could be explored in the future. An empirical and qualitative approach questioning practitioners and their stakeholders about their vision of the three concepts would be a useful extension of this conceptual and theoretical research.

In addition, the non-profit sector is heterogeneous and sub-sectoral studies are needed to extend the findings presented (Goerke, 2022). OSR remains a conceptual challenge in NPOs (Chaves Ávila & Monzón Campos, 2018) and requires further development (Olaya Garcerá et al., 2020), both from a sectoral perspective (Nevárez & Féliz, 2019) and in terms of new measures and tools (Alamo & Antonio, 2018).

The results also indicate that this field of research is still emerging, raising traditional theoretical questions: should scholars be inspired by or emancipated from research devoted to CSR in FPOs? Should traditional theories be adapted, or should new theoretical visions be formulated?

Research on isomorphisms and institutional pressure in OSR practices could also be relevant. In this vein, the mandatory nature of OSR in certain contexts (Nardo & Siboni, 2018) raises questions about the very notion of NPO commitment (volunteering being the core of OSR for Bivona, 2010) and the place of regulators, the authorities, and partners.

In conclusion, there are multiple reasons for the lack of interest in OSR research in NPOs: the ambiguous terminology (Lin-Hi et al., 2015), the potential pleonasm that the concept could create with the mission of NPOs (Lin-Hi et al., 2015), and a focus on NPO-FPO links via CSR (Phillips & Taylor, 2020). These reasons have been analysed and discussed in the present chapter. We can thus hope that this field of research will flourish and contribute to extending knowledge about OSR in NPOs in order to meet the pressing challenges raised by scarce resources and even the conjunctural crises they face.

Note

1 *Cambridge Business English Dictionary*, Online dictionary, consulted on October 18, 2023, https://dictionary.cambridge.org/dictionary/english/.

References

Alali, F., Chen, Z., & Liu, Y. (2019). Sustainability reporting in us government and not-for-profit organizations: A descriptive study. In C. R. Baker (Ed.), *Research on professional responsibility and ethics in accounting* (pp. 57–79). Emerald Publishing Limited. https://doi.org/10.1108/S1574-076520190000022005

Alamo, B., & Antonio, F. (2018). Organizational sustainability practices: A study of the firms listed by the corporate sustainability index. *Sustainability, 10*(1), 226. https://doi.org/10.3390/su10010226

Alonso-Cañadas, J., del Mar Gálvez-Rodríguez, M., del Carmen Caba-Pérez, M., & Saraite, L. (2019). Online disclosure of social responsibility strategies: Perceptions and reality among nonprofit organisations. In *Corporate social responsibility: Concepts, methodologies, tools, and applications* (pp. 1066–1085). IGI Global.

168 Guillaume Plaisance

Andreini, D., Pedeliento, G., & Signori, S. (2014). CSR and service quality in nonprofit organizations: The case of a performing arts association: CSR and service quality. *International Journal of Nonprofit and Voluntary Sector Marketing, 19*(2), 127–142. https://doi.org/10.1002/nvsm.1488

Arhin, A. A., Kumi, E., & Adam, M.-A. S. (2018). Facing the bullet? Non-governmental organisations' (NGOs') responses to the changing aid landscape in Ghana. *VOLUNTAS: International Journal of Voluntary and Nonprofit Organizations, 29*(2), 348–360. https://doi.org/10.1007/s11266-018-9966-1

Bansal, P., & Song, H.-C. (2017). Similar but not the same: Differentiating corporate sustainability from corporate responsibility. *Academy of Management Annals, 11*(1), 105–149. https://doi.org/10.5465/annals.2015.0095

Besel, K., Williams, C. L., & Klak, J. (2011). Nonprofit sustainability during times of uncertainty: Nonprofit sustainability during times of uncertainty. *Nonprofit Management and Leadership, 22*(1), 53–65. https://doi.org/10.1002/nml.20040

Bivona, E. (2010). Outlining long term corporate social responsibility strategies in nonprofit organizations: The case of a Colombian health care insurance. *Proceedings of the 6th International Conference on Applied Business Research, Dubai.*

Carroll, A. B. (1979). A three-dimensional conceptual model of corporate performance. *Academy of Management Review, 4*(4), 497–505. https://doi.org/10.5465/amr.1979.4498296

Casey, T. (2018). *Corporate Social Responsibility in Nonprofit Organizations: How Nonprofits Leverage CSR and Sustainability Reporting* [Master thesis]. University of San Francisco.

Ceptureanu, S.-I., Ceptureanu, E.-G., Orzan, M., & Marin, I. (2017). Toward a Romanian NPOs sustainability model: Determinants of sustainability. *Sustainability, 9*(6), 966–992. https://doi.org/10.3390/su9060966

Chaves Ávila, R., & Monzón Campos, J. L. (2018). La economía social ante los paradigmas económicos emergentes: Innovación social, economía colaborativa, economía circular, responsabilidad social empresarial, economía del bien común, empresa social y economía solidaria, *CIRIEC-España, revista de economía pública, social y cooperativa, 93*, 5–50. https://doi.org/10.7203/CIRIEC-E.93.12901

Chell, E., Spence, L. J., Perrini, F., & Harris, J. D. (2016). Social entrepreneurship and business ethics: Does social equal ethical? *Journal of Business Ethics, 133*(4), 619–625. https://doi.org/10.1007/s10551-014-2439-6

Chelladurai, P. (2016). Corporate social responsibility and discretionary social initiatives in sport: A position paper. *Journal of Global Sport Management, 1*(1–2), 4–18. https://doi.org/10.1080/24704067.2016.1177355

Cho, M., Park, S.-Y., & Kim, S. (2021). When an organization violates public expectations: A comparative analysis of sustainability communication for corporate and nonprofit organizations. *Public Relations Review, 47*(1), 101928. https://doi.org/10.1016/j.pubrev.2020.101928

Chung, N., Tyan, I., & Lee, S. J. (2019). Eco-innovative museums and visitors' perceptions of corporate social responsibility. *Sustainability, 11*(20), 5744. https://doi.org/10.3390/su11205744

Cornelius, N., Todres, M., Janjuha-Jivraj, S., Woods, A., & Wallace, J. (2008). Corporate social responsibility and the social enterprise. *Journal of Business Ethics, 81*(2), 355–370.

Dadić, L., & Ribarić, H. M. (2021). Improving the financial sustainability of nonprofit organizations through tourism-related activities. *Journal of Philanthropy and Marketing, 26*(2), e1692. https://doi.org/10.1002/nvsm.1692

Degli Antoni, G., & Portale, E. (2011). The effect of corporate social responsibility on social capital creation in social cooperatives. *Nonprofit and Voluntary Sector Quarterly, 40*(3), 566–582. https://doi.org/10.1177/0899764010362568

Dhanani, A., & Connolly, C. (2012). Discharging not-for-profit accountability: UK charities and public discourse. *Accounting, Auditing & Accountability Journal, 25*(7), 1140–1169. https://doi.org/10.1108/09513571211263220

Dixit, S. K. (2020). A new multiperspective emphasis on the public hospital governance. *International Journal of Healthcare Management, 13*(4), 267–275. https://doi.org/10.1080/20479700.2017.1403761

Elkington, J. (1998). Partnerships from cannibals with forks: The triple bottom line of 21st-century business. *Environmental Quality Management, 8*(1), 37–51. https://doi.org/10.1002/tqem.3310080106

Filho, W. L., Doni, F., Vargas, V. R., Wall, T., Hindley, A., Rayman-Bacchus, L., Emblen-Perry, K., Boddy, J., & Avila, L. V. (2019). The integration of social responsibility and sustainability in practice: Exploring attitudes and practices in higher education institutions. *Journal of Cleaner Production, 220*, 152–166. https://doi.org/10.1016/j.jclepro.2019.02.139

Gazzola, P., Ratti, M., & Amelio, S. (2017). CSR and sustainability report for nonprofit organizations. An Italian best practice. *Management Dynamics in the Knowledge Economy, 5*(3), 355–376.

Goerke, L. (2022). Trade unions and corporate social responsibility. *Annals of Public and Cooperative Economics, 93*(1), 177–203. https://doi.org/10.1111/apce.12313

Goodpaster, K. E. (2013). Tenacity: The American pursuit of corporate responsibility. *Business and Society Review, 118*(4), 577–605. https://doi.org/10.1111/basr.12022

Hogan, E. (2010). Does 'Corporate' responsibility apply to not-for-profit organizations? In S. O. Idowu & W. Leal Filho (Eds.), *Professionals' perspectives of corporate social responsibility* (pp. 271–288). Springer. https://doi.org/10.1007/978-3-642-02630-0_15

Idowu, S. O. (2008). An empirical study of what institutions of higher education in the UK consider to be their corporate social responsibility. *Environmental Economics and Investment Assessment II, I*, 263–273. https://doi.org/10.2495/EEIA080261

ISO. (2012). *Sustainability, sustainable development and social responsibility—ISO definitions and terminology* (2012–05; p. 7). International Organization for Standardization.

Jones, K. R., & Mucha, L. (2014). Sustainability assessment and reporting for nonprofit organizations: Accountability "for the Public Good". *VOLUNTAS: International Journal of Voluntary and Nonprofit Organizations, 25*(6), 1465–1482. https://doi.org/10.1007/s11266-013-9399-9

Kelly, D., & Lewis, A. (2009). Human service sector nonprofit organization's social impact. *Business Strategy Series, 10*(6), 374–382. https://doi.org/10.1108/17515630911005664

Langergaard, L. L. (2019). Interpreting 'the social': Exploring processes of social sustainability in Danish nonprofit housing. *Local Economy: The Journal of the Local Economy Policy Unit, 34*(5), 456–470. https://doi.org/10.1177/0269094219846626

Lee, W. (2017). Sustainability of nonprofit human service organizations in a neighborhood context. *Nonprofit Management and Leadership, 28*(1), 11–24. https://doi.org/10.1002/nml.21264

Lin-Hi, N., Hörisch, J., & Blumberg, I. (2015). Does CSR matter for nonprofit organizations? Testing the link between CSR performance and trustworthiness in the nonprofit versus for-profit domain. *VOLUNTAS: International Journal of Voluntary and Nonprofit Organizations, 26*(5), 1944–1974. https://doi.org/10.1007/s11266-014-9506-6

Manetti, G., & Toccafondi, S. (2014). Defining the content of sustainability reports in nonprofit organizations: Do stakeholders really matter? *Journal of Nonprofit & Public Sector Marketing, 26*(1), 35–61. https://doi.org/10.1080/10495142.2013.857498

Manfred, B., Bergman, Z., & Berger, L. (2017). An empirical exploration, typology, and definition of corporate sustainability. *Sustainability, 9*(5), 753. https://doi.org/10.3390/su9050753

170 Guillaume Plaisance

Mathras, D., Grinstein, A., Young, G. J., Thai, N. H., & Young, S. B. (2023). The value of core and noncore activity fit for corporate social responsibility: An expectation-based study of nonprofit hospitals. *Journal of Public Policy & Marketing*, *42*(2), 152–168. https://doi.org/10.1177/07439156221134803

Moldavanova, A. V., & Goerdel, H. T. (2018). Understanding the puzzle of organizational sustainability: Toward a conceptual framework of organizational social connectedness and sustainability. *Public Management Review*, *20*(1), 55–81. https://doi.org/10.1080/14719037.2017.1293141

Moldavanova, A. V., & Wright, N. S. (2020). How nonprofit arts organizations sustain communities: Examining the relationship between organizational strategy and engagement in community sustainability. *The American Review of Public Administration*, *50*(3), 244–259. https://doi.org/10.1177/0275074019884316

Montiel, I. (2008). Corporate social responsibility and corporate sustainability: Separate pasts, common futures. *Organization & Environment*, *21*(3), 245–269. https://doi.org/10.1177/1086026608321329

Nardo, M. T., & Siboni, B. (2018). Requirements and practices of social reporting in Italian not-for-profit organisations. In R. Tench, B. Jones, & W. Sun (Eds.), *Critical studies on corporate responsibility, governance and sustainability* (Vol. 12, pp. 299–317). Emerald Publishing Limited. https://doi.org/10.1108/S2043-905920180000012015

Neesham, C., McCormick, L., & Greenwood, M. (2017). When paradigms meet: Interacting perspectives on evaluation in the non-profit sector: Evaluation in the nonprofit sector. *Financial Accountability & Management*, *33*(2), 192–219. https://doi.org/10.1111/faam.12121

Nevárez, V. L., & Féliz, B. D. Z. (2019). La responsabilidad social en las dimensiones de la ciudadanía corporativa. Un estudio de caso en la manufactura agrícola. *CIRIEC-España, Revista de Economía Pública, Social y Cooperativa*, *97*, 179–211.

Olaya Garcerá, J. E., Rojas Muñoz, A. L., & Gutiérrez Vera, H. (2020). Responsabilidad Social en la Universidad Santiago de Cali. *Revista Venezolana de Gerencia*, *25*(3), 65–83. https://doi.org/10.37960/rvg.v25i3.33354

Omura, T., & Forster, J. (2014). Competition for donations and the sustainability of not-for-profit organisations. *Humanomics*, *30*(3), 255–274. https://doi.org/10.1108/H-12-2012-0026

Păceşilă, M., & Colesca, S. E. (2020). Insights on social responsibility of NGOS. *Systemic Practice and Action Research*, *33*(3), 311–339. https://doi.org/10.1007/s11213-020-09520-1

Palakshappa, N., & Grant, S. (2018). Social enterprise and corporate social responsibility: Toward a deeper understanding of the links and overlaps. *International Journal of Entrepreneurial Behavior & Research*, *24*(3), 606–625. https://doi.org/10.1108/IJEBR-05-2016-0131

Phillips, S., & Taylor, D. (2020). Corporate social responsibility in nonprofit organizations: The brokerage role of community housing mutuals. *Strategic Change*, *29*(4), 425–434. https://doi.org/10.1002/jsc.2354

Pope, S., Bromley, P., Lim, A., & Meyer, J. W. (2018). The pyramid of nonprofit responsibility: The institutionalization of organizational responsibility across sectors. *VOLUNTAS: International Journal of Voluntary and Nonprofit Organizations*, *29*(6), 1300–1314. https://doi.org/10.1007/s11266-018-0038-3

Riddel, R. C. (1999). Evaluating NGO development interventions. In D. Lewis (Ed.), *International perspectives on voluntary action: Reshaping the third sector* (pp. 222–241). Earthscan.

Smith, A. D. (2011). Corporate social responsibility implementation: Comparison of large not-for-profit and for-profit companies. *International Journal of Accounting & Information Management*, *19*(3), 231–246. https://doi.org/10.1108/18347641111169241

Throsby, D. (1995). Culture, economics and sustainability. *Journal of Cultural Economics,* *19*(3), 199–206.

Unerman, J., & O'Dwyer, B. (2010). Ngo accountability and sustainability issues in the changing global environment. *Public Management Review, 12*(4), 475–486. https://doi.org/10.1080/14719037.2010.496258

van Marrewijk, M. (2003). Concepts and definitions of CSR and corporate sustainability: Between agency and communion. *Journal of Business Ethics, 44*(2), 95–105. https://doi.org/10.1023/A:1023331212247

Veltri, S., & Bronzetti, G. (2014). Intellectual capital reporting in the Italian nonprofit sector. An image-building or an accountability tool? In E. Costa, L. D. Parker, & M. Andreaus (Eds.), *Advances in public interest accounting* (Vol. 17, pp. 251–278). Emerald Group Publishing Limited. https://doi.org/10.1108/S1041-706020140000017010

Waters, R. D., & Ott, H. K. (2014). Corporate social responsibility and the nonprofit sector: Assessing the thoughts and practices across three nonprofit subsectors. *Public Relations Journal, 8*(3), 19.

Weerawardena, J., McDonald, R. E., & Mort, G. S. (2010). Sustainability of nonprofit organizations: An empirical investigation. *Journal of World Business, 45*(4), 346–356. https://doi.org/10.1016/j.jwb.2009.08.004

Weidenbaum, M. (2009). Who will guard the guardians? The social responsibility of NGOs. *Journal of Business Ethics, 87*(S1), 147–155. https://doi.org/10.1007/s10551-008-9813-1

Yekini, L. S., & Yekini, K. C. (2020). NGO accountability on environmentalism: A literature review of relevant issues and themes. In K. C. Yekini, L. S. Yekini, & P. Ohalehi (Eds.), *Advances in environmental accounting & management* (pp. 139–155). Emerald Publishing Limited. https://doi.org/10.1108/S1479-359820200000009008

Zeimers, G., Anagnostopoulos, C., Zintz, T., & Willem, A. (2019). Examining collaboration among nonprofit organizations for social responsibility programs. *Nonprofit and Voluntary Sector Quarterly, 48*(5), 953–974. https://doi.org/10.1177/0899764019837616

Part IV

Governance and people: from human capital development to beneficiary focus

Introduction

Anne Goujon Belghit and Guillaume Plaisance

Traditionally, human capital is defined by a set of KSAOs: knowledge, skills, abilities and other characteristics (Ployhart & Moliterno, 2011; Ployhart et al., 2014). This definition is based on the idea, developed by Schultz (1961) and Becker (1964), that individuals are unequally endowed with the value of human capital. Human capital can be either specific or general. The former is intrinsically linked to an organisational context and refers to a set of knowledge, skills and abilities mobilised in a very specific professional environment. It thus enables the generation of unique and non-substitutable resources. The second refers to knowledge and skills that can be used in different situations (Hatch & Dyer, 2004; Ployhart et al., 2011). Goujon Belghit and Trébucq (2016) consider human capital to be an intangible asset located at the intersection of skills, creativity and organisational behaviour. However, the question of how to estimate this value remains. Should we rely on their education? Their level of training? Their health? Their mobility? Their skills and abilities? Their personality? What is the impact on organisational performance? How can human capital be managed at the organisational level?

At the organisational level, managers are particularly interested in management practices. Good human capital management practices create an intangible asset that is difficult to imitate or duplicate (Barney, 1991). According to resource theory, resources have value when organisations can implement effective strategies by exploiting market opportunities and controlling risks (Barney, 1991; Porter, 1985; Ulrich & Lake, 1991). Depending on the level of organisational maturity, management practices support and enhance individual performance (Curtis et al., 2012). However, the return on investment in human capital remains difficult to measure (Liu et al., 2014), although many studies show significant impacts on learning or performance (Hatch & Dyer, 2004). In reality, investment decisions

DOI: 10.4324/9781003460572-14

174   *Anne Goujon Belghit and Guillaume Plaisance*

are based on personal cognitive perceptions of reality rather than purely rational considerations (Coff & Raffiee, 2015). These investments are also risky, especially when "freshly" trained individuals decide to leave the organisation to "sell themselves elsewhere" (Peteraf, 1993). Nevertheless, they participate in social innovation (Defelix, 2019).

Human capital management is not limited to internal stakeholders: it also affects beneficiaries and fully involves funders or partner institutions. Goujon Belghit (2020) shows that in the social and medico-social sector, poor management of this human capital entails risks that need to be assessed in order to understand them better. It is therefore up to governance to consider the people who are the lifeblood of the organisation, as well as those who surround it.

In Chapter 10, Nathalie Dubost explains "how to retain volunteers" and the drivers of volunteer motivation. The relationship between a volunteer and an organisation is not based on a formal and written contract, but on some other more intangible aspects, such as the desire to feel useful at the level of society. There are several reasons that explain the motivation of volunteers to work for free for a non-profit organisation, such as the opportunity to acquire added value that can be exchanged on other markets, the need for recognition resulting from frustration at work or from the encounter with a specific organisation. Volunteering can be seen as the result of a process that can be divided into three main steps, such as personal predisposition, the decision to become a volunteer and the act of becoming a volunteer. This chapter concludes with a model that highlights the specificity of the relationship between a non-profit organisation and its volunteers, since it is not a simple encounter, but a series of regular and continuous actions that are repeated over time in order to consolidate the initial decision to become a volunteer.

In Chapter 11 asking "why meaning-making capabilities for non-profit executives?", Sungdae Lim develops a conceptual framework to identify the specificities of non-profit leadership. For ISO 37000:2021, it is crucial because "the governing body should set the tone for an ethical organisational culture. (…) Its own behaviours provide the model for the organisation's behaviour" (p. 25). Indeed, leaders play a central role in creating and managing shared meanings. In non-profit organisations, leaders manage the ongoing process of aligning and even reorienting the organisation's mission and values in order to increase the effectiveness of their activities in a given territory. Moreover, non-profit organisations face seemingly contradictory expectations to promote both community values and professional utilitarian performance. Leaders must therefore support organisational capital and generate social energy. The chapter proposes to mobilise a constructive-developmental theory of leadership, which could develop different links between meaning-making dynamics and individual developmental stages.

In Chapter 12, "authentic beneficiary engagement in aged care" is explored by Kylie Kingston, Sari Rossi, Belinda Luke and Alexandra Williamson. This chapter proposes a person-centred approach to care as part of non-profit governance and provides mechanisms for the governing body to increase its understanding of its beneficiaries. According to the ISO 37000:2021, "the governing body is responsible for and accountable to the organisation as a whole and is charged to continually act in the best interests of the organisation such that the organisational purpose is fulfilled over time" (p. 22). There is an urgent need for service providers to strengthen their accountability to their beneficiaries, as formal documents, policies and practices have failed to secure these rights. In the NPOs studied, older people should be actively involved both in their own care and in contributing to the life of the organisation, including its governance and the design, evaluation and improvement of quality care and services. The chapter explains the formal means of involving these specific stakeholders and the implementation of a formal complaints mechanism as an indicator of quality of care. Finally, the framework of this chapter revisits the classical approach to accountability.

References

Barney, J. (1991). Special theory forum the resource-based model of the firm: Origins, implications, and prospects. *Journal of Management, 17*(1), 97–98.

Becker, G. (1964). *Human capital: A theoretical and empirical analysis, with special reference to education.* University of Chicago Press.

Coff, R., & Raffiee, J. (2015). Toward a theory of perceived firm-specific human capital. *Academy of Management Perspectives, 29*(3), 326–341.

Curtis, B., Hefley, W. E., & Miller, S. A. (2012). *People CMM. Second edition. A framework for human capital management.* Addison Wesley, Pearson Education.

Defelix, C. (2019). Le capital humain, moteur sous-estimé de l'innovation. In A. Goujon Belghit, S. Trébucq, M. Bourgain, & A. Gilson (Eds.), *Capital humain: entre performance et bien-être au travail.* Eska.

Goujon Belghit, A., & Trébucq, S. (2016). Proposition d'une mesure du capital humain: entre comportement organisationnel, compétence et créativité. Le modèle des 3C de la chaire du capital humain et de la performance globale de Bordeaux. *Vie & Sciences de l'Entreprise, 2*(202), 145–165.

Goujon Belghit, A. (2020). La gestion du capital humain: maîtriser les risques en EHPAD. *Management & Avenir, 117*(3), 17–39.

Hatch, N. W., & Dyer, J. H. (2004). Human capital and learning as a source of sustainable competitive advantage. *Strategic Management Journal, 25,* 1155–1178.

Liu, X., van Jaarsveld, D. D., Batt, R., & Frost, A. C. (2014). The influence of capital structure on strategic human capital: Evidence from U.S. and Canadian firms. *Journal of Management, 40*(2), 422–448. https://doi.org/10.1177/0149206313508982

Peteraf, M. A. (1993). The cornerstones of competitive advantage: A resource-based view. *Strategic Management Journal, 14*(3), 179–191.

Ployhart, R. E., & Moliterno, T. P. (2011). Emergence of the human capital resource: A multilevel model. *Academy of Management Review, 36*(1), 127–150.

Ployhart, R. E., Van Iddekinge, C. H., & Mackenzie, W. I. Jr (2011). Acquiring and developing human capital in service contexts: The interconnectedness of human capital resources. *Academy of Management Journal, 54*(2), 353–368.

Ployhart, R. E., Nyberg, A. J., Reilly, G., & Maltarich, M. A. (2014). Human capital is dead; Long live human capital resources! *Journal of Management, 40*(2), 371–398.

Porter, M. (1985). *Competitive advantage: Creating and sustaining superior performance.* Free Press.

Schultz, T. W. (1961). Investment in human capital. *American Economic Review, 51*, 1–17.

Ulrich, D., & Lake, D. (1991). Organizational capability: Creating competitive advantage. *Academy of Management Perspectives, 5*(1), 77–92.

10 How to retain volunteers? A literature review and a managerial proposal of a volunteer journey

Nathalie Dubost

According to ISO 37000:2021, organisational viability requires that the governing body identifies the key resources that allow it to create sustained value for relevant stakeholders. Viability can be compared to the concept of maintenance defined as "the acquisition of resources, the retention of membership commitment, engagement in activities, and the attainment of goals after the organisation has been established" (Prestby & Wandersman, 1985, p. 289). Amongst these resources, volunteers are the human capital that is essential to the running and survival of non-profit organisations (Kim et al., 2019; Newby & Branyon, 2021). According to Ferrand-Bechmann (1992, p. 35), a volunteer is "any action that does not involve financial reward and is carried out without social constraint or sanction on the person who does not carry it out; it is an action directed towards others or towards the community with the desire to do good, to act in accordance with many societal values here and now".

Voluntary work in non-profit organisations is currently on the decline, due in particular to the health crisis (Akingbola, 2020; Plaisance, 2021). The viability challenge now is for non-profit organisations' governance bodies to get volunteers to return to their ranks so that they can continue to carry out their missions of solidarity and proximity.

This chapter provides a review of the literature on volunteer motivation, i.e. the reasons that lead an individual to become involved in a non-profit organisation at a given time (Prouteau & Wolff, 2004). Understanding volunteer motivation can help governing bodies of non-profit organisations to better target their canvassing and communication efforts, tailoring their message to the volunteers they wish to attract and retain, and hence ensure their viability (Bussell & Forbes, 2002; Wymer, 1997).

There are two main lines of research into volunteering. The first focuses on the needs of volunteers as the main driving force behind their involvement. The second models volunteering as a process, where various variables interact to understand long-term commitment. On the basis of these results, we recommend that non-profit organisations set up a volunteer journey as a way of attracting volunteers and building up their loyalty over the long term.

DOI: 10.4324/9781003460572-15

178 *Nathalie Dubost*

Volunteering as a source of various rewards

Here we present work from three disciplines: economics, sociology and social psychology. While the epistemological approaches, theoretical frameworks and methodologies differ, the common thread lies in the assumption that individuals become volunteers to satisfy a need, fill a gap and/or obtain a reward.

Volunteer motivation and economics

In their summary of economic models of volunteering, Prouteau and Wolff (2004) refer to the "production of collective goods" model, where the individual becomes a volunteer "in order to contribute to the provision of non-profit organisations services which have certain attributes of collective goods" and where "his or her participation is of interest to him or her only as a factor of production". The service provided by non-profit organisations may be exclusively for the benefit of others (this is known as an altruistic variant of the model) or for the volunteer himself: the author gives the example of a parents' crèche, where volunteers look after their own children and those of other parents who are members of non-profit organisations. This model is therefore based on a utilitarian vision of community involvement.

Another economic model, known as the "consumption of private goods model", shifts the focus away from the non-profit organisation's purpose and concentrates on the rewards that volunteers seek through their involvement: prestige, power and the pleasure of giving are the driving forces behind non-profit organisation involvement. Volunteers may also be looking for ways to improve their training and experience: this is known as the "investment model". One form of investment lies in the desire to create or expand a network of acquaintances through volunteering, a network that may prove useful later: this is known as investment in social capital, or even as "signposting" strategies, where the fact of listing their involvement with non-profit organisations on a *curriculum vitae* is an asset for the volunteer's career.

From an empirical point of view, the results of research provide a low degree of validity to these models: Prouteau and Wolff (2004) see the need to enrich these analytical frameworks. Furthermore, given the heterogeneity of volunteers (in terms of age, training, family situation, salaries, professional status, etc.) and the multidimensional nature of an individual's motivations, Prouteau and Wolff (2004) recommend conducting research on targeted populations, or even monographic approaches to gain greater analytical finesse. By opting for this methodology, the work proposed in sociology sheds some very interesting light on the subject.

Volunteer motivations and sociology

The research we have read clearly illustrates the shifting and evolving nature of volunteers' motivations, an aspect totally ignored by the economic sciences. For example, in her research into the political effects of involvement in non-profit organisations, Hamidi (2002) highlights the fact that volunteers do not necessarily have precise motivations at the outset.

It is not the idea of "getting involved", with all that this implies in terms of intentionality or the idea of a cause to be defended. In addition, Hamidi (2002) shows that the motivations of volunteers, far from being static, evolve over time: the factors that lead a volunteer to join a non-profit organisation are different from those that lead them to maintain their activity afterwards.

There is a fruitful stream of research in sociology on volunteering. At its congress in February 2004, the Association Française de Sociologie (French Association of Sociology) founded the "sociology of commitment, non-profit organisation life and volunteering" research group. Its aim is "to address the sociology of non-profit organisations, marked by the presence of volunteers who are often militant and inventive, to reflect on voluntary work alongside and in support of paid work, and on new forms of commitment and power to act at all stages of life and in various geographical and political areas" (www.afs-socio.fr/rt35.htm).

Looking at sports' non-profit organisations in France, Chevalier and Fleuriel (2008) show that it would be wrong to limit ourselves to a sacralised representation of voluntary work as a form of free and disinterested commitment to a cause. Volunteers are not a homogeneous group who share the same living conditions, the same causes and the same values: there is a division of voluntary work in sport, based on "invisible work" (all the tasks devolved to "performing" volunteers: the "toast-women" who run the competition refreshment stalls, the bar pickers, the stewards for the horse shows, the hostesses, etc.) and much more visible work which is carried out by the volunteers themselves) and the much more visible work of responsibility, management and representation carried out by elected or co-opted volunteers (the President, treasurer of the club, regional committee, federation, etc.). Although everyone agrees to pretend that the work, on the pretext that it is voluntary, is of the same nature in one case as in the other, it has to be said that the rewards expected, real or supposed, are not equivalent. In this respect, voluntary work can be an opportunity to acquire added value that can be exchanged on other markets, particularly professional markets.

For Hanafi (2006), volunteering can also satisfy a need for recognition that arises from frustration at work. Through fieldwork carried out in 2003 with an American charity that works to help women in difficulty find employment, she shows how involvement in non-profit organisations can meet the power needs of female managers whose upward social mobility has been compromised. In this context, being a volunteer helps to counteract the psychological and moral costs resulting from these women's confrontation with the "glass ceilings" of the professional world. Giving of oneself is seen as a safe haven and can serve as a driving force for a second career.

While this research clearly shows the many reasons for volunteering, it nevertheless focuses on the individual, his or her aspirations and history. However, volunteering involves an encounter with an organisation, the characteristics of which

180   *Nathalie Dubost*

can also have an influence on the motivation of volunteers. The act of volunteering presupposes that an entity, which is the recipient of an individual's aspirations, reinforces the desire to volunteer because of the signals it produces. In her analysis of two fair trade non-profit organisations, Gateau (2006) highlights the impact of the practices and values conveyed by a non-profit organisation on the motivation of volunteers to join and stay. After highlighting how each non-profit organisations differs from the other in its approach to Fair Trade (organisation, marketing, use of labels, etc.), the researcher shows that these two organisations attract heterogeneous volunteers who have "good reasons" for getting involved in one organisation or another.

As we can see, becoming a volunteer meets a variety of needs, specific to each life story. Given this diversity, work in social psychology will propose a synthesis of these various rewards using a typology.

Volunteer motivation and social psychology

Using research on a few hundred volunteers working in the health sector, Gidron (1978) identified three types of reward: social (seeking contacts and relationships with others), personal (feeling of personal fulfilment), and economic (building networks and gaining experience). The aspirations of volunteers change with age: younger people are motivated by the possibility of gaining professional experience, while older people are primarily interested in making contacts.

Fitch (1987) also proposes three categories of reward, which, while overlapping with Gidron's typology, assess whether the volunteer is acting primarily in his or her own interests or in the interests of others. He thus refers to altruistic motivations, selfish motivations and motivations of social obligation. Social obligation is defined as the feeling of owing a debt to society and comes under the two previous types of motivation (Table 10.1). Fitch (1987) developed a scale of 20 items, of which the following are a few examples.

In a study of student volunteers, Fitch (1987) found that the strongest motivation was of a selfish nature, followed in equal order by two motivations of an altruistic and selfish nature. Zweigenhaft et al. (1996) used the same scale, but with an older population: this time, the most frequently cited motivation related to a feeling of social obligation. This result confirms Gidron's hypothesis that younger volunteers are primarily looking for personal and economic rewards, which are selfish motivations.

Table 10.1 Examples of items of the motivation scales

Altruistic motivation	*Selfish motivation*	*Social obligation motivation*
I feel concerned for those less fortunate than myself	It's an opportunity to acquire new skills	I hope that someone would help me if I or a member of my family were in the same situation

How to retain volunteers? 181

For Cnaan and Goldberg-Glen (1991), volunteers do not act according to a particular category of motivation, but according to a combination of motivations that can be described as an overall reward. Based on a review of the literature, the researchers identified 28 motivations, which they tested on 258 volunteers. A series of factorial analyses showed that most of the motivations were grouped under a single factor: whereas theory distinguishes between two or three types of motivation, the empirical test tends to prove that volunteers' motivations are a unidimensional concept.

Clary et al. (1998) and Clary and Snyder (1999) used functionalism to understand the motivations that lead individuals to become volunteers and to remain volunteers for a certain period. According to this analytical framework, individuals may have the same attitudes but different motivations, hence its interest in understanding the complexity of volunteering. Using a detailed review of research on volunteers, Clary et al. (1998) propose six functions (or rewards) potentially fulfilled by volunteering: expression of values, understanding, social relations, career management, protection and self-development. Table 10.2 gives the definition of each function and an example of an item used to measure them.

To test the validity of their model, the researchers carried out various statistical treatments on the results obtained using their measurement instrument with several groups. The six dimensions (functions) of the model were found to be sufficiently reliable and stable over time, and the predictive validity was judged

Table 10.2 The six functions fulfilled by volunteering

Function (reward)	Definition	Examples of items
Expression of values	Individuals volunteer because it allows them to express values of altruism and humanity	"I think it's important to help others"
Understanding	The individual seeks to learn new things and exercise skills that he or she does not otherwise use	"Volunteering helps me to learn from experience in the field", "I learn about my own strengths"
Employee relations	Volunteering is a way of strengthening social relationships, being with friends and doing something that is valued by those around you	"The people I'm close to want me to volunteer"
Career management	Volunteering is a way of gaining experience, which is good for your career	"I can make new contacts that will help my career"
Protection	Volunteering helps to reduce negative feelings, such as guilt, or to resolve personal problems	"Volunteering makes me feel less alone"
Personal development	Volunteering helps boost self-esteem and gives you positive feelings	"I feel useful as a volunteer"

182   *Nathalie Dubost*

to be correct following laboratory research in which the researchers tested the effectiveness of messages from non-profit organisations in terms of the match between the type of motivation of the volunteer and the nature of the message.

Using this six-dimensional model (known as the Volunteer Functions Inventory or VFI), we can assess the importance of each function for volunteers: it seems that "expression of values", "understanding" and "personal development" are the most important functions, although the order varies from group to group (for example, "career management" is more important for younger volunteers than older ones). The "expression of values" function is said to have an amplifying effect on volunteer involvement: the more important this function is for the volunteer, the more frequently they get involved, and the more they show a desire to continue their involvement (Allison et al., 2002).

Following on from this work, Okun and Herzog (1998) looked at the relationship between volunteers' motivations and their age, showing that some motivations increase with age, while others decrease. Recently, Inglis and Cleave (2006) built on the work of Clary et al. (1998) to propose a framework for analysing the motivation of a category of volunteers: board members. The researchers came up with six categories of motivation, very similar in content to the six dimensions of the initial model.

It also appears that the debate about altruistic and selfish motivations is outdated in the sense that each function includes a part of both and that volunteering does not follow a purely other-oriented logic or a purely self-interested logic. The functionalist model makes it possible to trace the complexity and variety of motives for volunteering: for example, a volunteer may have several equally important motivations; similarly, an identical non-profit organisation activity will respond to different motivations depending on the volunteer interviewed. By way of illustration, based on a survey of 461 Italian volunteers, Marta et al. (2006) identify four groups of volunteers who differ in their profile in terms of the expression of values, career management, social relations and protection.

Finally, this model insists on the need to match the "benefit" a volunteer will derive with his or her motivation(s): when this match occurs, the volunteer is satisfied and expresses the intention to continue his or her activity in the longer term (Clary et al., 1998). Houle et al. (2005) confirm this general hypothesis by showing, following the results of a survey of 112 students, that volunteers differentiate well between the tasks proposed according to their motivations and, when they have the choice, choose the tasks for which they express a preference. From a practical point of view, the researchers recommend adapting the type of tasks volunteers are asked to carry out to their motivational profile.

It is debatable whether the six functions cover all the motivations of volunteers. Allison et al. (2002) compared the responses of 195 volunteers to two questionnaires: the first contained the VFI, and the second was an open questionnaire asking respondents to explain why they volunteered. After coding the answers to the second questionnaire, the researchers identified three additional motivations that the Clary et al. (1998) model did not consider: pleasure (17% of respondents), religion (9%) and teamwork (6%). Mowen and Sujan (2005) extended the work of Clary et al. (1998) by proposing a hierarchical model in which volunteers' motivations appear to be the result of personality variables which, by interacting with environmental variables, help to explain the propensity to volunteer: altruism, the need to be active and the need to learn emerge as fundamental variables for understanding volunteering.

Once we have listed the benefits that volunteers can derive from their participation in a non-profit organisation, however, we cannot answer the question of why some people become volunteers and others do not (Mowen & Sujan, 2005). This is why some researchers prefer to model the process that leads to volunteering, rather than focusing on the nature of the rewards.

Volunteering as the result of a process

According to Bales (1996), there are three stages in volunteering: the predisposition to become a volunteer, the decision to become a volunteer and the act of becoming a volunteer. Neely et al. (2022) add a fourth step which is continuance. The diversity of possible paths around this sequence would explain why the desire to become a volunteer is not always followed by action; in fact, we can think that contextual variables modulate each of the three stages. For example, knowing and appreciating a volunteer could act as an incentive to become a volunteer. Similarly, some individuals would like to volunteer, but would ultimately give it up because of conflicts arising from the difficulty of making this activity compatible with work and family (quoted in Bussell & Forbes, p. 250). This approach can be found in the model by Omoto and Snyder (1995), who include psychological and situational variables to explain who becomes a volunteer.

Warburton and Terry (2000) suggest using the theory of planned behaviour (TPB) to better understand the motivations of volunteers. According to this theory (Ajzen, 1991; Ajzen & Driver, 1991; Madden et al., 1992), individuals act according to the information they receive: thus, upstream of a behaviour, there is a logical sequence of cognitions that leads to an intention to act and then to the action itself. The intention to act is determined by three independent elements: the person's attitude towards the action (i.e. the person's positive or negative evaluation of the action), the subjective norm (i.e. the social pressure felt by the person to perform the action) and the perceived control of the action (i.e. the degree of control perceived to perform the action). The model can be summarised as in Figure 10.1.

This model helps to explain why an individual who has a positive attitude towards a behaviour and who thinks that this behaviour would be approved by people important to him will not necessarily carry it out: he may think that he lacks resources (skills, time, information, etc.) or that external factors (situation, environment, etc.) make it difficult to carry out this behaviour; as a result, the individual perceives that he has little control over the factors needed to carry

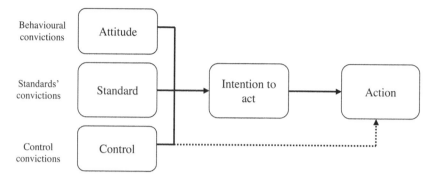

Figure 10.1 A model of volunteering according to the TPB
Source: Ajzen & Driver, 1991

out the behaviour and will not carry it out. Empirical studies have demonstrated the relevance of this theoretical framework for predicting various ethical behaviours, such as blood donation (Giles & Cairn, 1995) or giving nutritional advice to children (Astrom & Mwangosi, 2000).

Warburton and Terry (2000) carried out a two-stage study of older people (aged 65–74) living in Australia. In the first stage, using a questionnaire, the researchers measured the intention to volunteer and the three variables determining intention according to Ajzen's model:

- the respondent's favourable attitude towards volunteering (e.g. "how would you rate volunteering, from boring to interesting, from useful to useless, etc."),
- the subjective norm, i.e. how the respondent thinks those closest to him would react to his volunteering (e.g. "if I decided to volunteer, the people who are most important to me would approve of me"),
- perceived control over volunteering, i.e. the degree of difficulty perceived in volunteering (e.g. "it would be very difficult for me to volunteer in the next month").

Two other variables are also taken into account: the moral obligation, defined as the personal conviction of the merits of undertaking an action (e.g. "I would feel guilty if I didn't volunteer in the next month"), and the behavioural or descriptive norm, which reflects the respondent's perception of what those close to him or her do in terms of volunteering (e.g. "most people who are important to me volunteer"). It might be thought that seeing people close to you volunteering might encourage you to become a volunteer yourself: emotional closeness would lead to mimicry.

In the second stage (four to six weeks after the questionnaire was sent out), the researchers contacted the respondents by telephone and asked them if they had been involved in any voluntary activity since the questionnaire was sent out and how often. 240 responses were collected.

The results show that the intention to volunteer has a significant link with volunteering: in other words, the stronger the intention to volunteer, the more likely people are to volunteer. Intention is a crucial variable in the model, since no other variable (subjective and behavioural norms, moral obligation, perceived control) can predict volunteering. Upstream, the intention to volunteer is determined by all the variables except attitude towards volunteering: in other words, people who intend to volunteer perceive support from those around them (subjective norm), do not feel that it is difficult to volunteer (perceived control), feel morally obliged to volunteer (moral obligation) and have close friends who also volunteer (behavioural norm). On the other hand, the respondent's attitude towards volunteering is only indirectly linked to the volunteering action: moral obligation appears to be a mediating variable between attitude and action. Thus, having a positive attitude towards volunteering would reinforce the feeling of moral obligation, which in turn influences the intention to volunteer.

This research shows that it is necessary to take into account the social context in which volunteers evolve: we can see that people are motivated to volunteer not only because of their system of thought (moral obligation) but also because those around them approve of them and act in the same way. So, a study of volunteer motivation would not be complete if it only included individual variables.

Greenslade and White (2005) propose integrating the TPB with the theory of functionalism to better understand participation in voluntary activities. While the functional approach places more emphasis on social pressure through norms and perceived benefits, it neglects the weight of the determinants of the decision: to put it plainly, even if an individual perceives volunteering as an opportunity to reap "benefits" by expressing values, strengthening social relationships, increasing knowledge capital, etc., he or she will still not decide to become a volunteer. Greenslade and White (2005) compare the predictive powers of the two models (functionalist and expected behaviour) for volunteering. Using a two-stage survey of 81 Australian volunteers, the researchers showed that while both models significantly predicted volunteering, the TPB explained the highest percentage of variance (57% vs. 26%). Thus, they are individuals who (1) have a positive attitude towards volunteering, (2) perceive pressure from family and friends to volunteer, and (3) are confident about the possibility of giving a little of their time to volunteer intend to volunteer.

Similarly, the more people express the intention to volunteer, the more they will act. On the other hand, in the functionalist approach, only the "social relations" function has a significant link with volunteering: this result contradicts some research where the "expression of values", "understanding" and "personal development" functions appear to be the most important in explaining volunteering. In the end, this research clearly shows the usefulness of integrating several theories to understand the motivations of volunteers, but it should be noted that the concepts are sometimes very similar in content, even if they have different names: for example, the "perceived subjective norm" variable in the model

186   *Nathalie Dubost*

of planned behaviour has many points in common with the "social relations" variable; we should therefore be careful not to duplicate the same concepts when crossing several theories.

Penner (2002) defines volunteering as pro-social behaviour that is planned, long term in nature, aimed at people who are initially unknown and takes place in an organisational context. According to this definition, becoming a volunteer implies that the person concerned has considered the costs and benefits of volunteering. Similarly, this definition emphasises that volunteers carry out their activity independently of any implicit or explicit personal obligation: they do not act in the interests of one or more people close to them but wish to work for the greatest number. The researcher distinguishes two categories of variables to explain volunteering: individual variables and organisational variables (Figure 10.2). However, for Penner (2002), no single variable can explain volunteering; moreover, there are certainly interactions between all these variables: the influence of organisational variables on volunteer activity may be moderated by individual variables, and vice versa. Based on various research studies, Penner (2002) proposes a model to explain volunteering, which also includes the variable time.

The central variable in the model is the *decision to volunteer*. Upstream are the *situational factors*, i.e. the events: Penner uses the example of the 11 September attacks in the United States, which triggered a huge surge in volunteering. However, the dotted arrow between these situational factors and the decision to volunteer means that they have a much weaker impact than the other variables linked by a solid arrow.

Social pressure is a very strong determinant of the decision to volunteer. The more positive feedback the respondent receives from family and friends about volunteering, the greater the social pressure. The more this social pressure increases, the more likely the respondent is to decide to volunteer. Note that this concept of social pressure is very close to that of the subjective norm in the model of planned behaviour presented above. However, other variables will directly or indirectly modulate the link between social pressure and the decision to volunteer:

- *Demographic characteristics* (age, level of education, income, etc.). Numerous studies (Bussell & Forbes, 2002; Prouteau & Wolff, 2004) tend to show that certain socio-demographic variables are relevant in describing volunteers.
- *Three individual variables*, namely personal beliefs and values, prosocial personality (Penner et al., 1995) and motivations (Clary et al., 1998). The concept of prosocial personality, according to which there are personality traits specific to prosocial behaviour, including volunteering, is measured using a scale comprising an empathy dimension and a helpfulness dimension (Penner et al., 1995).
- An *organisational variable*, describing the attributes and practices of the organisation organising the volunteering (reputation, values, organisational justice, etc.).

How to retain volunteers? 187

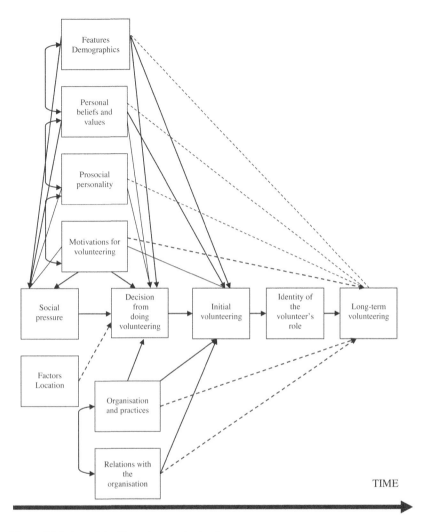

Figure 10.2 A model of long-term volunteering
Source: Penner, 2002

According to this model, demographic and individual characteristics will affect both the social pressure felt by the individual and the decision to volunteer. On the other hand, the organisational variable only affects the decision to volunteer: certain organisations would therefore be more attractive to future volunteers.

Then, once the decision has been made, what are the factors that influence *initial volunteering*, defined as the amount of time and effort a person puts in at the start of their voluntary involvement? Penner (2002) states that the demographic, individual and organisational variables presented above also help to understand the variations observed in initial volunteering. Another organisational variable, *relations with the organisation* (measured by satisfaction and involvement), has an impact on initial volunteering. In addition, although not shown in the diagram, there are links between individual and organisational variables: the impact of these variables is both direct and indirect.

The next step in the model is *volunteer role identity*, a concept developed by Piliavin et al. (2002). In this theoretical framework, an individual assumes multiple roles, one of which may be volunteering. If, at the outset, volunteering is explained by a social norm (expectation from parents or relatives), it gradually becomes "internalised" and adopted as a component of the self, an identity or role identity. This identity then explains *the volunteer's long-term commitment*, the final variable in the model. On this subject, Penner (2002) clearly shows that long-term volunteering depends essentially on the way in which the individual has assimilated the role of volunteer over time, rather than on individual characteristics or variables in the organisation to which he or she commits. Although the latter do have an impact on whether people continue to volunteer over the long term, as shown by the links in the model, this impact is much weaker than the link they have with initial volunteering. It is as if, over time, the variables that contributed to the initial commitment to volunteering gradually faded away, giving way to a role identity that would guarantee continued volunteering.

Finkelstein et al. (2005) empirically tested certain hypotheses arising from the model presented above. Using a survey of 302 volunteers working in a hospital, they found a very strong correlation between role identity and volunteer activity (measured by the frequency of the activity and how long it had been carried out), as well as between the social pressure felt by the volunteer and his or her volunteer activity, referred to as "perceived expectations". This suggests that active volunteers with a long-term commitment have strongly internalised their role as a volunteer and believe that those close to them expect them to continue to behave in this way. However, the researchers wonder about the causal link: is it a strong role identity that leads to sustained volunteering, or is it the fact of getting involved in volunteering that contributes to developing a strong identity? Longitudinal studies would be welcome to take this analysis further.

On the other hand, the link between volunteer motivations and volunteer activity is weak, and even surprising, since the correlations are negative. One explanation for this is that it is not so much the importance attached to a particular motive that explains long-term volunteering, but rather the degree to which these motivations are put into practice through volunteering. Kim et al. (2019) show that congruence between the volunteer's motivation and his experience is needed to improve retention.

Thinking and implementing the volunteer journey

Research shows that the viability challenge for non-profit organisations is not only to motivate volunteers to join them but also to build their loyalty and maintain their commitment over time. Appropriate communication campaigns are useful in highlighting the needs of volunteers and convincing them to give their time, but they alone cannot guarantee long-term commitment. The foundation of lasting commitment is a strong identity for the role of volunteer, and the question then becomes: what levers can be used to build and maintain this identity for the role of volunteer over time and to strengthen the viability of non-profit organisations?

Our proposal is to model the relationship between a non-profit organisation and its volunteers as a journey, and no longer as a "simple" encounter where the non-profit organisation's role is essentially to attract volunteers and capitalise on their motivation to commit over time. In practical terms, this volunteer journey is built on a series of regular and ongoing actions, repeated over time, to solidify the initial decision to volunteer (which can be explained by extrinsic motivations) and to develop an identification with the role of volunteer.

A variety of approaches can be devised, based on the six pillars of good practice in volunteer management devised by the France Bénévolat network, a national network dedicated to the volunteers' reception and guidance (https://www.francebenevolat.org/):

- **Clarifying needs:** Clearly define the mission, the role the volunteer will play in it and how it may relate to that of the employees, the way in which this mission contributes to the non-profit organisation's project and the qualities required for it.
- **Welcoming volunteers:** Welcoming a volunteer means first listening to them to understand their personal project and how they can join the non-profit organisations. It means showing them that they are "welcome" in the group, introducing them to the whole team, current projects, everyone's roles, etc.
- **Integrating volunteers:** A "sponsor" or "mentor" will facilitate the integration of volunteers by showing them how the non-profit organisations work, introducing them to their role, helping them to find the resources they need, answering any questions they may have, etc. Providing a "journey to integration" can help volunteers find the place that suits them best within the non-profit organisations.
- **Leading volunteers:** Leading volunteers means giving life to the joint action, the collective. It means exchanging ideas about the non-profit organisation's project, so that we can work together to find ways of improving.

190 *Nathalie Dubost*

It means sharing successes. It means creating a sense of belonging through "doing things together". And it also means paying attention to everyone, their motivations, their constraints, their desire to evolve ...

- **Volunteer training:** Volunteers come to non-profit organisations with their own skills, which they may wish to develop during their non-profit organisation's activities. The non-profit organisations must therefore support its volunteers in their training so that they can develop within the organisation or simply stay "in the loop". It should also be remembered that joint training can also help the group to develop.
- **Recognising volunteers:** Recognising volunteers means "making them want" to take part in the non-profit organisation's project. It means showing them the usefulness of their voluntary work, and the contribution each one makes to the collective result ... It also means thanking everyone, acknowledging their importance and offering moments of collective thanks, in a convivial atmosphere. It is a way for everyone to "grow" through volunteering.

As we can see, recognising the needs of volunteers (presented in the first part of this chapter) is the starting point for the volunteer's journey. Volunteering is an evolving process, where individual variables interfere, as well as variables relating to the volunteer's environment and non-profit organisations, as Penner's model illustrates. It is important for non-profit organisations to put in place a range of actions aimed at integrating and training volunteers, recognising their commitment, and thereby hoping for sustainable support over time.

Conclusion

Volunteers are an essential resource for non-profit organisations and are the key to their viability. This chapter has presented the main research on volunteer involvement and shown the need to approach the relationship between a non-profit organisation and its volunteers as an evolving process, where the identity of the volunteer role is built up gradually and forms the basis of a lasting commitment. From a managerial point of view, these results argue in favour of setting up a volunteer journey, made up of a series of actions and practices designed to integrate, train and recognise people's commitment.

References

Ajzen, I. (1991). The theory of planned behaviour. *Organizational Behaviour and Human Decision Processes, 50,* 179–211. https://doi.org/10.1016/0749-5978(91)90020-T

Ajzen, I., & Driver, B. L. (1991). Prediction of leisure participation from behavioural, normative and control beliefs: An application of the theory of planned behavior. *Leisure Science, 13*(3), 185–204. https://doi.org/10.1080/01490409109513137

Akingbola, K. (2020). COVID-19: The prospects for nonprofit human resource management. *Canadian Journal of Nonprofit and Social Economy Research, 11*(1), 16–20. https://doi.org/10.29173/cjnser.2020v11n1a372

How to retain volunteers? 191

Allison, L. D., Okun, M. A., & Dutridge, K. S. (2002). Assessing volunteer motives: A comparison of an open-ended and Likert rating scales. *Journal of Community & Applied Social Psychology, 12*, 234–255. https://doi.org/10.1002/casp.677

Astrom, A. M., & Mwangosi, I. E. (2000). Teachers' intentions to provide dietary counseling to children in Tanzanian primary schools. *American Journal of Health Behavior, 24*, 284–289. https://doi.org/10.5993/AJHB.24.4.4

Bales, K. (1996). Measuring the propensity to volunteer. *Social Policy and Administration, 30*(3), 206–226. https://doi.org/10.1111/j.1467-9515.1996.tb/00555.x

Bussell, H., & Forbes, D. (2002). Understanding the volunteer market: The what, where, who and why of volunteering. *International Journal of Nonprofit & Voluntary Sector Marketing, 7*(3), 244–257. https://doi.org/10.1002/nvsm.183

Chevalier, V., & Fleuriel, S. (2008). Travail bénévole et marché du travail sportif [Volunteer work and the sports labour market]. *Les Mondes du travail, 5*, 67–79.

Clary, E. G., & Snyder, M. (1999). The motivations to volunteer: Theoretical and practical considerations. *Current Directions in Psychological Science, 8*(5), 156–159. https://doi.org/10.1111/1467-8721.00037

Clary, E. G., Snyder, M., Ridge, R. D., Copeland, J., Stukas, A. A., Haugen, J., & Miene, P. (1998). Understanding and assessing the motivations of volunteers: A functional approach. *Journal of Personality and Social Psychology, 74*(6), 1516–1530. https://doi.org/10.1037/0022-3514.74.6.1516

Cnaan, R. A., & Goldberg-Glen, R. S. (1991). Measuring motivation to volunteer in human services. *Journal of Applied Behavioral Science, 27*, 269–284. https://doi.org/10.1177/0021886391273003

Ferrand-Bechmann, D. (1992). *Bénévolat et solidarité [Volunteering and solidarity]*. Syros Alternatives. ark:/12148/bpt6k33279805

Finkelstein, M. A., Penner, L. A., & Brannick, M. T. (2005). Motive, role identity, and prosocial personality as predictors of volunteer activity. *Social Behavior and Personality, 33*(4), 403–418. https://doi.org/10.2224/sbp.2005.33.4.403

Fitch, R. T. (1987). Characteristics and motivations of college students volunteering for community service. *Journal of College Student Personnel, 28*, 424–431.

Gateau, M. (2006). Quelle(s) stratégie(s) de distribution pour les produits équitables? Le cas Français ou la difficile alliance entre logique militante et logique commerciale [What distribution strategy(ies) for fair trade products? The French case or the difficult alliance between militant and commercial logic]. *Economie et solidarités, 37*(2), 109–122.

Gidron, B. (1978). Volunteer work and its rewards. *Volunteer administration, 11*(3), 18–32.

Giles, M., & Cairn, E. (1995). Blood donation and Ajzen's theory of planned behaviour: An examination of perceived behavioural control. *British Journal of Social Psychology, 34*, 173–188. https://doi.org/10.1111/j.2044-8309.1995.tb01056.x

Greenslade, J. H., & White, K. M. (2005). The prediction of above-average participation in volunteerism: A test of the theory planned behaviour and the volunteers' functions inventory in older Australian adults. *The Journal of Social Psychology, 145*(2), 155–172. https://doi.org/10.3200/SOCP.145.2.155-172

Hamidi, C. (2002). Les raisons de l'engagement associatif: Le cas de trois associations issues de l'immigration maghrébine [The reasons for nonprofit commitment: the case of three associations from North African immigrants]. *Revue française des affaires sociales, 4*, 149–165. https://doi.org/10.3917/rfas.024.0149

Hanafi, S. (2006). Dire le monde social: les sociologues face aux discours politiques, économiques et médiatiques [Articulating the Social World: Sociologists Confronting Political, Economic, and Media Discourses], 2ème congrès de l'Association Française de Sociologie, Bordeaux, 5-8 septembre.

192 *Nathalie Dubost*

Houle, B. J., Sagarin, B. J., & Kaplan, M. F. (2005). A functional approach to volunteerism: Do volunteer motives predict task preference. *Basic and Applied Social Psychology, 27*(4), 337–344. https://doi.org/10.1207/s15324834basp2704_6

Inglis, S., & Cleave, S. (2006). A scale to assess board member motivations in nonprofit organizations. *Nonprofit Management & Leadership, 17*(1), 83–101. https://doi.org/10.1002/nml.132

Kim, B. J., Kim, M. H., & Lee, J. (2019). Congruence matters: Volunteer motivation, value internalization, and retention. *Journal of Organizational Psychology, 19*(5), 56–70. https://doi.org/10.33423/jop.v19i5.2510

Madden, T. J., Scholder Ellen, P., & Ajzen, I. (1992). A comparison of the theory of planned behavior and the theory of reasoned action. *Personality and Social Psychology Bulletin, 18*(1), 3–9. https://doi.org/10.1177/0146167292181001

Marta, E., Guglielmetti, C., & Pozzi, M. (2006). Volunteerism during young adulthood: An Italian investigation into motivational patterns. *Voluntas: International Journal of Voluntary and Nonprofit Organizations, 17*, 221–232. https://doi.org10.1007/s11266-006-9015-3

Mowen, J. C., & Sujan, H. (2005). Volunteer behaviour: A hierarchical model approach for investigating its trait and functional motive antecedents. *Journal of Consumer Psychology, 15*(2), 170–182. https://doi.org/10.1207/s15327663jcp1502_9

Neely, A. R., Lengnick-Hall, M. L., & Evans, M. D. (2022). A process model of volunteer motivation. *Human Resource Management Review, 32*(4), 100879.

Newby, K., & Branyon, B. (2021). Pivoting services: Resilience in the face of disruptions in nonprofit organizations caused by COVID-19. *Journal of Public and Nonprofit Affairs, 7*(3), 443–460. https://doi.org/10.20899/jpna.7.3.443-460

Okun, M. A., & Herzog, A. R. (1998). Motivation to volunteer by older adults: A test of competing measurement models. *Psychology and Aging, 13*(4), 608–621. https://doi.org/10.1037/0882-7974.13.4.608

Omoto, A. M., & Snyder, M. (1995). Sustained helping without obligation: Motivation, longevity of service, and perceived attitude change among AIDS volunteers, *Journal of Personality and Social Psychology, 68*, 671–686. https://doi.org/10.1037/0022-3514.68.4.671

Penner, L. A. (2002). Dispositional and organizational influences on sustained volunteerism: An interactionist perspective. *Journal of Social Issues, 58*(3), 447–467. https://doi.org/10.1111/1540-4560.00270

Penner, L. A., Fritzsche, B. A., Craiger, J. P., & Freifeld, T. R. (1995). Measuring the prosocial personality. In J. Butcher & C. D. Spielberger (Eds.), *Advances in personality assessment*. Lawrence Erlbaum. https://doi.org/10.4324/9781315806228

Piliavin, J. A., Grube, J. A., & Callero, P. L. (2002). Role as resource for action in public service. *Journal of Social Issues, 58*(3), 469–485. https://doi.org/10.1111/0022-4537.t01-1-00027

Plaisance, G. (2021). French nonprofit organizations facing Covid-19 and lockdown: Maintaining a sociopolitical role in spite of the crisis and the political role in spite of the crisis of resource dependency. *Canadian Journal of Nonprofit and Social Economy Research, 12*(S1), 65–81. https://doi.org/10.29173/cjnser.2021v12nS1a411

Prestby, J. E., & Wandersman, A. (1985). An empirical exploration of a framework of organizational viability: Maintaining block organizations. *The Journal of Applied Behavioral Science, 21*(3), 287–305. https://doi.org/10.1177/002188638502100305

Prouteau, L., & Wolff, F. C. (2004). Les Motivations des bénévoles. Quel pouvoir explicatif des modèles économiques [Motivations of the volunteers. What is the explanatory power of economic models]? In D. Girard (Ed.), *Solidarités collectives. Famille et solidarités [Collective solidarities. Families and solidarities]* (pp. 197–211). L'Harmattan.

Warburton, J., & Terry, D. J. (2000). Volunteer decision making by older people: A test of a revised theory of planned behaviour. *Basic and Applied Social Psychology*, *22*(3), 245–257. https://doi.org/10.1207/15324830051036135

Wymer, W. W. (1997). Segmenting volunteers using values, self-esteem, empathy, and facilitation as determinant variables. *Journal of Nonprofit and Voluntary Sector Marketing*, *5*(2), 3–28. https://doi.org/10.1300/J054v05n02_02

Zweigenhaft, R. L., Armstrong, J., Quintis, F., & Riddick, A. (1996). The motivations and effectiveness of hospital volunteers. *The Journal of Social Psychology*, *136*(1), 25–34. https://doi.org/10.1080/00224545.1996.9923026

11 Why meaning-making capabilities for non-profit executives? Understanding the nature of non-profit leadership between the general and middle-range approaches

Sungdae Lim

Introduction

This is a theory-building template for non-profit leadership. Leadership can be understood as the influence process oriented towards setting and achieving certain goals. As ISO 37000:2021 – the international standard of governance of organisations, leadership is an essential enabling principle to make good governance of organisations. They stress the importance of organisational leadership in creating a value-based culture and facilitating trust and cooperation among those engaged. While the quest for a grand theory about the nature of leadership grows in organisation studies, non-profit leadership research has questioned whether the general accounts are effectively scaled to what is to be explored for the sectoral interest (Crosby & Bryson, 2005; Dym & Hutson, 2005; Herman, 2016; Lim et al., 2021; Ospina & Foldy, 2010; Ospina et al., 2012). Do they enrich theoretical applications to real-world leadership dynamics in the sectoral governance context or still leave out a substantial gap between theory and sector-specific practice? Non-profit organisations require a unique set of executive competencies in managing the organisational mission and most significant activities (Herman, 2016; Herman & Renz, 1997). Non-profit leaders create and align the specific meaning of their organisational reality and thus need to develop social construction skills in making sense of the particular actions, interests, and values of engaged actors around the organisation (Foldy et al., 2008; Lim et al., 2021).

The generalisability of leadership research needs to be scaled to the particular context of working dynamics while the contextual knowledge must be built on the fundamentals of social psychology and organisational behaviour (Ospina, 2017). Attention to these two emphases shows the importance and challenge of developing a middle-range theory of non-profit leadership. Although scholars have long theorised meaning-making leadership and its assumptions for decades (McCauley et al., 2006; Smircich & Morgan, 1982), their general approach has yet to determine how non-profit leaders, in the sectoral governance context, construct organisational realities while managing multiple constituents (Lim et al., 2021).

DOI: 10.4324/9781003460572-16

It is important to bring theory building upon these unique considerations. This book chapter thus elaborates on the meaning-making nature of non-profit leadership and proposes a middle-range theory for non-profit executives as the principal governing body. Constructive-developmental theory of leadership (Day et al., 2009; McCauley et al., 2006) underlies the conceptual framing while also highlighting the executive centrality assumption in non-profit management. This chapter connects the separate works of literature and addresses the conceptual void.

This work first calls for attention to the merit of middle-range theories employing the sectoral context with service-driven outcomes and values while also founded on social psychology fundamentals. Since the arena of leadership is generally underdeveloped in the non-profit literature, this template fills and addresses the lacuna with a special focus on why executive meaning-making capabilities are important to non-profit organisations. The main body of this chapter then reviews and answers the following questions: What is the nature of leadership specific to the non-profit sector? Who are non-profit leaders responsible for governance? How does their leadership develop with what tool to use? This chapter then discusses implications and future analytical frameworks to enrich knowledge and practice.

Theorising leadership for non-profit organisations: Is that a quest for a grand theory?

Many observers have suggested that leadership in organisations is apparently the most-studied subject in social sciences. Generations of leadership scholars have continued to refine various theoretical approaches. In the history of scholarly works, leadership scholarship found various types of interventions of social effects, which result in variations and changes in leadership outcomes and types. The literature on leadership linked successful narratives of skills (e.g., Bartone et al., 2007; Kearns et al., 2015; Lord & Hall, 2005; Mumford et al., 2000), behaviours (e.g., Bass, 1998; Fleishman et al., 1991; Yukl, 2012), relations (e.g., Ospina & Uhl-Bien, 2012; Uhl-Bien, 2006), and contingencies to leadership effectiveness.

Given the accumulation of scientific knowledge, scholars have explored whether a grand theory of leadership is achieved, equipped with explanatory power for general executive practices. Many current leadership studies are committed to developing frameworks that encompass as many theories as possible into an integrative body (Day et al., 2009; DeRue et al., 2011; Dulebohn et al., 2012). For example, DeRue et al. (2011), in their meta-analytic behavioural model of leadership, suggest that leader behaviours are direct visible leadership types and determine multidimensional leadership effectiveness. In developing the integrative behavioural model of leadership effectiveness, they include all significant leadership theories – transformational leadership, transactional leadership, participative leadership, servant leadership, directive leadership, and passive leadership, which

196 *Sungdae Lim*

finally leads to choosing one of the four types of leader behavioural orientations for the situational effectiveness. One might conclude that these efforts may try to assemble central themes of knowledge into a comprehensive framework. By outlining thematic maps for further applicability of a grand theory, recent leadership studies provide approaches to bridging mutually consistent discussions of multifaceted theories in an effort to achieve integration in the literature.

Nevertheless, the research has also led to inconsistent conceptions and implications of the leadership construct. As stated by Stogdill (1974, p. 259), "There are almost as many definitions of leadership as there are persons who have attempted to define the concept". For example, the term – *leadership* – in theories of relational leadership and transformational leadership, by comparison, does not indicate the same unit of analytic subjects (see Bass, 1998; Uhl-Bien, 2006). Similarly, *leader(s)* is considered either a person with top authority, one with popularity or rich networks, individuals in a group, a group of low-ranked followers, or perhaps something belonging to no one person as only existing in relational properties. The lack of consensus on the fundamental assumptions and components of the concept, along with the vast amount of literature, indicates the complexity and difficulty in grounding a general approach to the nature of organisational leadership (Avolio et al., 2009).

The need for a middle-range theory of non-profit leadership

While the quest for a grand theory grows in organisation studies, non-profit leadership scholarship – with the sectoral cluster of strategic foci and leadership effectiveness – has questioned whether these general theories successfully illuminate what is to be explored for the non-profit sector (Crosby & Bryson, 2005; Dym & Hutson, 2005; Herman, 2016; Ospina et al., 2012). Do the major schools enrich applications to real-world leadership practices in the sectoral governing context or still leave out a substantial gap? The need for sector-specific theories is increasingly recognised as such middle-range theories are expected to revitalise the use of concepts and assumptions drawn from general organisation studies in framing how particular practices form leadership for desirable outcomes that are contextualised in non-profit missions.

Research on non-profit leadership has mostly focused on practical leadership roles and outcomes applied to the service fields and their professionals. Dym and Hutson (2005) set mission and value alignment as leadership outcomes in non-profit organisations. How individual leaders manage the ongoing alignment and realignment process of organisational mission and values is considered the distinctive leadership quality in the non-profit sector. The goodness of fit in value orientations for certain services is a fundamental measure of individual leadership effectiveness in non-profit organisations. Crosby and Bryson (2005) suggest that leadership in the non-profit sector essentially works for the common good through tackling social problems that face the corresponding non-profits.

Why meaning-making capabilities for non-profit executives? 197

Building upon a shared-power assumption that social problems are so complex that single actors involved cannot solve the problems effectively, they theorised policy entrepreneurial team leadership pointing to collective capacity to coordinate solutions for the complex and intertwined social problems. In Ospina et al.'s (2012) social-change leadership theory, the purpose of leadership in community-based organisations is to contribute to making desirable social change as the mission achievement of the organisations. These studies apparently prioritise articulating observable leadership roles and outcomes drawn from the mission and service characteristics.

One common strength of the middle-range approach is its emphasis on pragmatic characteristics of management strategies and challenges, especially as applied to day-to-day practices. For example, unique and pressing leadership issues in the non-profit sector such as executive succession (Balser & Carmin, 2009), founder's syndrome (Block & Rosenberg, 2002; Carman & Nesbit, 2013), executive centrality (Heimovics et al., 1995; Herman, 2016), and boards' lack of expertise (Brown & Guo, 2010) have been particularly identified and discussed by non-profit leadership studies. This practical orientation concerns the unique challenges faced by those responsible for managing non-profits. Influence mechanisms and their contexts vary depending on the contextualised outcome characteristics, distinct from profit-oriented organisations.

By applying contextual work settings of the non-profit sector, scholars further aspire to connect leadership models to sector-distinct management and service challenges and demands. An extensive review of leadership research and theory may present the need for a bridge between sector-distinct issues in practice and social psychology assumptions in theory that underlie the identification of effective practices, problem-solving processes, and competencies in the non-profit context (c.f., Foldy et al., 2008; Ospina et al., 2012). Public leadership scholarship recently experienced contrasting streams of thought about its intended audience (Ospina, 2017; Van Wart, 2013). One recognised dilemma among public leadership academics lies in an emphasis on the publicness of public leadership research as opposed to joining the comprehensive conversation about the nature of leadership across sector boundaries (Morse, 2010; Vogel & Masal, 2015). Ospina (2017), emphasising the social psychological basis in leadership research, expresses concern over recent public leadership literature inclined towards a disciplinary self-referential ethos with little groundedness in the literature on organisational behaviour. One might see this would result in "the insufficient embeddedness of this domain within leadership studies" (Ospina, 2017, p. 284). The same concern applies to the research on non-profit leadership. This book chapter thus extends the body of scholarship with the intent to link theory to non-profit contexts.

I propose that the scale of generalisability of leadership research needs to be appropriately focused on the particular context of interest and unique dynamics for that context although emphasis within the dynamics must be built on the

198   *Sungdae Lim*

fundamentals of organisational behaviour (Lim et al., 2021). Attention to these two emphases can produce both practical and theoretical implications applied to the nature of non-profit leadership.

Proposition 1. Non-profit leadership is better identified by middle-range theories that aim to frame sector-distinct leadership roles and outcomes in practice while theoretically grounded on the foundational literature on organisational behaviour.

Leadership roles for the non-profit sector

The unique missions featured by non-profit organisations are diverse but converge into values that are variously public-serving, voluntaristic, and member-serving (Frumkin, 2002). The missions and community engagement aspects of non-profits bring distinct characteristics that describe how non-profits should form and perform effective leadership (Crosby & Bryson, 2005; Dym & Hutson, 2005; Lim et al., 2021; Ospina et al., 2012), that is, they possess a challenging scope of management.

Firstly, non-profits confront seemingly contradictory expectations to promote both community values and professional utilitarian performance simultaneously. They seek social goals that create core identities while also developing operational strategies. Santos (2012) contrasted how non-profits undertake value creation (i.e., strategic focus on social value returns) as well as value appropriation (i.e., strategic focus on financial returns). Frumkin and Andre-Clark (2000) argued that non-profits face strategic limitations in both markets and communities in positioning their strategy between commitment to values and commitment to performance. Similarly, Knutsen and Brower (2010) illuminated the dual accountability system inherent in the non-profit sector – labelled as *expressive* and *instrumental* accountabilities. These accountabilities correspond to social value creations and operational concerns, respectively. Their review reveals that non-profit organisations are challenged to serve both dimensions of rationale.

Herman and Renz (2008) emphasised the importance of identifying performance outcomes at both organisational and community levels. The expressive role of non-profits suggests that their diverse social value orientations eventually converge on a united value guardian entity as a whole for the community (Kramer, 1981), whereas promoting instrumental outcomes of the values comes into contention with strategy development (Moore, 2000). Salamon and associates (2000) extend these expressive and instrumental dimensions to wide-ranging roles of non-profit leadership: advocacy, expression, community building, and service provision and innovation.

Particular leadership roles have been suggested to address the dual and often contrasting community-business orientations. Nanus and Dobbs (1999) suggested six leadership roles in managing a non-profit organisation to address the dual accountabilities: *visionary and strategist, politician and campaigner, coach*, and *change agent*. They contend that non-profit leaders should assume all six leadership roles to promote organisational capital and generate social energy, as well as to produce social goods simultaneously. Carlson and Donohoe (2010) and Herman (2016) suggest similar leadership roles that are effective in non-profit management to address both civic engagement and business strategies. Social entrepreneurship has received much attention as an approach that combines the dual goal orientation system of non-profit organisations (Weerawardena & Mort, 2012).

Another noteworthy leadership challenge facing the non-profit sector is making sense of the social-change roles of the non-profit, which are made more complex because they are intertwined with the difficulty of managing value-based orientations (Allyn, 2011; Bryson, 2016). The challenge in making sense of non-profit social-change roles is that multiple audiences hold discordant conceptions of mission and service orientations (Herman & Renz, 1997), that is, while non-profits' unique accountabilities require them to practice a coherent set of expressive values and community-serving roles based upon the organisation's primary values and activities, they often encounter complexities in defining and aligning the expressive dimension (Allyn, 2011). Organisational mission in the non-profit sector provides "the social justification for its existence" and draws a value-enhancing approach to the non-profit's interactions with and expressions to the community (Bryson, 2016, p. 247). However, mission conceptions for a non-profit organisation vary depending on the engaged actors' traits and responsibilities, and the external conditions in which the non-profit operates (Berlan, 2018).

Berlan (2018) suggests five dimensions of personal mission conceptions of non-profit professionals – issue of focus, activity and role, target population, target area, and value and ideal conceptions. Aligning different conceptions about the five dimensions for a dominant configuration is an important unique predictor of organisational capacity in the non-profit sector (Dym & Hutson, 2005). When non-profit managers create alignment around the mission conceptions, they generate capacity that strengthens the ongoing social construction process of the non-profit's social roles and community engagement (Dym & Hutson, 2005). Shared values and goals are suggested and renewed when leaders attempt to manage the ongoing isomorphic process of matching mission with services.

Similar to the internal dissimilarities in mission conceptions, non-profit management is subject to divergent value-creation forces from various groups of people in a community of practice such as donors, governments, community leaders, volunteers, and governing boards (Herman & Renz, 1997). The primary demands on a single social service organisation are complex and intertwined. For this reason, Herman and Renz (2008) suggest that non-profit executive effectiveness should be based on the coordination dynamics of competing forces and interests that seek public benefits and voluntary commitment and expressions differently. Coordinating specific programme priorities and strategic foci depends on how an organisation defines its expressive goal orientation.

200 *Sungdae Lim*

Herman and Renz (2008) note that a universally applicable social construction is rarely achieved that is agreed upon by the engaged stakeholders.

Non-profit leaders thus face divergent value criteria in conceiving of organisational identity (Young, 2003). To balance this divergence around identity, effective leaders use a political frame of organisational reality construction in which they integrate the complex and intertwined mission, finance, and management strategies into a coherent form (Heimovics et al., 1993, 1995). They employ and integrate perspectives from multiple constituencies in the social construction process (Herman, 2016). Non-profit leaders negotiate various value criteria to make them coherent in a social construction domain for their organisations.

As noted, Crosby and Bryson (2005) suggest policy entrepreneurial leadership to address the complexity, interdependence, and interrelatedness inherent in social problems that face the non-profit sector. Those who attempt to solve such problems should perform visionary, political, and ethical leadership roles. In a time sequence of tackling social problems, visionary leadership roles articulate the meaning of particular public problems. After identifying and constructing the problem's meaning, political leadership adopts and implements policies, programmes, and projects that are incorporated into solutions. Finally, ethical leadership roles coordinate disputes over combining different solution units. They propose that policy entrepreneurship integrates these leadership roles and performs an effective coordination practice for the common good. Crosby and Bryson (2005) describe the leadership practice as "a shared-power phenomenon that embraces many individuals, organisations, and institutions" (p. xxiii). This integrative leadership is considered an approach to making sense of multidimensional mission and service operations and bridging them (Crosby & Bryson, 2012).

Conceptual framing: Meaning-making leadership for non-profit executives

Meaning-making nature in non-profit leadership

Scholarly efforts to underscore the range of leadership roles in managing the dual strategic foci and multiple value creation orientations reveal the meaning-making nature of non-profit leadership. Meaning-making leadership is defined as the construction and management of shared meaning for the organisation (Smircich & Morgan, 1982). Governing an organisation depends on how the leader creates and manages the shared meaning for the organisation. As a leader, one makes sense of the organisational reality and shares the organisational sensemaking concerning its mission, goals, and most significant activities with other engaged actors. The leader motivates employees, mobilises resources, and sets up and performs strategic actions based on the shared organisational reality (Foldy et al., 2008; Lim et al., 2021). Meaning-making is thus responsible for building coherent meaning structures in social interactions with engaged actors from the organisation and the community. Therefore, non-profit leadership performance hinges on how to build and manage a coherent form of organisational activities.

Contrary to general business organisations that may have a definite and unified system of goal orientation, non-profit organisations are subject to varying interpretations of goals and strategies, even among those inside the organisation. From a mission-oriented approach, Berlan (2018) suggests the isomorphic process of mission conceptions among internal members in a non-profit that leads their varying mission conceptions to a unified form with the identified five dimensions of mission. The meaning-making approach sees leadership practices as the ongoing social construction process of organisational reality in all matters (Lim et al., 2021).

Meaning-making in non-profits performs two broad operations. Firstly, it relates to making a coherent orientation on the organisation's mission through the most significant activities that are all aligned. Meaning-making leadership seeks to match the non-profit's ultimate social justification through the day-to-day services and programmes. The other theme about meaning-making leadership relates to making sense of the organisational activities that are communicated with both internal and external audiences, which constantly change. Their social role and community demands remain fluid and context-dependent, meaning sensemaking sources, methods, and engaged actors ever change. Therefore, communicating the value and strategic orientations should be an ongoing practice in non-profits.

Recent theory development of non-profit leadership identifies the meaning-making nature to frame antecedents and outcomes of effective leadership within social-change contexts. Ospina et al. (2012) developed social-change leadership theory from a relational approach. It suggests that three leadership practices – *reframing discourse*, *bridging difference*, and *unleashing human energies* – and four core leadership activities – *organising*, *public policy advocacy*, *community building*, and *service provision* – enhance the shared power capacity of non-profits that lead to social change as mission achievement. This leadership theory advances social constructionism for addressing the complex community challenges. Ospina and her colleagues articulated the development process of collective leadership capacity for social change (Ospina & Foldy, 2010; Ospina et al., 2012). Social-change leadership contributes to identifying relational properties in addressing non-profit service dynamism.

As noted, Dym and Hutson's (2005) alignment leadership articulates the meaning-making process of effective leaders in non-profit organisations. Starting from an individual leader's sensemaking of the organisation's mission, goals, and activities, the leader increasingly broadens the range of aligned meaning structures with other stakeholder groups, the market, and the community. The alignment then becomes an ongoing realignment process that depends on the individual leader's interactions with the organisation and the organisational context regarding four arenas of organisational sensemaking – basic nature, underlying principles, means, purpose, and direction (Dym & Hutson, 2005). This alignment

202   *Sungdae Lim*

map may lead to developing cycles of management of shared meaning when the leader, the organisation, the community, and the market are all aligned.

Executive centrality in social construction

Reviewing the nature of non-profit leadership reveals the need for developing meaning-making capabilities in the social construction process of organisational realities (Heimovics et al., 1995; Herman & Renz, 1997; Lim et al., 2021). An emphasis on the non-profit sector's meaning-making leadership roles necessitates paying attention to skilled executive competencies in aligning various interpretations about the internal and external environments that constantly change, between all engaged. Much research suggests executive centrality in non-profit governance, indicating that chief executives' competencies primarily settle on leadership practices (Foldy et al., 2008; Lim et al., 2021). Executive centrality as a non-profit's unique characteristic underpins the dynamics of managing the multiple forms of organisational identity (Balser & Carmin, 2009; Herman, 2016).

Noting that the forces of sensemaking for non-profit organisations are centrally driven by executive leaders, the meaning-making nature of non-profit leadership can be explored in greater depth by looking into applicable executive leadership skills (Lim et al., 2021). Theory and research need to identify not only what executive competencies make a difference in practice but also how the competency dimensions are determined. The exploration draws from assumptions of leader competency development (Day et al., 2009). A useful extension of this work might be a study that examines cognitive and identity attributes in greater detail, especially those that underlie the competency development of non-profit executives.

Constructive-developmental approach to meaning-making capabilities

Constructive-developmental theory of leadership suggests various linkages between meaning-making dynamics and individual development stages (Kegan, 1980; McCauley et al., 2006). Constructivism assumes that individuals, as the agents of understanding and arranging experiences, perceive and construct the meaning of reality (Cobb, 1996; Kegan, 1982; von Glasersfeld, 1995; Vygotsky, 1978). These constructivist theorists hold that individuals construct and reconstruct the worlds of experiences through their cognitive and social interaction processes. Their primary concern with the psychological development is the individuals' interactions with others and engagement in social activities. For example, Bauersfeld (1988) defines learning as "the subjective reconstruction of societal means and models through negotiation of meaning in social interaction" (p. 39). In the ongoing reality construction processes, knowing, learning, and meaning-making continuously take place by the individuals' function of human developmental psychology. Social activities and interactions are the sites through which the negotiation of individual meaning-making occurs (Vygotsky, 1978).

From a leader-centric lens on non-profit leadership, the executive leader is seen as the one performing leadership with responsibility (Heimovics et al., 1993, 1995). This approach assumes that it is the individual leader who initiates and manages meaning-making shared with engaged actors under organisational power-based conditions and environmental contingencies. Those individuals, including the leader, possess their own cognitive processes through which they understand and construct worlds of experiences. As such, persons are capable of perceiving, learning, and reflecting on their own meaning-making of the surrounding reality (Bruner, 1990; Kegan, 1980, 1982). The leader develops leadership skills to understand and arrange the multiple frames of meaning-making in the organisation and suggests a shared form of organisational reality within a corresponding community context (Foldy et al., 2008; Lim et al., 2021).

Lim et al. (2021, p. 311) define leadership as the leader's motivational force drawing members into concerted action. This may be, in a sense, considered the leader's sense giving given to the social processes of organisational sensemaking (Foldy et al., 2008; Maitlis, 2005). Although leaders are embedded within particular contexts and relations with others, their practices primarily concern social construction of the organisational activities and manage the shared meaning (Drath, 1990). The meaning-making process thus relies on the leader's ability to construct and reflect on the aligned professional experiences and interactions for those engaged in shared conceptions (Humphreys et al., 2012). The unit of analysis is individual leaders in social action. Smircich and Morgan (1982) present this point of view by stating "[E]ffective leadership depends upon the extent to which the leader's definition of the situation, ..., serves as a basis for action by others" (p. 262). I propose that how a non-profit leader manages the social construction process of the organisation determines leadership effectiveness in promoting mission achievement and service outcomes. Meaning-making capabilities of non-profit executives are the essence of their leadership.

Leadership development theories have extensively determined a number of hierarchical structures for individual cognitive and identity development processes by which particular leadership skills and competencies are fruitfully achieved (Cunliffe & Coupland, 2012; Day & Sin, 2011; Maclean et al., 2012; Pye, 2005). The research on leadership development touches upon hierarchically structured cognitive mental structures as the basis for further identity and skill development processes. It further emphasises the connection between leader sensemaking stages presented by identity and practice skills development and the corresponding leadership development (Day et al., 2009). Day and Sin's (2011) three-level competency model of leader development shows that a set of necessary leadership capabilities are established and developed fundamentally from the individual leader's invisible cognitive and identity development processes and ensuing action dynamics. Therefore, leadership competency for a non-profit

204   *Sungdae Lim*

leader is understood as a resultant skill set that is directly visible to others but developed by one's underlying cognitive and identity-based processes.

Proposition 2. Non-profit leadership is characterised by the executive's developmental competency to manage the shared meaning of the organisation.

Interpretive leadership skill

The observations about executive centrality in the meaning-making nature suggest that individual non-profit leaders' meaning-constitutive capabilities characterise their leadership competency (Foldy et al., 2008; Lim et al., 2021). These capabilities then turn out to converge on the acquisition of a single human skill (Anderson, 1982, 1985). Vygotsky argued that the individual mind is "a set of specific capabilities, each of which is, to some extent, independent of the others and is developed independently" (p. 83). Building on these constructivist theorists' assumptions about psychological development processes, I assert that the meaning-making capabilities of non-profit leaders jointly constitute a single human skill. This chapter echoes the theory of *interpretive leadership skill* for meaning-making leadership of non-profit executives (Lim et al., 2021).

The interpretive leadership skill conceptualisation is drawn from traditional definitional works for interpretive procedures of cognitive skill acquisition (Anderson, 1982, 1985). Being *interpretive* indicates the individual's declarative and procedural forms of knowledge compilation. The interpretive procedures, by which the knowledge is both declaratively and procedurally acquired, enhance the individual's interpretive skill. Anderson (1982) provided a detailed account of the two forms of knowledge that collectively characterise one's interpretive skill acquisition.

Declarative knowledge is an individual understanding of what factual things and functions exist. It is derived from Ryle's (1949) distinction of *knowing-that* (Johnson-Laird, 1983). In contrast, procedural knowledge is setting one's own trial and error for how the functions work better. It is referred to as *knowing-how* (Johnson-Laird, 1983). In order to interpret a course of action, one needs to discover the range of meanings that are communicated in a community of practice and frame hypothetical strings into a plausible reality structure. The discovering process refers to *knowing-that* and the framing process refers to *knowing-how*. Constructivism scholarship suggests that interpretation is certainly a skilled performance dimension of the individual mind because it involves the ongoing learning process of how to apply sociocultural contexts into one's sensemaking (Cobb, 1996) through the leader's cognitive and identity-based reality construction processes (Lim et al., 2021). The cognitive process corresponds to the individual's mental model of sensemaking (Vandenbosch & Higgins, 1996), and the identity-based process represents one's leader identity and self-regulation mindset (Day & Sin, 2011; Day et al., 2009).

I define interpretive leadership skill as the leader's ability to discover, coordinate, and reflect multidimensional forms of organisational reality construction.

It consists of independent but interactive three meaning-making capabilities – *contextual astuteness, self-reflective capacity,* and *coordination capacity.* The three capabilities imply interactive dynamics such that leaders discover which particular contextual situations and operations exist at a specific time, engage in the social construction of the organisational reality in a way that provides coordination to the engaged participants, and reflect on one's meaning-making practices. While contextual astuteness corresponds to the conception of declarative knowledge of interpretation, coordination capacity and self-reflective capacity represent two forms of procedural knowledge.

How individual leaders precisely discover the function, resources, and environments of the organisation characterises their contextual astuteness. The procedural knowledge dimension of interpretive leadership skill needs to establish a know-how structure for constructing and managing shared meaning for the non-profit. Therefore, learning the procedural knowledge in the meaning-making dynamics should not only perform its role of trial-and-error procedures based on the current know-how structure (i.e., coordination capacity) but also trace and reflect on context changes in the mission and services (Schwandt, 2005). Dewey (1910) defines reflective thinking as an act of searching or investigation to bring further facts that may prove or nullify the current assumptions. Therefore, this chapter suggests self-reflective capacity and coordination capacity as the two forms of the ongoing meaning-making procedural process for interpretive leadership skill. Through joint interactions of these meaning-making capabilities, interpretive leadership skill enables the non-profit leader to better engage in the ongoing social construction dynamics for comprehension, reflections, and alignments of the complex and multidimensional mission and service contexts for the non-profit.

Proposition 3. Interpretive leadership skill is the essential executive competency in the meaning-making nature of non-profit leadership, composed of contextual astuteness, coordination capacity, and self-reflective capacity.

Key takeaways

The conceptual framing is summarised by three points. Firstly, managing shared meaning –labelled *meaning-making leadership* – is the essence of non-profit leadership as non-profit leaders encounter unique challenges in serving both expressive and instrumental accountabilities and in aligning variously interwoven expectations of the mission and services from engaged actors that constantly change. Secondly, meaning-making leadership in non-profits is centrally exerted by those with executive authority. Thirdly, *interpretive leadership skill,* as the ability to discover, coordinate, and reflect on forms of organisational reality construction, consists of three meaning-making capabilities – *contextual astuteness, coordination capacity,* and *self-reflective capacity –* and is the executive competency for addressing non-profit challenges.

Discussion

The discussion of this chapter concerns the implications made by the main sections, presented in Table 11.1. It first provided the conceptual overview of the meaning-making nature of non-profit leadership and the executive competency in managing the shared meaning of organisational reality. As defined, meaning-making reflects the leader's power-based reality construction by which the leader draws people into concerted action. The importance of meaning-making leadership in non-profit organisations is especially captured by the difficulty in setting and addressing the targeted social cause with varying and ever-changing conceptions and expectations of the mission and services.

Table 11.1 Meaning-making capabilities for non-profit executives in theory and practice

Themes	Implications
Leadership	• Influential interactions to lead others to the goal orientation • The complexity and difficulty in grounding a general approach to the nature of organisational leadership
Need for a middle-range theory of non-profit leadership	• Lack of general theories applied to leadership practices in the sectoral governing context • Pressing topics for non-profit leadership such as leadership succession, founder's syndrome, executive centrality, and boards' lack of expertise • The need for a bridge between sector-distinct issues in practice and social psychology assumptions in theory that underlie the identification of effective practices, problem-solving processes, and competencies
Non-profit leadership challenges	• Dual expectations: expressive and instrumental accountabilities • Complexities in practising a coherent set of social-change roles that satisfy divergent value orientations and demands • Leadership roles to address these challenges
Meaning-making as the sector-specific application to non-profit leadership	• Meaning-making leadership defined as the management of shared meaning for the organisation • Leader to make sense of the organisational reality and share the organisational sensemaking concerning its mission, goals, and most significant activities with other engaged actors. The leader motivates employees, mobilises resources, and sets up and performs strategic actions based on the shared organisational reality • Such roles reveal the meaning-making nature of non-profit leadership
Executive centrality for leadership property	• Executive centrality as a non-profit's unique feature • Meaning-making leadership expected to show an applicable executive competency developed by one's underlying cognitive and identity-based processes (constructive-developmental approach)
Interpretive leadership skill	• Interpretive leadership skill as the essential executive competency in which three interactive meaning-making capabilities – contextual astuteness, coordination capacity, and self-reflective capacity – are combined to determine leadership effectiveness
Evidence for practice	• Utility of ongoing management of value orientations for effective service provision models

Why meaning-making capabilities for non-profit executives? 207

For this conceptual work, I discussed linkages between the general theory development of leadership and the sector-specific leadership challenges and roles for non-profits. The extensive review of leadership research and theory across multi-sectoral scholarship has accentuated the need for an in-depth investigation of the meaning-making nature that requires executive competencies. This led to the utility of middle-range theories of non-profit leadership. I proposed that, in order to advance understanding of leadership in non-profits, it is important to further examine key contextual capabilities that are also theoretically well drawn from social psychology foundations and assumptions.

Secondly, this conceptual framing, founded on the selected dimension of leadership, advanced the model of interpretive leadership skill as a non-profit executive competency composed of contextual astuteness, coordination capacity, and self-reflective capacity that are combined to determine leadership effectiveness in addressing sector-distinct challenges. Non-profit leadership depends on executive leaders' interpretive leadership skill, specifically how they construct and arrange the shared meaning for the organisation's social-change roles and service orientations. The importance of meaning-making leadership in non-profit organisations is stressed with regard to the identified sector-distinct challenges. The varying and often conflicting strategic foci between operational performance and social value creation, and varying demands on the organisational value orientation and criteria together require a leadership competency for framing and communicating the organisational reality. Building upon the theory of declarative and procedural knowledge in the interpretive process (Anderson, 1982), this chapter suggests interpretive leadership skill is the competency for non-profit executives. The skill-based approach identified the meaning-constitutive capabilities.

This chapter also described the development process of interpretive leadership skill, as grounded in social psychology, and thus offers a reasonable extension of non-profit leadership research. Interpretive leadership skill enables the non-profit leader to better engage in the ongoing social construction process through comprehension, reflections, and alignments of the mission and service contexts for the non-profit. It presents this essential executive role in non-profit governance.

Therefore, this conceptual work theoretically discovered the substantive mechanisms of non-profit leadership that have been scarcely brought by the scholarship. The effort to connect separate bodies of knowledge extends our accumulated understanding of how to address managerial challenges and roles in the meaning-making nature. This work thus adds a useful middle-range application.

Practically, this chapter proposes a strategy for exercising effective roles in non-profit management. Linking value-oriented expressions with outcome-oriented performance has always been a major managerial goal in the non-profit sector (Bish & Becker, 2016; Brown & Guo, 2010; Frumkin & Andre-Clark, 2000). Non-profit executives' convincing expressive value orientations can be a driving force for arranging and managing complex and fluid interpretations of organisational missions and significant activities. The leader's understanding of

208 *Sungdae Lim*

the expressive roles of the organisation leads to a well-organised form of mission-service matches, that is, the identification of the particular meaning-making nature of each non-profit broadens the utility of expressive values to develop organisational strategies. I expect this may form the groundwork to develop more effective organisational strategies.

Conclusion

I acknowledge limitations. Firstly, this conceptual work lacks empirical support. The interpretive leadership skill construct needs to be confirmed through construct validation studies. Its three meaning-making sub-dimensions combined to form the single competency have to be supported by valid factor analyses for the matched measurement model. Follow-up studies will also need to examine the comprehensive model of the development process and its influence mechanisms. Secondly, the non-profit context discussed in this chapter only pertains to the US context. I anticipate future research will bring abundant other cultural settings and add to the knowledge in non-profit leadership.

To conclude, meaning-making is the sector-specific application of non-profit leadership. Interpretive leadership skill, in combination of the identified meaning-making capabilities, is proposed as the executive competency. The theoretical elaboration may advance practice by refining the utility of aligned value orientations to develop operational strategies and promote desirable outcomes.

References

Allyn, D. (2011). Mission mirroring: Understanding conflict in nonprofit organizations. *Nonprofit and Voluntary Sector Quarterly, 40*(4), 762–769. https://doi.org/10.1177/0899764010370869

Anderson, J. R. (1982). Acquisition of cognitive skill. *Psychological Review, 89*(4), 369–406. https://psycnet.apa.org/doi/10.1037/0033-295X.89.4.369

Anderson, J. R. (1985). *Cognitive psychology and its implications.* W. H. Freeman and Company.

Avolio, B. J., Walumbwa, F. O., & Weber, T. J. (2009). Leadership: Current theories, research, and future directions. *Annual Review of Psychology, 60*, 421–449. https://doi.org/10.1146/annurev.psych.60.110707.163621

Balser, D. B., & Carmin, J. (2009). Leadership succession and the emergence of an organizational identity threat. *Nonprofit Management and Leadership, 20*(2), 185–201. https://doi.org/10.1002/nml.248

Bartone, P. T., Snook, S. A., Forsythe, G. B., Lewis, P., & Bullis, R. C. (2007). Psychosocial development and leader performance of military officer cadets. *The Leadership Quarterly, 18*(5), 490–504. https://doi.org/10.1016/j.leaqua.2007.07.008

Bass, B. M. (1998). *Transformational leadership: Industrial, military, and educational impact.* Lawrence Erlbaum.

Bauersfeld, H. (1988). Interaction, construction, and knowledge: Alternative perspectives for mathematics education. In T. Cooney & D. Grouws (Eds.), *Effective mathematics teaching* (pp. 27–46). National Council of Teachers of Mathematics.

Why meaning-making capabilities for non-profit executives? 209

Berlan, D. (2018). Understanding nonprofit missions as dynamic and interpretative conceptions. *Nonprofit Management and Leadership*, *28*, 413–422. https://doi.org/10.1002/nml.21295

Bish, A., & Becker, K. (2016). Exploring expectations of nonprofit management capabilities. *Nonprofit and Voluntary Sector Quarterly*, *45*(3), 437–457. https://doi.org/10.1177/0899764015583313

Block, S. R., & Rosenberg, S. (2002). Toward an understanding of founder's syndrome: An assessment of power and privilege among founders of nonprofit organizations. *Nonprofit Management and Leadership*, *12*(4), 353–368. https://doi.org/10.1002/nml.12403

Brown, W. A., & Guo, C. (2010). Exploring the key roles for nonprofit boards. *Nonprofit and Voluntary Sector Quarterly*, *39*(3), 536–546. https://doi.org/10.1177/0899764009334588

Bruner, J. (1990). *Acts of meaning*. Harvard University Press.

Bryson, J. M. (2016). Strategic planning and the strategy change cycle. In D. O. Renz & R. D. Herman (Eds.), *The Jossey-Bass handbook of nonprofit leadership and management* (4th ed., pp. 240–273). John Wiley & Sons.

Carlson, M., & Donohoe, M. (2010). *The executive director's guide to thriving as a nonprofit leader* (2nd ed.). Jossey-Bass.

Carman, J. G., & Nesbit, R. (2013). Founding new nonprofit organizations syndrome or symptom? *Nonprofit and Voluntary Sector Quarterly*, *42*(3), 603–621. https://doi.org/10.1177/0899764012459255

Cobb, P. (1996). Where is the mind? A coordination of sociocultural and cognitive constructivist perspectives. In C. T. Fosnot (Ed.), *Constructivism: Theory, perspectives, and practice* (pp. 3–7). Teachers College Press.

Crosby, B. C., & Bryson, J. M. (2005). *Leadership for the common good: Tackling public problems in a shared-power world* (2nd ed.). Jossey-Bass.

Crosby, B. C., & Bryson, J. M. (2012). Integrative leadership and policy change: A hybrid relational view. In M. Uhl-Bein & S. M. Ospina (Eds.), *Advancing relational leadership research: A dialogue among perspectives* (pp. 303–333). IAP.

Cunliffe, A., & Coupland, C. (2012). From hero to villain to hero: Making experience sensible through embodied narrative sensemaking. *Human Relations*, *65*(1), 63–88. https://doi.org/10.1177/0018726711424321

Day, D. V., & Sin, H. P. (2011). Longitudinal tests of an integrative model of leader development: Charting and understanding developmental trajectories. *The Leadership Quarterly*, *22*(3), 545–560. https://doi.org/10.1016/j.leaqua.2011.04.011

Day, D. V., Harrison, M. M., & Halpin, S. M. (2009). *An integrative approach to leader development: Connecting adult development, identity, and expertise*. Routledge.

DeRue, D. S., Nahrgang, J. D., Wellman, N. E. D., & Humphrey, S. E. (2011). Trait and behavioral theories of leadership: An integration and meta-analytic test of their relative validity. *Personnel Psychology*, *64*(1), 7–52. https://doi.org/10.1111/j.1744-6570.2010.01201.x

Dewey, J. (1910). *How we think: A restatement of the relation of reflective thinking to the educative process*. Heath.

Drath, W. H. (1990). Managerial strengths and weaknesses as functions of the development of personal meaning. *The Journal of Applied Behavioral Science*, *26*(4), 483–499. https://doi.org/10.1177/0021886390264006

Dulebohn, J. H., Bommer, W. H., Liden, R. C., Brouer, R. L., & Ferris, G. R. (2012). A meta-analysis of antecedents and consequences of leader-member exchange integrating the past with an eye toward the future. *Journal of Management*, *38*(6), 1715–1759. https://doi.org/10.1177/0149206311415280

Dym, B., & Hutson, H. (2005). *Leadership in nonprofit organizations*. Sage Publications.

210 Sungdae Lim

Fleishman, E. A., Mumford, M. D., Zaccaro, S. J., Levin, K. Y., Korotkin, A. L., & Hein, M. B. (1991). Taxonomic efforts in the description of leader behavior: A synthesis and functional interpretation. *The Leadership Quarterly, 2*(4), 245–287. https://doi.org/10.1016/1048-9843(91)90016-U

Foldy, E. G., Goldman, L., & Ospina, S. (2008). Sensegiving and the role of cognitive shifts in the work of leadership. *The Leadership Quarterly, 19*(5), 514–529. https://doi.org/10.1016/j.leaqua.2008.07.004

Frumkin, P. (2002). *On being nonprofit: A conceptual and policy primer.* Harvard University Press.

Frumkin, P., & Andre-Clark, A. (2000). When missions, markets, and politics collide: Values and strategy in the nonprofit human services. *Nonprofit and Voluntary Sector Quarterly, 29*(1_suppl), 141–163. https://doi.org/10.1177/0899764000291S007

Heimovics, R. D., Herman, R. D., & Coughlin, C. L. J. (1993). Executive leadership and resource dependence in nonprofit organizations: A frame analysis. *Public Administration Review, 53*(5), 419–427. https://doi.org/10.2307/976342

Heimovics, R. D., Herman, R. D., & Jurkiewicz, C. L. (1995). The political dimension of effective nonprofit executive leadership. *Nonprofit Management and Leadership, 5*(3), 233–248. https://doi.org/10.1002/nml.4130050303

Herman, R. D. (2016). Executive leadership. In D. O. Renz & R. D. Herman (Eds.), *The Jossey-Bass handbook of nonprofit leadership and management* (4th ed., pp. 167–187). John Wiley & Sons.

Herman, R. D., & Renz, D. O. (1997). Multiple constituencies and the social construction of nonprofit organization effectiveness. *Nonprofit and Voluntary Sector Quarterly, 26*(2), 185–206. https://doi.org/10.1177/0899764097262006

Herman, R. D., & Renz, D. O. (2008). Advancing nonprofit organizational effectiveness research and theory: Nine theses. *Nonprofit Management and Leadership, 18*(4), 399–415. https://doi.org/10.1002/nml.195

Humphreys, M., Ucbasaran, D., & Lockett, A. (2012). Sensemaking and sensegiving stories of jazz leadership. *Human Relations, 65*(1), 41–62. https://doi.org/10.1177/0018726711424320

Johnson-Laird, P. N. (1983). *Mental models.* Harvard University.

Kearns, K. P., Livingston, J., Scherer, S., & McShane, L. (2015). Leadership skills as construed by nonprofit chief executives. *Leadership & Organization Development Journal, 36*(6), 712–727. https://doi.org/10.1108/LODJ-11-2013-0143

Kegan, R. (1980). Making meaning: The constructive-developmental approach to persons and practice. *The Personnel and Guidance Journal, 58*(5), 373–380. https://doi.org/10.1002/j.2164-4918.1980.tb00416.x

Kegan, R. (1982). *The evolving self: Problem and process in human development.* Harvard University Press.

Knutsen, W. L., & Brower, R. S. (2010). Managing expressive and instrumental accountabilities in nonprofit and voluntary organizations: A qualitative investigation. *Nonprofit and Voluntary Sector Quarterly, 39*(4), 58–610. https://doi.org/10.1177/0899764009359943

Kramer, R. M. (1981). *Voluntary agencies in the welfare state.* University of California Press.

Lim, S., Brower, R. S., & Berlan, D. G. (2021). Interpretive leadership skill in meaning-making by nonprofit leaders. *Nonprofit Management and Leadership, 32*(2), 307–328. https://doi.org/10.1002/nml.21477

Lord, R. G., & Hall, R. J. (2005). Identity, deep structure and the development of leadership skill. *The Leadership Quarterly, 16*(4), 591–615. https://doi.org/10.1016/j.leaqua.2005.06.003

Maclean, M., Harvey, C., & Chia, R. (2012). Sensemaking, storytelling and the legitimization of elite business careers. *Human Relations, 65*(1), 17–40.

Maitlis, S. (2005). The social processes of organizational sensemaking. *Academy of Management Journal*, *48*(1), 21–49. https://doi.org/10.5465/amj.2005.15993111

McCauley, C. D., Drath, W. H., Palus, C. J., O'Connor, P. M., & Baker, B. A. (2006). The use of constructive-developmental theory to advance the understanding of leadership. *The Leadership Quarterly*, *17*(6), 634–653. https://doi.org/10.1016/j.leaqua.2006.10.006

Moore, M. H. (2000). Managing for value: Organizational strategy in for-profit, non-profit, and governmental organizations. *Nonprofit and Voluntary Sector Quarterly*, *29*(1_suppl), 183–208. https://doi.org/10.1177/0899764000291S009

Morse, R. S. (2010). Integrative public leadership: Catalyzing collaboration to create public value. *The Leadership Quarterly*, *21*(2), 231–245. https://doi.org/10.1016/j.leaqua.2010.01.004

Mumford, M. D., Zaccaro, S. J., Harding, F. D., Jacobs, T. O., & Fleishman, E. A. (2000). Leadership skills for a changing world: Solving complex social problems. *The Leadership Quarterly*, *11*(1), 11–35. https://doi.org/10.1016/S1048-9843(99)00041-7

Nanus, B., & Dobbs, S. M. (1999). *Leaders who make a difference: Essential strategies for meeting the nonprofit challenge*. Jossey-Bass.

Ospina, S. M. (2017). Collective leadership and context in public administration: Bridging public leadership research and leadership studies. *Public Administration Review*, *77*(2), 275–287. https://doi.org/10.1111/puar.12706

Ospina, S. M., & Foldy, E. (2010). Building bridges from the margins: The work of leadership in social change organizations. *The Leadership Quarterly*, *21*(2), 292–307. https://doi.org/10.1016/j.leaqua.2010.01.008

Ospina, S. M., & Uhl-Bien, M. (2012). Mapping the terrain: Convergence and divergence around relational leadership. In M. Uhl-Bien, & S. M. Ospina (Eds.), *Advancing relational leadership research: A dialogue among perspectives* (pp. xix–xlvii). IAP.

Ospina, S. M., Foldy, E. G., El Hadidy, W., Dodge, J., Hofmann-Pinilla, A., & Su, C. (2012). Social change leadership as relational leadership. In M. Uhl-Bien & S. M. Ospina (Eds.), *Advancing relational leadership research: A dialogue among perspectives* (pp. 255–302). IAP.

Pye, A. (2005). Leadership and organizing: Sensemaking in action. *Leadership*, *1*(1), 31–49. https://doi.org/10.1177/1742715005049349

Ryle, G. (1949). *The concept of mind*. Hutchinson.

Salamon, L. M., Hems, L. C., & Chinnock, K. (2000). The nonprofit sector: For what and for whom? Comparative nonprofit sector project working paper no. 37. Johns Hopkins Center for Civil Society Studies.

Santos, F. M. (2012). A positive theory of social entrepreneurship. *Journal of Business Ethics*, *111*, 335–351. https://doi.org/10.1007/s10551-012-1413-4

Schwandt, D. R. (2005). When managers become philosophers: Integrating learning with sensemaking. *Academy of Management Learning & Education*, *4*(2), 176–192. https://doi.org/10.5465/amle.2005.17268565

Smircich, L., & Morgan, G. (1982). Leadership: The management of meaning. *The Journal of Applied Behavioral Science*, *18*(3), 257–273. https://doi.org/10.1177/002188638201800303

Stogdill, R. M. (1974). *Handbook of leadership*. Free Press.

Uhl-Bien, M. (2006). Relational leadership theory: Exploring the social processes of leadership and organizing. *The Leadership Quarterly*, *17*(6), 654–676. https://doi.org/10.1016/j.leaqua.2006.10.007

Vandenbosch, B., & Higgins, C. (1996). Information acquisition and mental models: An investigation into the relationship between behaviour and learning. *Information Systems Research*, *7*(2), 198–214. https://doi.org/10.1287/isre.7.2.198

Van Wart, M. (2013). Administrative leadership theory: A reassessment after 10 years. *Public Administration*, *91*(3), 521–543. https://doi.org/10.1111/padm.12017

212 *Sungdae Lim*

Vogel, R., & Masal, D. (2015). Public leadership: A review of the literature and framework for future research. *Public Management Review*, *17*(8), 1165–1189. https://doi.org/10.1080/14719037.2014.895031

von Glasersfeld, E. (1995). *Radical constructivism: A way of knowing and learning.* Falmer Press.

Vygotsky, L. S. (1978). *Mind in society: The development of higher psychological processes.* Harvard University Press.

Weerawardena, J., & Mort, G. S. (2012). Competitive strategy in socially entrepreneurial nonprofit organizations: Innovation and differentiation. *Journal of Public Policy & Marketing*, *31*(1), 91–101. https://doi.org/10.1509/jppm.11.034

Young, D. R. (2003). Organizational identity in nonprofit organizations: Strategic and structural implications. *Nonprofit Management and Leadership*, *12*(2), 139–157. https://doi.org/10.1002/nml.12202

Yukl, G. (2012). Effective leadership behavior: What we know and what questions need more attention. *The Academy of Management Perspectives*, *26*(4), 66–85. https://doi.org/10.5465/amp.2012.0088

12 Authentic beneficiary engagement in the aged care sector

Advancing non-profit governance through care

Kylie Kingston, Sari Rossi, Belinda Luke, and Alexandra Williamson

Introduction

The International Standard on Governance of Organizations – ISO 37000:2021 (ISO Technical Committee, 2022) details core governance outcomes of Responsible Stewardship, Effective Performance, and Ethical Behaviour. Embedded within these, *Stakeholder engagement* is identified as an enabling governance principle and a fundamental component of effective accountability. ISO 37000:2021 stipulates the "governing body should ensure that the organisation's stakeholders are appropriately engaged and their expectations considered" (The British Standards Institution, 2021, p. 24). Additionally, ISO 37000:2021 emphasises the importance of understanding stakeholders' rights and *identifying* and *prioritising* stakeholders, whilst acknowledging stakeholder types, groupings and relevance will vary across organisations.

Engaging with beneficiary stakeholders is increasingly acknowledged as a component of effective accountability. For example, in the human services sector there is increased positioning of beneficiary stakeholders as central, with terminology such as "person-centred care" (Kitwood, 1993, 1997, 2012; Seah et al., 2022, p. 6; World Health Organization, 2018; Yee et al., 2021) and "patient-centric care" (Aye et al., 2020; Productivity Commission, 2017), suggesting that care revolves around the beneficiary stakeholder. Prioritising a person-centred care approach as part of non-profit organisations' (NPOs') governance can provide mechanisms for the governing body to:

- Increase understanding of its beneficiary stakeholders
- Establish and maintain effective relationships with beneficiary stakeholders

This is especially the case for NPOs representing and providing services to vulnerable members of the community. Strong relationships with beneficiary stakeholders and a person-centric focus may boost understanding of beneficiaries' expectations, thus informing organisational decision-making to

DOI: 10.4324/9781003460572-17

support the purpose of the organisation, and better meeting beneficiaries' accountability needs.

Despite the increased advocacy for a person-centred care-based approach to the delivery of human services, accountability within the non-profit sector remains typically focussed 'upwardly', towards donors, funders, or government (Najam, 1996; O'Leary, 2017). These are stakeholders known to have power to hold the organisation and its board to account. This power is typically related to economic power. Conversely, whilst an NPO's beneficiaries may have a *right* to receive an account (Marini et al., 2017; O'Leary, 2017; Yasmin et al., 2021) from the organisation, that right typically has to be granted by someone in a more powerful position. In this context beneficiaries have restricted ability to elicit information capable of fulfilling the receipt of an account on their terms (Miller, 2002). Therefore, notwithstanding ISO 37000:2021 advocating organisational governance that understands the "rights and expectations of the stakeholder groups" (British Standards Institute, 2021, p. 16), a rights-based approach to governance appears to fall short of meeting care-based needs.

The purpose of this chapter is to conceptualise a care-based approach to organisational governance that might better support the meeting of beneficiaries' accountability needs. Moving beyond a rights-based approach to governance may enable the actualisation of ISO 37000:2021's principle of *Stakeholder engagement* in circumstances where stakeholders lack the ability to demand that their rights are met, which is often the case with beneficiary groups.

We focus our study within the aged care setting due to the importance of embracing models of governance that lead to the empowerment and engagement of beneficiary stakeholders. Within this context we conceptualise a care-based approach to organisational governance that might better support the meeting of aged care beneficiaries' accountability needs. To assist our theorisation, we draw upon the perspective of an *ethics of care*, which recognises a fundamental responsibility towards others (Gilligan, 1993) and is explained further in the next section. Following this, a literature review concerning stakeholder engagement and accountability within the aged care sector is provided. This review leads toward the articulation of a care-based accountability framework to support the principle of *Stakeholder engagement* described within ISO 37000:2021 and enhance accountability toward beneficiaries.

An ethics of care

Care, in its noun form, denotes the provision of attention, concern, support, or aid towards the well-being, health, safety, or happiness of an individual, group, or living being (Hadadian-Chaghaei et al., 2022). It includes a range of actions and attitudes that demonstrate empathy, responsibility, and consideration for the needs and feelings of others. As a verb, to care involves showing interest and concern, or giving attention to someone or something (Hadadian-Chaghaei et al., 2022).

Authentic beneficiary engagement in the aged care sector 215

It means taking action to ensure the well-being, protection, or improvement of a person, object, or situation. Caring can include activities, behaviours, or expressions that reflect attentiveness and consideration. In a broader philosophical framing, care refers to a moral or ethical stance that emphasises interconnectedness, empathy, and responsibility toward other individuals, communities, or the environment (Hadadian-Chaghaei et al., 2022). This perspective underscores the significance of relationships, understanding, and nurturing in fostering a compassionate and equitable society.

Stemming from the work of Carol Gilligan (1993), *ethics of care* "primarily consider human relations that grow out of needs for care to be fundamental to human existence" (Tronto, 2008). Ethics of care concerns caring about, caring for, caring with, caregiving, and care receiving (Johansson & Wickström, 2023; Tronto, 1998). Here care is both a practice and a politics that promotes care's radical potential and refutes neoliberal logics of individualism and profitability (Thompson, 2022). Ethics of care represents a way of thinking that is embedded in relationships (Adhariani & Siregar, 2018; Reiter, 1997; Rentfro & Hooks, 2006), where care can be seen as a "quality of spaces that are produced relationally" (Raghuram et al., 2009, p. 6).

Qualities of ethics of care are presented in Table 12.1 and juxtaposed against those within a rights or justice-based view of ethics. Notably, ethics of care is embedded within entangled connections, acknowledging pluralistic responsibility across species and ecologies, and reflective of a feminist approach to ethics (Gilligan, 1993). Conversely, an ethics of rights draws upon rules-based principles, rationality, and hierarchy. An ethics of rights decontextualises in order to attempt to create universal conditions of fairness and consistency and flourishes within a neoliberal economic view focussed on the individual.

Table 12.1 Qualities of ethics of care and ethics of rights/justice

Ethics of care	*Ethics of rights/justice*
• Relationships	• Rules/principles
• Feminist	• Masculine
• Interconnections	• Hierarchy
• Contextual	• Universality
• Relational practices	• Fairness
• Ecologies	• Neoliberal principles
• Multispecies	• Human centred
• Empathy	• Autonomy
• Emotion	• Rationality
• Responsibility	• Rules
• Applied situations	• Abstract situations
• Activity	• Consistency
• Pluralistic	• Individualistic

216   *K. Kingston, S. Rossi, B. Luke, and A. Williamson*

Tronto (1998) argues that an analysis of care provides a framework for political change. Here care is recognised as being inherently political and never neutral (Carstens, 2020), within relationships that are socially and politically situated (Branicki, 2020). Care therefore involves power relations and is fraught with conflict as different stakeholders' needs struggle to be both described and recognised (Tronto, 1998).

Whilst commonly considered within disciplines such as social work, politics, and healthcare, ethics of care remains relatively novel within the business literature (Adhariani & Siregar, 2018). However, ethics of care with its focus on the needs of multiple stakeholders (linking to stakeholder theory) (Adhariani & Siregar, 2018) offers a valuable way to consider the needs of beneficiaries within organisational contexts, which contrasts rights-based and neoliberal modes of governance and organisation (Branicki, 2020).

Practices incorporating ethics of care have been considered in various contexts such as auditor independence (Reiter, 1997), regulatory reporting (Adhariani & Siregar, 2018), and accounting (Dellaportas, 2019). Here, 'connected accounting' involves the construction of accounting-related "information stemming from concern and care in the protection of others". Branicki's (2020) application of ethics of care enabled the theorisation of a radical feminist alternative to the rationalist forms of crisis management that were privileged in response to the COVID-19 pandemic. Horton (2021) considered a framework based upon ethics of care to evaluate the infrastructural and relational spaces produced by financialisation within residential care facilities for older people. At a basic level, these papers illustrate the entanglement of accounting and other rationalist techniques within a complex, interdependent, plural, and relational existence.

We draw upon ethics of care to explore alternatives to a rights-based view of non-profit organisational governance and accountability, alternatives which might better support the engagement of beneficiary stakeholders. In doing so, we remain committed to the value of rights (for example across all aspects of the United Nation's sustainable development goals). However, we acknowledge the limitations of a solely rights-based approach to ethics, where aspirational goals may do little to address the immediate or even longer-term needs of others without the power to ensure their rights are met within complex organisational contexts. One such context is NPOs providing services to beneficiaries and specifically those NPOs that provide services to older people.

Care and the engagement of beneficiary stakeholders in aged care services

Aged care services sector

We situate our conceptualisation of a care-based approach to governance within the aged care sector due to the recognised urgent need for these service providers to strengthen accountability towards their beneficiaries (Chen et al., 2022).

Authentic beneficiary engagement in the aged care sector   217

Within an Australian context, this urgent need has arisen despite the existing Australian Government's Charter of Aged Care Rights (2019) which advocates for the rights of older people including that they are free from abuse, are heard, and are listened to within institutional care contexts. Whilst formal acknowledgement of these issues is documented, policy and practice have failed to ensure these rights have been actualised. Aged care recipients represent a particularly vulnerable group of beneficiary stakeholders, and the Australian aged care sector has faced considerable scrutiny in recent years (Department of Health and Aged Care, 2023). Strengthening engagement with and accountability towards this group of beneficiary stakeholders presents a salient and pressing challenge.

Services provided within the aged care sector include support for older people to maintain independent living within their own home (home care), and residential facilities that provide full-time care (residential care) (Sutton et al., 2022). Whilst 'older people' are typically defined as 65 years or older, the average age of those in Australian residential aged care is 85 years (Australian Institute of Health and Wealth, 2021). Over half (53%) of the residents in Australian aged care facilities are living with dementia (Siette et al., 2021) and two thirds are women (Australian Institute of Health and Wealth, 2021).

In 2018 the Australian *Royal Commission into Aged Care Quality and Safety* (hereafter Royal Commission) was established following what former Australian Prime Minister Scott Morrison termed as "a *disturbing trend* of abuse and non-compliance" throughout the aged care sector (Hutchens, 2018). In the lead up to the Royal Commission being established, the *Inquiry into the Quality of Care in Residential Aged Care Facilities in Australia* was conducted. The resulting Inquiry report outlined that mistreatment of older Australians could be either direct or indirect:

> Mistreatment in this context is often referred to as 'elder abuse', which is defined by the World Health Organization (WHO) as 'a single, or repeated act, or lack of appropriate action, occurring within any relationship where there is an [unmet] expectation of trust which causes harm or distress to an older person'. Further, this abuse may be 'financial, physical, psychological and sexual ... [and] can also be the result of intentional or unintentional neglect'.
>
> (Parliament of Australia, 2018, p. 1.5)

Engagement of beneficiary stakeholders in the aged care sector

Prior to 2019, service quality within this context was predominately assessed based on clinical indicators and organisational outcomes (Chen et al., 2021; Cleland et al., 2021). In 2019 the first iteration of quality standards for aged care was introduced in Australia, and in March 2023, in response to recommendations made by the Royal Commission, revised standards were published.

Echoing international assertions of the need to prioritise individualised care and promote patient empowerment, several of the standards have themes of beneficiary empowerment, engagement, and person-centredness. Of the seven standards, 'Standard 1: The Person' and 'Standard 2: The Organisation' particularly highlight the older person as an active participant in both their own care and in contributing to the organisation, including its governance and the "design, evaluation and improvement of quality care and services" (Department of Health and Aged Care, 2023, p. 11). The person-centred care approach is included in the Revised Aged Care Quality Standards as Outcome 1.1:

> The provider understands and values the older person, including their identity, culture, ability, diversity, beliefs and life experiences. Care and services are developed with, and tailored to, the older person. Care and services are provided in a way that upholds the rights of older people and cultivates their relationships and social connections.
>
> (Department of Health and Aged Care, 2023)

Engagement enables "people to take an active role in deciding about and planning their own care" (Bastiaens et al., 2007, p. 34). Engagement and participation enable "people to influence decision-making processes and to get involved in the actions that affect their lives" (Casado et al., 2020, p. 878). However, engagement may be challenging for groups of people such as the elderly (Casado et al., 2020), especially as the way that an older person individually perceives engagement varies. Engagement may be viewed as receiving information and being part of caring relationships rather than being actively involved in decision-making (Bastiaens et al., 2007). Furthermore, the degree to which the personhood of the older person is supported, and the extent that they can express personal preferences and have these respected is considered a central indicator of quality care (Milte et al., 2016). Wishes and needs vary,[1] as does *how* the older person expresses their wishes and needs (Schweighart et al., 2022).

Within aged care contexts, caring relationships are typically close and intimate which resonates with the interdependent and relational aspects underpinning an ethic of care (Petriwskyj et al., 2018). For example, Petriwskyj et al. (2018) observed more informal and interactional forms of engagement between staff and beneficiaries which helped to build relationships and connections through everyday interactions. In that study a staff member observed beneficiaries "didn't look happy" (p. 1365), highlighting the importance of a care-based quality of engagement and observation of beneficiaries' well-being.

Formal means of engagement through evaluative opportunities include mechanisms such as complaints and compliments registers, client (beneficiary) experience surveys, and less frequently, client (beneficiary) consultation forums (Petriwskyj et al., 2018). Having a formal complaint mechanism in place is viewed as an indicator of *quality of care* (Cleland et al., 2021). However, in

Authentic beneficiary engagement in the aged care sector 219

a case study of a large Australian aged care provider, Petriwskyj et al. (2018) observed that formal mechanisms were organisation reliant and driven, where power rests with staff to act in response to feedback, rather than being client (beneficiary) driven. Studies also report aged care beneficiaries, and their families often fear potential repercussions if they raise concerns (Cleland et al., 2021; COTA Australia, 2018).

Predominately, extant literature determines quality in aged care on the basis of clinical and organisational outcome measurement, rather than what is actually of value to the residents (Milte et al., 2016). Aged care recipients are often excluded from having their voices heard (Petriwskyj et al., 2018), yet "the incorporation of the 'voice' of consumers into the concept of quality residential care is needed" (Milte et al., 2016, p. 10).

Older people are often stereotyped according to the four D's – dependency, disease, disability, and depression (Chapin & Cox, 2002) and face specific barriers restricting engagement and participation. Barriers identified by Casado et al. (2020) include:

- Exclusionary structures and institutional practices that give power and control to professionals
- Fear (due to power differences)
- Lack of confidence and distrust in own value or competence

In the same study, Casado et al. (2020) identified enablers to participation which involve a person-centred approach. These enablers include having conversations about life choices which encourage a sense of empowerment and well-being and the recognition that *even* the elderly desire autonomy. One way that older people may be involved with decision-making regarding their own care is through advance care planning. This is a co-ordinated communication and planning process that ideally captures the older person's values and their preferences for future decision-making when they are no longer able to (Detering et al., 2019).

The voices of older people (along with carers and practitioners) and their lived experiences were prioritised in a two-year participatory action research project conducted by Andrews et al. (2020). The research responded to a range of identified challenges facing older people with high-support needs, including challenges around: sharing responsibility with older people (e.g., in making decisions and promoting collective well-being), strengthening the individual and collective voice of older people, and recognising that 'little things' as well as significant innovations can make a big difference (Andrews et al., 2020, p. 601). The research used dialogue and storytelling to facilitate the involvement of older people in care. Whilst the project initially followed a learning, evaluation, and planning (LEAP) framework[2] it also allowed for unplanned fluid developments and adopted a 'community of enquiry' approach that involved a range of stakeholders. The researchers describe that many of the positive outcomes[3] "came about through a responsive, dialogic and emergent approach" (Andrews et al., 2020, p. 609).

Care within the aged care sector

The consideration that organisational rules and policies (in keeping with a rights-based approach) may be at odds with care-based needs is discussed by Molterer et al. (2020) who identify this as two different *logics of care* (a *professional* logic of care and a *relational* logic of care). Findings from the ethnographic field study conducted in a residential aged care facility consider ways to integrate day-to-day needs of the older person. Molterer et al. (2020) suggest that neither logic of care is good nor bad and that often a negotiation is required, termed a 'tinkering process' which is defined as "a matter of 'intuitive deliberation', 'situated assessment' and/or 'affective juggling' between different care practices and their inherent 'goods'" (Molterer et al., 2020, p. 96). These findings support the value of both ethics of care and ethics of rights approaches when considering engagement of and accountability to older people in aged care contexts.

Bowers et al. (2001) identified three definitions of care: care-as-service; care-as-relating; and care-as-comfort. Aged care residents viewing care-as-service were more likely to make verbal complaints to the supervisory staff when they grew impatient with waiting, which resulted in temporary staff responsiveness despite potentially annoying care staff (Bowers et al., 2001). Residents who viewed care-as-relational appeared less likely to make complaints, however when reacting to wait times they were more likely to strengthen interpersonal relationships by undertaking tasks independently, even at the risk of physically endangering themselves. The third group of residents, those viewing care-as-comfort, were also unlikely to make complaints. For assistance in meeting basic needs such as toileting, or making adjustments (e.g., moving a pillow or changing the temperature), these "residents often selected 'waiting until I can't stand it' as the most reasonable, albeit agonising option" (Bowers et al., 2001, p. 544). Hence, engaging with, and understanding beneficiaries' perspectives of care along with their unique care preferences is essential in order to provide effective care.

Different understandings of care also correspond to differences in how aged care beneficiaries might provide evaluations of the services they receive and how they are understood and subsequently labelled within organisations (Bowers et al., 2001). For example, when care is viewed as a purchased service, beneficiaries might be understood and referred to as customers or clients; whereas when care is understood as relational, beneficiaries might be understood as participants. Further nuance to the labelling of beneficiaries arises in response to the different service provision types. For example, where beneficiaries live in residential care services, they might be referred to as residents, whereas the same service provider might consider their in-home beneficiaries to be clients.

Regardless of the 'label', the principle statement guiding *Stakeholder engagement* in ISO 37000:2021 is that "the governing body should ensure that the organization's stakeholders are appropriately engaged, and their expectations considered" (p. 12). Yet the discussion above highlights the multifaceted engagement needs of older people in aged care contexts, the difficulty of understanding their expectations, and the complexity of knowing what 'appropriate' engagement looks like. What is clear, however, is the importance (and frequent lack) of appropriate care within this sector.

Person-centred care terminology was introduced by Kitwood (1993, 1997) and represents a shift away from a task-focussed biomedical approach (Seah et al., 2022; Yee et al., 2021). The term was initially used when referring to the care of people living with dementia and emphasises relationships and communication, "the maintenance of personhood as being central" (Brooker, 2003, p. 12). Observing that person-centred care was interpreted in varying ways across different contexts, Brooker (2003) developed the Values, Individualised, Perspective, Social (VIPS) framework. This refers to: a 'value' base, an 'individualised' approach, understanding the personal 'perspective', and promotion of the 'social psychology' or 'social environment' (Brooker, 2012; Seah et al., 2022). To mitigate the possibility of the person being "viewed as an individual static object" (Tieu et al., 2022, p. 1), person-centred care must "be based on a dynamic concept of personhood that integrates the relevant social, relational, temporal and biographical dimensions" (Tieu et al., 2022, p. 1).

Literature across the human services sector emphasises the importance of a person-centred approach to care (World Health Organization, 2018). The phrase *quality of care* is often used synonymously with person-centred care (Chen et al., 2021), with a person-centred focus in delivering care contributing to its quality. An expected outcome of quality of care is increased quality of life (Alonazi & Thomas, 2014); quality of care being the extent to which health-based services "increase the likelihood of desired health outcomes" (World Health Organization, n.d.). To achieve quality of care, services should be effective, safe, and people-centred. To be optimally beneficial, care should be timely, efficient, equitable, and integrated (Chen et al., 2021; World Health Organization, n.d.). The components of quality can be conceptualised as dimensions that are in relation to each other (Malley et al., 2019). Whilst people-centred (as a quality dimension) is described as a "positive experience that is both caring and responsive", effectiveness is understood as "care that promotes a good quality of life and is based on best practice" (Malley et al., 2019, p. 1). Malley et al. (2019) assert that understanding the relationship between dimensions is helpful from both a policy and a practice perspective to balance experiences of care with quality of life outcomes, and to maximise any one of the dimensions may require a degree of trade-off.

In a literature review examining *quality of care* indicators for older people living in aged care, Cleland et al. (2021) identified nine key themes:

- Respect and dignity
- Spiritual, cultural, religious, and sexual identity
- Aged care staff skills
- Relationships with aged care staff
- Informed choices
- Social relationships and the community
- Supporting older people's health and well-being
- Safety and comfort
- Ability to make complaints and provide feedback

In terms of beneficiary stakeholder engagement, these themes emphasise the importance of relationships (including with aged care staff and the community), and the ability to be involved with informal evaluations (e.g., making complaints or providing feedback). Hence, quality of life is enhanced through recognising and respecting an individual's identity and care needs, including the need to be heard.

A care-based accountability and stakeholder engagement framework

Figure 12.1 presents a traditional organisation-centric framework for understanding non-profit accountability. This framework depicts different directions of stakeholder accountability as inwardly, upwardly, sideways, and downwardly to the beneficiary stakeholder group. We contend that this way of viewing non-profit

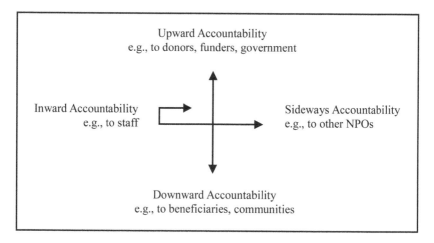

Figure 12.1 Directions of accountability (adapted from Kingston et al., 2020)

Authentic beneficiary engagement in the aged care sector 223

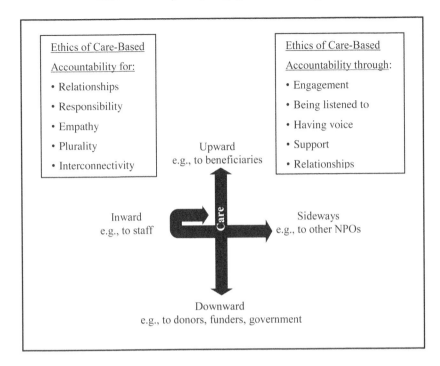

Figure 12.2 A care-based accountability framework for enhanced engagement of beneficiaries

accountability is embedded within a predominantly economic perspective from where the need for rights often arises. Here accountability presents as hierarchical, universal, and rational. We seek to challenge this view of NPO accountability and to instead embed accountability within perspectives of care. This is particularly important given care is a largely missing element from formal understandings of organisational governance and accountability.

Figure 12.2 illustrates a variation to the traditional NPO accountability framework when viewed from a perspective that prioritises beneficiaries and a care-based focus of accountability to them. Prioritising care changes the positioning of stakeholders such that beneficiaries move to the upward position, where care is most pressing. The reconsideration of accountability directions aligns with the prioritisation of mission, the reason NPOs exist, and explicitly emphasises the importance of care within the broader mission focus.

Repositioning traditionally more powerful stakeholders such as government, funders, and regulators to a downward accountability position reflects the different focus of this accountability. From this care-based focus, if an NPO's mission is achieved and its services are effectively delivered with the appropriate level of care, downward accountability would then involve reporting this to the

224   *K. Kingston, S. Rossi, B. Luke, and A. Williamson*

downward stakeholder groups. Thus, consideration of accountability where care is prioritised, rather than economic power, facilitates reassessment regarding accountability directions and priorities.

Within Figure 12.2, *processes* of beneficiary accountability and what an NPO becomes accountable *for* from a care-based perspective are also considered. Here beneficiary accountability becomes enabled through engagement, having a voice that is listened to and acted upon, support, and relationships. Care-based accountability moves towards organisations being accountable for the relationships they enable, their responsibility for care and empathy, and their fostering of plurality and interconnectivity. This framework supports enhanced governance through prioritising stakeholder engagement (accountability 'through').

Considering accountability from a care-based perspective has implications for theory and NPO practice. Implications for theory include not only the repositioning of beneficiary (and other) stakeholders within directional understandings of accountability but also a reassessment of how accountability to them might be more effectively addressed. In particular, an ethics of care involves a relational approach to accountability, based on genuinely relating to another. It reflects accountability to mission, and considers accountability for the other (Roberts, 1991), based on their needs and terms.

Implications for NPOs in practice include the consideration of care through a lens of ethics which combines the apparent simplicity of attending to the needs of others with a sense of duty or intended purpose. This conceptual combination reminds us of the importance of aged care services providing both a fundamental principle (care) and an ethical stance typically associated with professional services.

Conclusion

NPOs are accountable to many different stakeholder groups. Focussing on directions of accountability based on economic flows through an organisation (e.g., in Figure 12.1) risks overlooking other ways accountability might be prioritised, and consideration of the importance of accountability for what and through what means. This chapter has highlighted the importance of considering beneficiary accountability through the lens of an ethics of care, to foster organisational governance that values relationships and responsibility, to foster beneficiary engagement.

Whilst neoliberal principles and the valuation of rights are well established, there is also an acknowledgement that policy and practice have not achieved the intended outcomes in sectors such as aged care. Similar concerns have been noted in a wide range of social and environmental issues. Seeing things differently, through a prioritisation of care, and adoption of an ethics of care lens has the potential to change this. Yet the process of change relies not only on seeing things differently, but also doing things differently, and this chapter hopes to provoke such thought and action. This presents great scope for further research

Authentic beneficiary engagement in the aged care sector 225

embedded within organisational contexts to understand how NPOs are able to meet the needs of their beneficiaries such that care-based accountability flows.

Clearly the importance of care is not restricted to the aged care sector. It is arguable that care is at the core of most NPOs, whether that be human care in childcare, education, healthcare, or disability care sectors, or animal or environmental care across other sectors. For this reason, the care-based framework for accountability developed within this chapter has potential significance beyond aged care settings and offers opportunities for further research to enable it to be refined and embedded in practice. Further research could seek to explore what care means to beneficiaries within different non-profit sectors. After all, how care-based accountability is actualised across the non-profit sector will be necessarily different and dependent upon individual contexts.

Notes

1 Schweighart et al. (2020) identified the following 12 wishes and needs of older people: (1) activities, leisure, and daily routine; (2) autonomy, independence, choice, and control; (3) death, dying, and end-of-life; (4) economics; (5) environment, structural conditions, meals, and food; (6) health condition; (7) medication, care, treatment, and hygiene; (8) peer relationship, company, and social contact; (9) privacy; (10) psychological and emotional aspects, security, and safety; (11) religion, spirituality; and (12) sexuality.
2 The LEAP framework includes an exchange model of assessment which was used which balanced the views of service beneficiaries, relatives, the organisation, and multidisciplinary assessors in a four-part exchange with the following stages: (1) exchange information, (2) negotiate, (3) agree outcomes, and (4) record outcomes.
3 Outcomes of the project included pinpointing organisational policies that were at odds with the research findings (i.e., evidence from the older persons and from the frontline staff perspectives). This is prompting organisational policy change. Further the project outcomes result in the development of a new approach called the Developing Evidence-Enriched Practice (DEEP) approach which has since been adapted in several social care contexts in Wales.

References

Adhariani, D., & Siregar, S. V. (2018). How deep is your care? Analysis of corporations' "caring level" and impact on earnings volatility from the ethics of care perspective. *Australasian Accounting, Business and Finance Journal, 12*(4), 43–59. http://dx.doi.org/10.14453/aabfj.v12i4.4

Alonazi, W. B., & Thomas, S. A. (2014). Quality of care and quality of life: Convergence or divergence? *Health Services Insights, 7.* http://doi.org/10.4137/HSI.S13283

Andrews, N., Gabbay, J., Le-May, A., Miller, E., Petch, A., & O'Neill, M. (2020). Story, dialogue and caring about what matters to people: Progress towards evidence-enriched policy and practice. *Evidence & Policy, 16*(4), 597–618. https://doi.org/10.1332/174426420X15825349063428

Australian Government, Aged Care Quality and Safety Commission. (2019). *Charter of Aged Care Rights.* https://www.agedcarequality.gov.au/older-australians/your-rights/charter-aged-care-rights

Australian Institute of Health and Wealth. (2021). *Aged care*. Australian Government. https://www.aihw.gov.au/reports/australias-welfare/aged-care

Aye, Y. M., Liew, S., Neo, S. X., Li, W., Ng, H.-L., Chua, S.-T., Zhou, W.-T., Au, W.-L., Tan, E.-K., & Tay, K.-Y. (2020). Patient-centric care for Parkinson's disease: From hospital to the community. *Frontiers in Neurology, 11*, 502. https://doi.org/10.3389/fneur.2020.00502

Bastiaens, H., Van Royen, P., Pavlic, D. R., Raposo, V., & Baker, R. (2007). Older people's preferences for involvement in their own care: A qualitative study in primary health care in 11 European countries. *Patient Education and Counseling, 68*(1), 33–42. https://doi.org/10.1016/j.pec.2007.03.025

Bowers, B. J., Fibich, B., & Jacobson, N. (2001). Care-as-service, care-as-relating, care-as-comfort: Understanding nursing home residents' definitions of quality. *The Gerontologist, 41*(4), 539–545. https://doi.org/10.1093/geront/41.4.539

Branicki, L. J. (2020). COVID-19, ethics of care and feminist crisis management. *Gender, Work & Organization, 27*(5), 872–883. https://doi.org/10.1111/gwao.12491

British Standards Institute. (2021). *BS ISO 37000:2021: Governance of organizations. Guidance*. British Standards Institute.

Brooker, D. (2003). What is person-centred care in dementia? *Reviews in Clinical Gerontology, 13*(3), 215–222. https://doi.org/10.1017/S095925980400108X

Brooker, D. (2012). Understanding dementia and the person behind the diagnostic label. *International Journal of Person Centered Medicine, 2*(1), 11–17. https://doi.org/10.5750/ijpcm.v2i1.167

Casado, T., Sousa, L., & Touza, C. (2020). Older people's perspective about their participation in health care and social care services: A systematic review. *Journal of Gerontological Social Work, 63*(8), 878–892. https://doi.org/10.1080/01634372.2020.1816591

Carstens, D. (2020). *An ethics of immanence: Posthumanism and the politics of care*. In Bozalek, V., Zembylas, M., & Tronto, J. C. (Eds.), *Posthuman and political care ethics for reconfiguring higher education pedagogies* (pp. 79–90). Routledge.

Chapin, R., & Cox, E. O. (2002). Changing the paradigm: Strengths-based and empowerment-oriented social work with frail elders. *Journal of Gerontological Social Work, 36*(3–4), 165–179. https://doi.org/10.1300/J083v36n03_13

Chen, G., Ratcliffe, J., Milte, R., Khadka, J., & Kaambwa, B. (2021). Quality of care experience in aged care: An Australia-wide discrete choice experiment to elicit preference weights. *Social Science & Medicine, 289*, 114440. https://doi.org/10.1016/j.socscimed.2021.114440

Chen, J., Harrison, G., & Jiao, L. (2022). Rights-based accountability in aged care organisations: The roles of beliefs and boundary controls. *Australian Journal of Public Administration, 81*(3), 492–511. https://doi.org/10.1111/1467-8500.12538

Cleland, J., Hutchinson, C., Khadka, J., Milte, R., & Ratcliffe, J. (2021). What defines quality of care for older people in aged care? A comprehensive literature review. *Geriatrics & Gerontology International, 21*(9), 765–778. https://doi.org/10.1111/ggi.14231

COTA Australia. (2018). *Project report: Measuring quality and consumer choice in aged care*. https://policycommons.net/artifacts/3686815/project-report/4492734/

Dellaportas, S. (2019). The role of accounting in mediating empathic care for the "other". *Accounting, Auditing & Accountability Journal, 32*(6), 1617–1635. https://doi.org/10.1108/AAAJ-02-2017-2860

Department of Health and Aged Care. (2023). *Revised aged care quality standards: Draft for Pilot*. https://www.health.gov.au/sites/default/files/2023-05/strengthened-aged-care-quality-standards-pilot-program.pdf

Detering, K. M., Buck, K., Sellars, M., Kelly, H., Sinclair, C., White, B., & Nolte, L. (2019). Prospective multicentre cross-sectional audit among older Australians accessing health and residential aged care services: Protocol for a national advance care directive prevalence study. *BMJ Open, 9*(10), e031691. http://dx.doi.org/10.1136/bmjopen-2019-031691

Gilligan, C. (1993). *In a different voice: Psychological theory and women's development.* Harvard University Press.

Hadadian-Chaghaei, F., Haghani, F., Taleghani, F., Feizi, A., & Alimohammadi, N. (2022). Nurses as gifted artists in caring: An analysis of nursing care concept. *Iranian Journal of Nursing and Midwifery Research, 27*(2), 125–133. https://doi.org/10.4103/ijnmr.ijnmr_465_20

Horton, A. (2021). Liquid home? Financialisation of the built environment in the UK's "hotel-style" care homes. *Transactions of the Institute of British Geographers, 46*(1), 179–192. https://doi.org/10.1111/tran.12410

Hutchens, G. (2018). *Scott Morrison announces royal commission into aged care after string of scandals.* https://www.theguardian.com/australia-news/2018/sep/16/morrison-to-announce-royal-commission-into-aged-care-after-string-of-scandals#:~:text=The%20Morrison%20government%20will%20establish,nursing%20homes%20across%20the%20country

ISO Technical Committee. (2022). *ISO 3700:2021 governance of organizations – Guidance.* British Standards Institute. https://committee.iso.org/files/live/sites/tc309/files/ISO%2037000%20slides/ISO%2037000%20Governance%20of%20organizations%20-%20Guidance%20-%20v1%202022%20web.pdf

Johansson, J., & Wickström, A. (2023). Constructing a 'Different' strength: A feminist exploration of vulnerability, ethical agency and care. *Journal of Business Ethics, 184*(2), 317–331. https://doi.org/10.1007/s10551-022-05121-1

Kingston, K. L., Furneaux, C., de Zwaan, L., & Alderman, L. (2020). From monologic to dialogic: Accountability of nonprofit organisations on beneficiaries' terms. *Accounting, Auditing & Accountability Journal, 33*(2), 447–471. https://doi.org/10.1108/aaaj-01-2019-3847

Kitwood, T. (1993). Towards a theory of dementia care: The interpersonal process. *Ageing & Society, 13*(1), 51–67. https://doi.org/10.1017/S0144686X00000647

Kitwood, T. (1997). *Dementia reconsidered: The person comes first.* Open University Press.

Kitwood, T. (2012). Dementia reconsidered: the person comes first. In J. Katz, S. Peace, & S. Spurr (Eds.), *Adult lives: A life course perspective* (1st ed., pp. 89–99). Bristol University Press. https://doi.org/10.2307/j.ctt1t895q0.15

Malley, J., D'Amico, F., & Fernandez, J.-L. (2019). What is the relationship between the quality of care experience and quality of life outcomes? Some evidence from long-term home care in England... *Social Science & Medicine, 243*, 112635. https://doi.org/10.1016/j.socscimed.2019.112635

Marini, L., Andrew, J., & van der Laan, S. (2017). Tools of accountability: Protecting microfinance clients in South Africa? *Accounting, Auditing & Accountability Journal, 30*(6), 1344–1369. https://doi.org/10.1108/AAAJ-04-2016-2548

Miller, C. (2002). Toward a self-regulatory form of accountability in the voluntary sector. *Policy & Politics, 30*(4), 551–566. https://doi.org/10.1332/030557302760590378

Milte, R., Shulver, W., Killington, M., Bradley, C., Ratcliffe, J., & Crotty, M. (2016). Quality in residential care from the perspective of people living with dementia: The importance of personhood... *Archives of Gerontology and Geriatrics, 63*, 9–17. https://doi.org/10.1016/j.archger.2015.11.007

Molterer, K., Hoyer, P., & Steyaert, C. (2020). A practical ethics of care: Tinkering with different 'Goods' in residential nursing homes. *Journal of Business Ethics, 165*(1), 95–111. https://doi.org/10.1007/s10551-018-04099-z

Najam, A. (1996). NGO accountability: A conceptual framework. *Development Policy Review, 14*(4), 339–354. https://doi.org/10.1111/.1467-7679.1996.tb00112.x

O'Leary, S. (2017). Grassroots accountability promises in rights-based approaches to development: The role of transformative monitoring and evaluation in NGOs... *Accounting, Organizations and Society, 63,* 21–41. https://doi.org/10.1016/j.aos.2016.06.002

Parliament of Australia. (2018). *Inquiry into the Quality of Care in Residential Aged Care Facilities in Australia.* Retrieved from https://www.aph.gov.au/Parliamentary_Business/Committees/House/Health_Aged_Care_and_Sport/AgedCareFacilities/Report/section?id=committees%2freportrep%2f024167%2f25942

Petriwskyj, A., Gibson, A., & Webby, G. (2018). What does client 'engagement' mean in aged care? An analysis of practice. *Ageing and Society, 38*(7), 1350–1376. https://doi.org/10.1017/S0144686X17000095

Productivity Commission. (2017). *Impacts of health recommendations, shifting the dial: 5 year productivity review, supporting paper No. 6.* Retrieved from https://www.pc.gov.au/inquiries/completed/productivity-review/report

Raghuram, P., Madge, C., & Noxolo, P. (2009). Rethinking responsibility and care for a postcolonial world. *Geoforum, 40*(1), 5–13. https://doi.org/10.1016/j.geoforum.2008.07.007

Reiter, S. (1997). The ethics of care and new paradigms for accounting practice. *Accounting, Auditing & Accountability Journal, 10*(3), 299–324. https://doi.org/10.1108/09513579710178098

Rentfro, R., & Hooks, K. L. (2006). Ethics of care and decisions of financial statement preparers to manage earnings. In *Research on professional responsibility and ethics in accounting* (Vol. 11, pp. 127–148). Emerald Group Publishing Limited.

Roberts, J. (1991). The possibilities of accountability. *Accounting, Organizations and Society, 16*(4), 355–368. https://doi.org/10.1016/0361-3682(91)90027-C

Schweighart, R., O'Sullivan, J. L., Klemmt, M., Teti, A., & Neuderth, S. (2022). Wishes and needs of nursing home residents: A scoping review. *Healthcare, 10*(5), 84. https://doi.org/10.3390/healthcare10050854

Seah, S. S. L., Chenoweth, L., & Brodaty, H. (2022). Person-centred Australian residential aged care services: How well do actions match the claims? *Ageing & Society, 42*(12), 2914–2939. https://doi.org/10.1017/S0144686X21000374

Siette, J., Knaggs, G. T., Zurynski, Y., Ratcliffe, J., Dodds, L., & Westbrook, J. (2021). Systematic review of 29 self-report instruments for assessing quality of life in older adults receiving aged care services. *BMJ Open, 11*(11), e050892. https://doi:10.1136/bmjopen-2021-050892

Sutton, N., Ma, N., Yang, J. S., Lewis, R., Brown, D., Woods, M., McEwen, C., & Parker, D. (2022). *Australia's aged care sector: Full-year report (2021–22).* UTS Ageing Research Collaborative, The University of Technology Sydney. http://hdl.handle.net/10453/163697

The British Standards Institution. (2021). *Governance of organizations – Guidance (BS ISO 37000).* https://bsol.bsigroup.com/Search/Search?searchKey=ISO+37000&OriginPage=Header+Search+Box&autoSuggestion=false

Thompson, S. (2022). *Caring housing futures: A radical care framework for understanding rent control politics in Seattle,* USA. *Antipode...* https://doi.org/10.1111/anti.12874

Tieu, M., Mudd, A., Conroy, T., Pinero de Plaza, A., & Kitson, A. (2022). The trouble with personhood and person-centred care. *Nursing Philosophy, 23*(3), e12381. https://doi.org/10.1111/nup.12381

Tronto, J. (2008). The ethics of care: Personal, political, and global. By Virginia Held. New York: Oxford University Press, 2006. *Hypatia, 23*(1), 211–217. https://doi:10.1017/S0887536700017876

Tronto, J. C. (1998). An ethic of care. *Generations Journal, 22*(3), 15–20. https://www.proquest.com/scholarly-journals/ethic-care/docview/1990240640/se-2?accountid=13380

World Health Organization. (2018). *Delivering quality health services: A global imperative.* OECD Publishing. https://www.who.int/publications/i/item/9789241513906

World Health Organization. (n.d.). *Quality of care.* Retrieved September 26, from https://www.who.int/health-topics/quality-of-care#tab=tab_1

Yasmin, S., Ghafran, C., & Haslam, J. (2021). Centre-staging beneficiaries in charity accountability: Insights from an Islamic post-secular perspective. *Critical Perspectives on Accounting, 75.* https://doi.org/10.1016/j.cpa.2020.102167

Yee, J., Souza, M., Horta, N., & Kartoz, C. (2021). Person-centered care for older adults living in long-term care facilities: A systematic literature review. *Journal of Public Health Issues and Practices, 5*(2), 184.

Conclusion

Guillaume Plaisance and Anne Goujon Belghit

At the end of this book, we are convinced that to develop governance in non-profit organisations (NPOs), practitioners and scholars will find here an original and comprehensive approach based on 12 analytical frameworks. This book indeed had three main aims.

The first was academic: to offer empirical and conceptual studies in order to construct analytical frameworks dedicated to NPOs. They should enable scholars interested in the subject to position their research on the basis of these propositions. Our book offers a set of 12 frameworks that cover all the dimensions of ISO 37000:2021 and provide a new perspective on the notion of governance. These 12 frameworks are intended to be discussed, used, adapted, challenged and tested by scholars in our field of research. We hope that all disciplines concerned with NPOs, such as economics, management science, sociology, political science and many others, will be able to use our proposals to shed new light on the theoretical and practical issues that governance raises for NPOs.

Our second objective was aimed at practitioners, as we wanted to provide frameworks for reflection for professionals in the non-profit sector to facilitate the management and development of governance processes. However, these frameworks should not fall into the easy trap of best practices. It is our hope that these 12 frameworks will enable organisations themselves to reflect on their practices and possibly lead to the adoption of governance structures and processes that are more appropriate to their organisational reality. Once again, these 12 frameworks can be re-discussed and debated by professionals and the non-profit sector, which will undoubtedly be able to enrich them and advance knowledge of the sector.

Finally, this book had a major scientific objective, which is to operationalise and adapt the various dimensions of ISO 37000:2021 to the governance of NPOs. To our knowledge, this international standard has hardly been used in the non-profit sector. However, its ambitions in terms of adaptability and consideration of contingencies are clearly in line with the challenges and difficulties that the sector may face. We hope, therefore, that this book will be the first step in the re-appropriation by NPOs of international standards usually adopted

DOI: 10.4324/9781003460572-18

Conclusion 231

by the public sector or the private for-profit sector. It is worth noting the efforts made by international standard setters to take into account, at least in ISO 37000:2021, specific contexts such as NPOs.

Table C.1 summarises, for each of the chapters, the different dimensions covered by ISO 37000:2021 and the proposed frameworks.

This book is more than a scientific and practical reflection on non-profit governance. By bringing together authors from different backgrounds, who jointly propose original and innovative points of view on the different dimensions of organisational governance as it is understood today by ISO 37000:2021, we wanted to contribute to the evolution of the paradigm dedicated to NPOs.

Part I demonstrated that NPOs and their governance cannot be based solely on the traditional vision of control. It is a special sector in the sense that it has fewer resources than other sectors and its organisational methods are fundamentally different from those of the public sector or the private for-profit sector. The chapters in this section began by arguing for collaboration between the actors involved in NPOs and, of course, between the organisation itself and its stakeholders. These chapters have also argued for comprehension, on the one hand, of the sector, which cannot be treated like any other (because it has a strong social and societal impact, but also because its resources and operations are specific), and on the other hand, of each of the organisations, which face strong contingencies. Finally, these chapters have argued in favour of adaptation, so that stakeholders, as powerful as they may be, recognise that the demands made upon other private for-profit organisations, for example, are not always applicable to all NPOs. It is also important to recognise the polarisations and differences within the sector. In short, the main lesson from Part I is to adapt and adjust to the specific characteristics of the non-profit sector.

This paradigm shift suggests moving away from a control-based approach to a cognitive and behavioural vision of NPOs. This implies a number of changes in practice. Part II looks in more detail at how this paradigm shift is being implemented. This means moving away from the dynamics of regulation and towards much more differentiated strategies specific to each organisation. The chapters in Part II look at translation practices, mergers that enable organisations to meet requirements and the value of collaboration in evaluating an organisation. It is only on the basis of these new practices that the impact of NPOs will increase.

The affirmation of this fact raises a number of questions. What is value creation? What is performance? What is impact in the non-profit sector? Part III proposed to reflect on these questions and to try to understand the new dimensions of performance implied by this paradigm shift. The challenge is not simply to ensure financial viability, but to move towards stabilisation in order to achieve a form of sustainability. There is also a need to recognise the importance of the responsibilities of NPOs, which can become models for organisations in other sectors. However, we need to be careful of the semantic inflation that surrounds these issues, which is why it has been necessary to understand and study the

Table C.1 Statement of the dimensions of ISO 37000:2021 covered by the chapters and the proposed frameworks

Chapter	ISO 37000:2021	Framework
From traditional to collaborative governance: A stakeholder environment framework	Oversight	A better understanding of collaborative governance mechanisms and their relevance to NPOs
Implementing and maintaining an effective risk management system in non-profit organisations: A conceptual framework	Risk governance	A diamond dedicated to risk management in the non-profit sector
The role of public actors in the governance of French non-profit organisations: Proposing an integrated governance analysis framework	Effective performance Ethical behaviour Responsible stewardship	Towards the co-construction of governance mechanisms, between disciplinary issues and a cognitive approach
New rules: How funding and control tools shape the relationships between social actions actors	Stakeholder engagement Viability and performance over time	Finding a better balance between governance and performance in contractual relations between funders and NPOs
What strategic processes to meet the challenges of democratic governance? The case of mergers between NPOs	Strategy	Revisiting the strategic process in NPOs using a problematisation approach
Alliances for outcome evaluation and theory of change to generate impact: Integrating network level and organisational level effort via organisational learning	Value generation Stakeholder engagement Data and decisions	The renewal of evaluation in the non-profit sector, thanks to a collaborative approach that values learning
Drama-free finance: Structures and strategies for stability and growth in non-profit organisations	Viability and performance over time	Stabilising NPOs and their funding to enable their potential growth (and thus increase their positive impact on communities and society)
Double or tandem movement? The emergence and evolution of non-profit social responsibility	Social responsibility	An articulation of emerging requirements for NPOs, particularly in terms of responsibilities
Social responsibility and sustainability in non-profit organisations: Towards a semantic and conceptual precision	Social responsibility Viability and performance over time	A conceptual puzzle about performance, based on the notions of viability, social responsibility, sustainability and OSR
How to retain volunteers? A literature review and a managerial proposal of a volunteer journey	Viability and performance over time	A model that promotes long-term volunteering
Why meaning-making capabilities for non-profit executives? Understanding the nature of non-profit leadership between the general and middle-range approaches	Leadership	An explicitation of meaning-making capabilities for non-profit executives in theory and practice
Authentic beneficiary engagement in the aged care sector: Advancing non-profit governance through care	Accountability	A care-based accountability framework for enhanced engagement of beneficiaries

difference between organisational social responsibility practices, the concept of social responsibility and sustainability.

However, all these changes, all these developments in practice as well as in thinking and philosophy, can only be achieved if people are involved, mobilised and committed to NPOs. Part IV has therefore sought to understand and study human capital and people. Leadership adapted to the non-profit context, human resource practices that consider human capital as people before considering them as resource providers, accountability that goes beyond a purely regulatory, disciplinary or control-based vision to offer beneficiaries a new way of expressing themselves – these are the different dimensions that the chapters in Part IV have proposed to study. They constitute the conditions that must be met in order to achieve the paradigm shift proposed in this book. Beneficiaries and society remain the compass of NPOs. In this respect, the whole of non-profit governance is being rethought in terms of its processes, its operations, its actors, its goals, its objectives and its purpose.

Perhaps we can even hope that these reflections dedicated to NPOs can inspire the work and practices dedicated to business and the public sector. As organisations face ever more profound and disruptive challenges, the non-profit sector undoubtedly has much to contribute, not only in managing these changes but also in helping other organisations in their transitions.

Index

Note: Page numbers in **bold** and *italics* refer to tables and figures, respectively.

absorptive capacity 101
accountability 13, 48, 49, 52–54; directions of *222*; to stakeholders 100
accounting standards 17, 70
active learning 110
actorhood 149
actor-network theory (ANT). 84
adaptation 9
adverse selection 56
advocacy-based social impact 107
aged care services 216–222; in Australia 216–217; barriers in 219; care within 220–222; caring relationships and 218; engagement of beneficiary stakeholders 217–220; mistreatment in 217; quality in 220; standards for 218
agency theory 9, 50
Agle, B. R. 14
Ajzen, I. 184
Al-Amri, K. 33
alignment leadership 201–202
alignment theory of change, non-profit learning through 112–113
Allison, L. D. 182
Amslem, T. 72
Anderson, J. R. 204
Andre-Clark, A. 198
Andreini, D. 154, 157
Andrews, N. 219–220
Anheier, H. K. 1
Arnold, V. 33
Arshad, R. 36
auditing 57
auditing standards 17

Australian Government's Charter of Aged Care Rights (2019) 217
Australian *Royal Commission into Aged Care Quality and Safety* (2018) 217

Bales, K. 183
Bansal, P. 156
Basecamp 112
Bauersfeld, H. 202
Beaujolin-Bellet, R. 85
Belghit, G. 1
Believing in Forever 111
beneficiary stakeholders: engagement in aged care services 214, 216–222; ethics of care 214–216; relationships with 213
benefit corporations 149
benefits theory 126
Berlan, D. 199, 201
Berle, A. 2
Bernet, J. 72
Bivona, E. 156
Blau, P. 2
Boisselier. P. 66
Bowen, H. 143
Bowers, B. J. 220
Bowman, W. 125
Branicki, L. J. 216
Brooker, D. 221
Brouard, F. 10
Brower, R. S. 198
Bryson, J. M. 196, 200
Bui, D. G. 37
Bundy, J. 34

Index 235

capital projects budgeting 131
Carama, D. 111
care: within aged care services
220–222; definitions of 220;
different understandings of 220–221;
person-centred 221
care-based accountability framework *222*,
222–224, *223*
career management 182
Carlson, M. 199
Carroll, A. B. 158
Casado, T. 219
cash flow management 127
cash reserves 127–129, **128**
catalyst theory of change 104;
non-profit learning through 112
Chandler, A. 2, 65
Charreaux, G. 62
Chatman, J. A. 37
Chelladurai, P. 156, 157
Chen, J. 32–33, 37
Chevalier, V. 179
Chiapello, È. 70
clarifying needs 189
Clary, E. G. 181–183
Cleave, S. 182
Cleland, J. 222
Clerkin, R. M. 107
Cnaan, R. A. 181
cognitive approach of governance 9,
50–51
collaboration 9, 35, 41
collaborative governance 60; barriers
of 24–25; definition of 13, **19**, 19–20;
engaging forum 23; examples of 24;
fragmentation of accountability 24–25;
high transaction costs 24; ingredients
of 20–23; interdependency 21;
joint purpose and motivation 21;
leadership, engagement and commitment
to 22; loss of autonomy 24–25;
mechanism framework 25, *25*; need
for organisations to collaborate 18–19;
other ingredients 23; power balance
and sharing 22; resources and capacity
23; system and process of 20, 23–24;
trusting relationship 21–22
Committee Of Sponsoring Organisation
of the Treadway Commission (COSO)
31; latest version of 32
communication 35

communication strategies 101
communities of practices 108–109
comprehension 9
connected accounting 216
consistency 36
constructive-developmental theory
of leadership 195, 202–204
constructivism scholarship 204
contextual astuteness 205
cooperation 35
Cooper, K. R. 103
coordination capacity 205
Cornelius, N. 156
Cornforth, C. 3
corporate entities 148
corporate social responsibility (CSR) 32,
140, 143–144; mediating effect of 34;
roles in 145–147, **146**
cost savings 33
COVID-19 1, 103, 125, 216
Crosby, B. C. 196, 200
cross-sector learning 108–109
"C type" corporations 149
culturally sustainable development 157–158

data collection 100; for performance
evaluation 106–107
Davydov, Y. 33
Day, D. V. 203–204
De Andrés-Alonso, P. 58
decision to volunteer 186; demographic
characteristics 186; individual
variables 186; organisational
variable 186
declarative knowledge 204, 207
democratic actions 71
de Quevedo-Puente, E. 34
DeRue, D. S. 195
directions of accountability *222*
directive leadership 195
disciplinary approach of governance 50
Dixit, S. K. 157
Dobbs, S. M. 198–199
Doctors without Borders 141
Donnelly-Cox, G. xvi
Donohoe, M. 199
double loop learning 101–102;
and theory of change 109–113
double movement 140–143, *141*, *142*
dual accountability system 198;
leadership roles in 198–199

236 *Index*

Duchek, S. 123
Dym, B. 196, 201

economic dimension 120
education reform 104–105
elder abuse 217
Elkington, J. 158
emergency (or "operating") reserves 129–130
endowment funds 130–132; capital projects budgeting 131; internal control 131–132; moving average payout from 130–131, **131**; windfall policy 130
engagement: of beneficiary stakeholders in aged care services 217–220; complaints and compliments in 219–220; formal means of 219–220; *see also* stakeholder engagement
engaging forum 23
enterprise risk management (ERM) 29; COSO's definition of 32; degree of maturity of 32; essential components of 31–32; holistic approach to 30–32; link between value creation and 34; modern portfolio theory 31; quality of 34; research in implementation of 32–34; risk culture 37–38; use of external experts and 36
entrepreneurship *vs.* fears of marketisation 125–126
environmental dimension 120
ethics of care 214–216; application of 216; framework upon 216; practices incorporating 216; qualities of **215**, 215–216; rights-based approach to 216
executive centrality in social construction 202
executive leader 203
executive succession 197
expressive accountability 198
external governance mechanisms 13, 16–17
external stakeholders 103
Exxon 144

Fabre, P. 71
Fama, E. F. 66
Farjaudon, A.-L. 70, 79
Ferrand-Bechmann, D. 177

Filho, W. L. 154–155, 157
financial capacity 125
financial dimension 120
financial growth 132–136; borrowing, growing, and paying off debt over time 135–136; deficit spending to grow operations 133; investing financial assets 134; paying off debt, and growing unrestricted net assets 132–133; portfolio asset class policy 134; reducing costs 134–135; savings and 133–134; seizing rare, advantageous opportunities 135; and stability over time **136**, 136–137; strategic investment internal grants 135
financial management, key strategies in 124
financial performance 33
financial resilience 123
financial stabilisation 127–132
financial transparency 49
financial vulnerability 165
financing by public procurement 78
Finkelstein, M. A. 188
Fitch, R. T. 180
Fleuriel, S. 179
for-profit movement 145–148
France Bénévolat network 189
Freeman, E. R. 144
Freeman, R. E. 65
French non-profit organisations 1–2; integrated governance analysis framework of 48–60; key stakeholders in 49
French organic public finances law (Loi Organique relative aux Lois de Finances (LOLF)) 51–52
Friedman, M. 144
"From traditional to collaborative governance: a stakeholder environment framework" 10
Frumkin, P. 198
functional dimension 70
funding competition 100
Furneaux, C. 129

Gateau, M. 180
Gazzola, P. 156
gender equality 70
Gendron, Y. 72

Index

generalisability of leadership research 194–195, 197–198
Generally Accepted Accounting Principles (GAAP) 17
general theory development of leadership 207
Ghani, E. K. 36
Gidron, B. 180
Gilbert, P. 70
Gilligan, C. 215
globalisation 140, 149, 150
Goldberg-Glen, R. S. 181
Gordon, L. A. 33
Goujon Belghit, A. 173–174
Gouldner, A. W. 2
governance: and performance, link between 119; system and its environment 17, *18*; *see also* stakeholder governance
grand theory of leadership 195–198
GreenHouse17 110–111
Greenslade, J. H. 185
Griffin, B. 37, 38
grouping movements 88

Habermas, J. 87
Hamidi, C. 179
Hanafi, S. 179
Herman, R. D. 198–200
Herzog, A. R. 182
Hood, C. 49
Horton, A. 216
Houle, B. J. 182
human capital: defined 173; management 174
Hutson, H. 196, 201

Idowu, S. O. 157
imbalance between governance and performance *80*
incorporation 41–42
Ingals, C. 65
Inglis, S. 182
initial volunteering 187
innovation 72
innovation culture 37
Inquiry into the Quality of Care in Residential Aged Care Facilities in Australia 217
institutionalisation of contractual funding 53

instrumental accountability 198
integrated approach of governance 51
integrated governance framework *60*
integrating volunteers 189
integration 42
integrative leadership 200
intention to volunteer 185
interdependency 21
internal auditors 35
internal control 131–132
internal governance mechanisms 13, 15–16
internal stakeholders 103
international nongovernmental organisations 141
International Organization for Standardization (ISO) 154, 156–157
inter-organisational restructuring (IOR) and mergers 88–97; case study 89–90; case study results 90–94; merger as quest for organisational legitimacy 90–91; organisational design and enrolment 91–93; organisational design as support for institutional work 93–94; reasons for failure of 88–89; strategic implications of 88; in voluntary sector 88
interpretive leadership skill 204–205, 207
Irvin, R. A. 129
ISO 37000:2021 standards 3, 5, 10, 213; different dimensions and proposed frameworks of **232**; of financial governance role 123; for non-profit organisations 83–84; in practice of NPO strategy 83, 96

Jensen, M. C. 66
Jenson, M. C. 2
John, K. 37

Kaarbøe, K. 33
Kitwood, T. 221
Knutsen, W. L. 198
Kreutzer, K. 3

Langergaard, L. L. 156
lateral learning 111
leadership: Bauersfeld definition of 202; development theories 203–204; engagement and commitment 22; Lim definition of 203; *see also* *specific leadership*

238 *Index*

leading volunteers 189–190
learning, evaluation, and planning (LEAP) framework 219
learning theory of change 104; non-profit learning through 110–111
Lee, C. 107
Lew, C. C. 38
Lim, S. 203
literature 103
logics of care 220
long-term volunteering *187*
Lu, H. 33

macro-environment 14
Malley, J. 221
management control systems 70
management practices, social actions and 71–72
management tools 70; use of 79
Marival, C. 88
Marta, E. 182
Mathras, D. 164
Mauss, M. 2
McCauley, C. D. 195
meaning-making leadership 200–202, **206**
Means, G. 2
Meckling, W. H. 2
Meidell, A. 33
meso-level conflicts 104
meta-analytic behavioural model of leadership 195
Mintzberg, H. 2
Moldavanova, A. V. 157, 164
Molterer, K. 220
monthly cash forecast **128**
Morales, J. 70, 79
moral hazard 56
Morgan, G. 203
Morrison, S. 217
Mountain Association 112–113
Mowen, J. C. 183
My Brother's Keeper 112

Nanus, B. 198–199
Naseem, T. 34
Neely, A. R. 183
neoliberal management 72
new public management (NPM): "3 Es" rule of 52; analysing corporate governance in 50–51; impact on mechanisms deployed

50–54; movement and philosophy of 59–60
new public management (NPM) principles 49; deployment of 60; dissemination of 49–50, 52–55, 56; impact of 50–54; rise of 51–52
New York Times 144
non-profit accountability 103
non-profit and for-profit movements 145–147; overlap through ecumenical frameworks 148–149; towards more progressive practices 147–148
non-profit finance research: entrepreneurship *vs.* fears of marketisation 125–126; financial growth 132–136; financial stabilisation 127–132; financial stability and growth over time **136**, 136–137; monthly cash forecast **128**; optimal reserves 126–127; overhead costs 124–125; resource dependency and mission drift 125; revenue diversification and risk minimisation 126; stabilisation and growth 127; trends in 124–127
non-profit landscape, power to restructure 77–78
non-profit leaders: leadership competency for 203–204; leadership roles of 198–199
non-profit leadership: alignment leadership 201–202; challenges in 199; constructive-developmental theory of 202–204; executive centrality in social construction 202; interpretive leadership skill 204–205, 207; issues in 197; leadership roles 198–199; meaning-making nature in 200–202, **206**; mission and value alignment as 196; need for middle-range theory of 196–198; research on 196–197; theory-building template for 194–195
non-profit learning pathways 105–109, *106*; challenges in 107; creating communities of practices via lateral learning 108–109; formal learning via normative pressure 107–108; institutional pressure underlying 105–106, *106*; network level influence 107–108; through alignment theory of change 112–113; through catalyst theory of change 112; through learning

theory of change 110–111; through policy theory of change 111; through project theory of change 109–110

non-profit management literature 106

non-profit managers, public funders and 55–57

non-profit organisations (NPOs): accountability framework 222–223, *223*; adoption of ERM in 30–34; allocation of resources to 71–72; as "armed arms" 1; control tools of 71; definitions of 1, 3; disciplinary approach 9; distinction between OSR, social responsibility, and sustainability in 158–162, *162*; effective performance 6; effects of 6; employees control over 17; ethical behaviour 6; financial performance in 123–124; framework for analysing governance of *60*; in France 1–2; funding for 53; global approach to 3; governance logics at work in 55–57; governance of 2–4, 49, 230–231; governance principles 4; governance system and its environment 17, *18*; governance with action of funders 50–54; guidelines for practitioners 86–87; implementation of risk management in 34–38; implications of distinction for theory and practitioners 163–166, *165*; indirect funding for 48; integrated approach in governance of 58–60; inter-organisational restructuring (IOR) and mergers 88–97; ISO 37000:2021 standards for 3, *5*, 10, 83–84; issue of governance of 61–62; leadership roles for 198–200; leaders of 59; meaning-making leadership in 207; need for 1–2; need for an integrated, co-constructed approach 56–60; need for specific risk management framework for 38–43; "normalization" of 88; principles of 50–54; public funders in governance of 48; reasons for implementing governance mechanisms in 9; relationship between State and 72, 75–76, 78–79; responsible

stewardship 6; revenue portfolio design 126; risk management in 29–43; role of public funders and 52–54; roles of 71; social actions of 69–80; with social missions 73–78; social responsibility and sustainability in 154–157; stakeholder governance in 65–66; strategic process within 94–97, *95*; survival strategy in 54; theorising leadership for 195–198; tools for managing public policies 76–77; voluntary work in 177–190

non-profit risk management diamond (NP-RM Diamond) 38–43, *39*; collaboration 41; incorporation 41–42; integration 42; levels of **42**

norm of reciprocity 2

notion of performance 120

NPO practitioner guidelines: adaptive responsiveness to external dynamics 97; stakeholder engagement and inclusivity 97; strategic clarity and articulation 96

NPO strategy: analytical tools for 84–88; institutional nature of 87–88; in its institutional context 87–88; practical and collective dimension of 84–85; "practical turn" in 85, 86; as a translation process 86–87

Okun, M. A. 182

older people: four D's of 219; quality of care for 222

Omoto, A. M. 183

OneLex 111

operational dimension 120

optimal reserves 126–127

O'Reilly, C. A. 37

organisational actorhood 124

Organisational assessment 112

organisational culture, defined 37

Organisational decision-making 100, 101

Organisational design 104

organisational effectiveness 48

Organisational goals 100

organisational identity 200

Organisational learning theory 101; importance of 102; to non-profit sector 103; and purpose-oriented networks **101**, 101–104; single loop *versus*

240 *Index*

double loop perspectives in 101–102; two perspectives of **102**
organisational mission 199
organisational reality 203
organisational social responsibility (OSR) 30, 161; definition of 155; distinction between social responsibility, sustainability and 158–162, *162*; goal of 156; interchangeability between OSR and sustainability 157–158; link between OSR and sustainability 157–158; in NPO 155–162, **159**
organisational viability 177
Organisation for Economic Co-operation and Development (OECD) countries 48
Ortega-Rodríguez, C. 9
Osman, A. 38
Ospina, S. M. 197, 201
Ott, H. K. 155
outcome evaluation, and theory of change 100–113
outcome-oriented culture 37
overhead costs 124–125
oversight approach 50
owner-shareholder 2

Pan, Y. 38
participative leadership 195
passive leadership 195
peer learning 108–109; vertical learning *vs.* 108–109
Penner, L. A. 186–188
Pérez-Cornejo, C. 34
performance evaluation 13; data collection for 106–107
performance outcomes 198
person-centred care 213, 221
Petriwskyj, A. 218–219
Pfeffer, J. 52
Piliavin, J. A. 188
Pilon, M. 10
Plaisance, G. 123, 125
Polanyi, K. 140–141
policy theory of change 104; non-profit learning through 111
Pope, S. 124
portfolio rebalancing 134
positive attitude 183
power balance and sharing 22

Power, M. 34
private regulation 152
procedural knowledge 207
professional logic of care 220
project-based social impact 106–107
project theory of change 104; non-profit learning through 109–110
Prouteau, L. 178
public funders: action of, in governance of NPO 58; factors justifying use of monitoring mechanisms by 55; perceptions of non-profit managers and 55–57; role of 52–54
public leadership scholarship 197
purpose-oriented networks **101**, 101–104

quality of care 218, 221; for older people 222

rationalisation of organisational life 149
reciprocity 2
recognising volunteers 190
relational factors 100
relational logic of care 220
reliability 36
Renz, D. O. 3, 4, 198–200
resource dependency and mission drift 125
resources and capacity 23
revenue diversification and risk minimisation 126
Ring, P. J. 37
risk culture 40; defined 37; as the term 37–38
risk governance 39–40
risk management: capacity 41; contingent approach to 41–43; in non-profit organisations 29–43; organisational culture in 35; process 40–41; role of culture in adoption and use of 37–38; "silo" approach to 29
Ryle, G. 204

Salamon, L. M. 1, 58, 198
Salancik, G. R. 52
Santos, F. M. 198
Schmidt, G. 85
Schwab, K. 142
scientisation 149–150

Index 241

self-reflective capacity 205
servant leadership 195
service-based social impact 107
shadow businesses 156
shared motivation 21
shared understanding 21
Sheedy, E. 37, 38
Shergold, P. 20
Shumate, M. 103
Sierra Club 147
Siloam Health 110
single loop learning 101–102
Sin, H. P. 203–204
Smircich, L. 203
Snyder, M. 181, 183
social actions: construction of 74–75;
   management practices and 71–72;
   of non-profit organisations 69–80
social actors 149
social-change leadership theory 197, 201
social dimension 120
social entrepreneurship 199
social impact: definition of 106;
   types of 106–107
social innovation 30, 77
social justice 147
social mobility 179
social pressure 186
social psychology 207
social relations 186
*The Social Responsibilities of the
   Businessmen* (Bowen) 143
social responsibility 5, 13, 162;
   definition of 155, 157, **159–160**;
   distinction between OSR,
   sustainability and 158–162, *162*;
   issue of 156; notion of 164;
   see also social responsibility movement
social responsibility movement: from
   accountability to transparency 150;
   corporate social responsibility (CSR)
   140, 143–144; double movement
   140–143, *141*, *142*; examples of
   dimensions of **151**; overview of
   139–140; scandals of 142–143;
   tandem movement 143–149, **146**
"The Social Responsibility of Business
   Is to Increase Its Profits" 144
societal dimension 120
solidarity actions 71
Song, H.-C. 156

SPARK (Small non-profit Peer
   Accelerating Rural eastern Kentucky)
   112–113
stakeholder engagement 4, 13;
   care-based accountability framework
   for 222–224, *223*; in ISO 37000:2021
   213–214, 221
stakeholder governance 65–66
stakeholders 14–15, 103; defined 14;
   external 103; internal 103
stakeholder theory 216
Steinberg, R. 125
Stewardship theory 9
stock market 33
Stogdill, R. M. 196
*Strategic Management: A Stakeholder
   Approach* (Freeman) 144
strategy-as-practice perspective 85
structural dimension 70
Sujan, H. 183
survival financing 78
sustainability 162; definition of 155,
   160–161; distinction between social
   responsibility, OSR and 158–162,
   162
sustainable development 13, 30
system alignment 104

tandem movement 143–149, **146**;
   in macrosociological context
   149–150
Terry, D. J. 183–184
theorising leadership for NPO 195–198
theory of change: and double loop
   learning 109–113; and outcome
   evaluation 100–113
theory of change framework 104–105
theory of planned behaviour (TPB) 183,
   184
three-level competency model of leader
   development 203
three lines model: difficulties in applying
   35–37; principles of 36
Toepler, S. 58
Total 144
transactional leadership 195
transformational leadership 195
transparency 36
Trébucq, S. 173
Tronto, J. C. 216
trusting relationship 21–22

242 *Index*

United Nations Centre on Transnational
Corporations 145

Valéau, P. 71–72
value-based orientation 199
value creation 198, 231
value generation 13
Values, Individualised, Perspective,
Social (VIPS) framework 221
Viscelli, T. R. 33
visionary leadership 200
Volunteer Functions Inventory (VFI) 182
volunteering: Ajzen's model 184;
defined 186; functions (rewards) by
180, **181**; implementing 189–190;
initial 187; intention to 185; lines of
research in 177–178; long-term *187*;
in non-profit organisations 177–190;
Penner model 186–188; reasons for
179–180; respondent's attitude towards
185; as result of a process 183–188;
as a source of various rewards 178–183;
stages in 183; TBP and 183, *184*
volunteer management 189–190
volunteer motivation: and economics 178;
Gidron's hypothesis 180; Gidron's
typology 180; motivation scales **180**;
and social psychology 180–183;

and sociology 178–180; and volunteer
activity 188
volunteer role identity 188
volunteer's long-term commitment 188
volunteer training 190
Vygotsky, L. S. 204

Warburton, J. 183–184
Waters, R. D. 155
Weber, M. 149
welcoming volunteers 189
White, K. M. 185
Willems, J. 3
Williamson, O. E. 2
Wilsker, A. L. 126
windfall policy 130
Wirtz, P. 62
within-sector learning 108–109
Wolff, F. C. 178
working capital requirement (WCR) 1
World Economic Forum 142
World Health Organization (WHO) 217
Wright, N. S. 157, 164

Young, D. R. 126

Zeimers, G. 154, 156–157
Zweigenhaft, R. L. 180